MW01242116

Tokyo Tales –
My Journey

Cohen-Okubo Suzy

Tokyo Tales - My Journey
Cohen-Okubo Suzy

Cover design: Lia Joffe
Graphic design: Sigalit Eshet

Copyright © 2022 Cohen-Okubo Suzy

No part of this book may be reproduced, copied, photocopied, recorded, translated, stored in a database, or transmitted in any manner or by any means, whether electronic, optical or mechanical (including photocopy, recording, Internet and e-mail). Commercial use of any kind of the content of this book is strictly prohibited without an authorization detailed in writing by the author.

Table of Contents

Introduction

At the end of January 2020, for a few days I accompanied a group of Israeli tourists who had debarked from the Diamond Princess. Two days after we said our farewells, the news reported that one of the passengers from Hong Kong had been diagnosed with Covid-19. It was the first we had heard of the coronavirus outbreak in the Chinese province of Wuhan.

There had been fifteen Israeli passengers aboard the ship, and the Israeli media began reporting the event, especially after the Japanese Ministry of Health ordered all the passengers to remain quarantined on board the ship for two weeks. The order was met with silence in Japan but caused a panic in Israel, and all the tourists who were planning to come to Japan for the cherry blossom season cancelled their reservations. Between the cherry blossoms and the Tokyo 2020 Olympics scheduled for the following summer, it should have been our most profitable year. The void that opened up in the center of my usually busy life was an uninvited and surprising challenge which I soon realized was a gift from the universe, and I used the unexpected free time to write this book.

A New Life

Twenty-nine years ago, on my 24th birthday, I made a spontaneous decision not knowing how life-changing it would become. I quit my secretarial job in a construction company, sold my Citroën and boarded a plane to Thailand. From the day I finished my military service in the Israeli Defense Forces people were telling me about "the magic of Thailand." Most of these stories came from Israelis who had gone off to what was known as "the great adventure after the army." I knew exactly where I wanted to go: the Far East. What attracted me was the chance to get away, take time off and rethink the direction my life was going in. Thoughts became a practical search for information, and in the meantime I learned that Sandy, a good friend I got to know during basic training in the army, was planning her own great adventure. Based on my research I suggested tropical Thailand; she liked the idea and said she would join me. We spent the time before the flight planning what to visit and see. We agreed not to spend too much time visiting the temples in Bangkok, but rather to just island-hop and relax.

At the end of 1992 we landed in Bangkok and four days

later left for the islands. Our first target was Koh Phangan, an obligatory stop for all Israelis. We took a night bus to a port, then a ferry to Koh Samui and from there we caught another ferry that took us to Koh Phangan. We met a lot of young Israeli tourists on the ferry, among them an interesting girl named Sherry, who told us she was planning to go to Japan.

"I'm looking for someone to travel with," she said. At that precise moment something lit up in me, and I felt I found a way to expand the limits of time and space. I knew Thailand would never be enough, and I had to see more of what the world had to offer. During the ferry trip I listened to Sherry's stories about Japan with mounting excitement. At the time I had no idea how I would do it or how I would tell Sandy I was changing my plans, but I knew I wanted to know more about Japan.

Sherry said she had met a young man in Bangkok who had relatively cheap rooms for rent in a guesthouse in Tokyo. She was planning to live there and in the meantime find work to finance the rest of her trip. She kept talking and I kept asking questions, and I gradually realized we had truly bonded, and that she would be my ideal partner to travel to Tokyo with.

Once the ferry arrived at the shore and we parted I kept thinking about everything she had told me. I liked the idea of being able to earn money in Japan, and I knew a lot of Israelis had worked there either in the hospitality industry or in sales. However, first I needed a visa to enter the country. Sherry told me the Japanese authorities sometimes banned certain Israelis from entering Japan. We agreed to meet in Bangkok a few days before the flight so we could buy tickets and warm clothes for the cold winters in the land of the rising sun.

In the meantime, I was looking forward to spending two weeks sunbathing on the beaches in Thailand. It is said you really get to know someone when you are with them 24/7 and far from home, and it became obvious to me that there was so much more to Sandy than what I had seen when we were in training together. The hard life we shared in boot camp had overshadowed her funny, cynical outlook on life. Her stories about her army service and subsequent job with an airline company were hilarious, and I was amazed she had kept her sense of humor. She grew up with 12 brothers and sisters, and her stories about them had me laughing for hours. She made new friends easily, was open-minded and loved having a good time. The time we spent together brought us even closer and we became best friends.

Every evening we rented a motor scooter and drove to the other side of the island to eat at a sea-side restaurant. We couldn't have asked for more. We both like Thai food, especially the desserts, crepes filled with fruit and dripping with a sweet sauce, or the Thai version of granola with freshly-picked tropical fruits. We were happy all the time, and Sandy was doubly happy because it was her first time abroad. I asked her to come to Japan with me, but she had to go back to work and didn't want to give up her job with the airline. Our two weeks together had been wonderful, and I felt terrific, I was tanned, relaxed and happy. Eventually we said our sad farewells.

Tokyo, Japan

"You will have the time of your life in Japan and won't ever want to leave," said an Israeli guy who was staying in a bungalow near ours with his German girlfriend. His descriptions left me more eager than ever to see the country. "If I could get permanent residence I would live there forever, but I've been in and out of the country so often I'm afraid to try again," he said.

I was astounded that an Israeli, whose mentality was so different, could live there for long. He was so wrapped up in his own enthusiasm about Japan he failed to notice my surprise, but eventually I became less apprehensive.

"No one has any problems with language," he assured me. "The Japanese speak and write English very well. If you need something, just write it down and show it to someone, and they will understand." I asked questions well into the night and he patiently answered every one of them. Sometimes he laughed and told me to calm down: once I'd got there everything would work out for the best.

I had no way of knowing how I would get along with Sherry. I didn't know much about her beyond our common desire to get away from home and arrive in Japan, but I hoped for the best. As planned, we met in Bangkok, excited but somewhat apprehensive because of the stories about Israelis who had been detained for questioning by the immigration authorities. The repeated advice we got from those who'd been there was to say we were only coming for a visit and as proof show them our wallets with only one credit card and enough cash for one month. With luck they would grant us three-month visas. Following further suggestions by Israelis, I was going to wear a newly-purchased pair of tailored black slacks and a button-down white shirt to make a good impression on the authorities at the airport. Finally, we had to find somewhere to live and have a ride pick us up from the Shinjuku railway station. Once that was all sort out there was only one thing left, which I was dreading most: calling home.

My father picked up the phone. I gave him a brief outline of my most recent adventures, and said, "Tomorrow I'm flying to Japan. I'm going to look for work and make enough money to keep traveling."

He said, "Is money a problem? How much do you need?" His intentions were good but I didn't want his help. "No," I said, "everything is fine. Don't worry, I want to work and I heard they pay well in Japan."

He wanted to know when I was coming home. "I really don't know. In the meantime, everything's great and I want to keep traveling."

"Take care of yourself," he said "and don't forget to call at least once a week so I won't worry."

I promised to call every weekend, just to be able to hang up as soon as possible. I also didn't bother to tell him that the past month had been the happiest of my life and that I didn't want to go home, I wasn't in the least homesick, not for "home" and not for Israel. I'll get back to that later. But in the meantime I embraced my happiness, I was thankful I could continue on my journey and put distance between myself and everything I had known before.

As we landed in Tokyo my heart was pounding and I broke out in cold sweat. The minutes waiting to go through immigration and customs seemed like hours. We couldn't decide whether or not to wait in the same line, and in the end, we chose to stand in different lines in case one of us was held up or turned away. I arrived at the passport control and handed over my passport for inspection. The clerk looked at me carefully, looked at my passport, stamped it and waved me through. That was all it took. It was the same for Sherry. We had been so worried, and now everything was fine, but we kept our giggles to ourselves because we were afraid someone would think it meant we had fooled them.

Once we were outside, we smiled from ear to ear. "We did it, we are in Japan." It was like a dream come true. Almost. We were stopped for customs, where they carried out a very thorough inspection of all our belongings. They emptied our bags and at the bottom of mine they found some small bright grains that looked suspicious. I told the officer in front of me that I was pretty sure it was nothing more than sand from one of the Thai islands, but he was not convinced. He put them in a test tube and I began to feel very uneasy. He poured some clear liquid into the test tube and waited for what seemed to me like an eternity. The test tube remained clear, I was innocent and cleared, and he gave me permission to repack my bag, take my things and leave.

We took the express train directly from the airport to Shinjuku station. Now that the trauma of the airport was history we could finally relax and take in the surroundings. Once we were off the platform the city seemed to welcome us with open arms. The streets were full of Christmas decorations, little colored lights decorated the store windows, each one with holiday messages, and the streets were strikingly clean. People smiled at us and wished each other a happy new year in a language we didn't understand. Women in fashionable dresses and men in suits added touch to the magical atmosphere. We felt we had arrived in a prosperous, modern, progressive country. We found a telephone and called Claude, a Frenchman Sherry knew, and reserved rooms in his guesthouse. He explained how to get to the meeting place at the station. We asked him how he would identify us in the crowd and he laughed and said, "Don't worry, as long as you don't look Japanese I won't miss you."

We found a place to sit and wait, while watching people passing by. I was amazed. I had never seen so many people moving in a public place in such a calm, orderly fashion. It almost seemed as if they were floating within the Christmas decorations along all the hundreds of Japanese words written in neon lights. I had fallen in love with Tokyo at first sight. I felt happiness bubbling up inside me and knew this was the place I was meant to be in. This feeling was reinforced in me later by many accounts, none of which more than my discovery that the Japanese were truly hospitable people, and polite, which made me feel far more comfortable than I felt in Thailand, where I had experienced a sense of pressure. Tokyo was clean and orderly, and I found it enchanting and appealing.

Claude found us easily. We shook hands, and he smiled and said, "Welcome to Tokyo." He spoke Hebrew with a thick French accent. We smiled back. While he was helping us put our luggage into the trunk of his car we complimented him on his Hebrew, and he said he had been on a kibbutz for two years. He had family in Israel and he loved the country, he said, and had a lot of Israeli friends in Japan.

The further we drove away from the airport the less urban the scenery became. We passed through old, crowded neighborhoods with narrow streets and buildings that looked like ancient pagodas. Claude said the neighborhood was called Nakano City. We drove for about 20 minutes and then turned into a narrow alley and parked next to the guesthouse. It was an old structure made of wood. Next to the entrance were several pairs of shoes and Claude asked us to remove ours. We did as we were told and followed him up the stairs to the second floor.

At the top of the staircase he opened a door and let us into a large room. It had a kitchenette with a sink, a small cupboard, a gas ring and kitchen utensils, as well as a closet for cloths, a TV with a cassette player, futons, down comforters, a space heater and an old radio-tape recorder. A door in one wall led to a large porch. Rent was $500 per person per month, but he said we could pay him after we received our first paycheck.

"Let's go meet the other tenants," he said. As we

followed him, he said everyone took turns cleaning the common areas and throwing out the garbage. "You share the kitchen, shower and toilets. If there are any problems give me a call and I will be right over."

We met most of the other tenants in the kitchen. They were sitting around a large stove in the middle of the room, drinking coffee. Claude introduced us: Sharon and Angie from England, Sarah, Kate and Mark from Australia, John from Canada, and Sophie and Louis from France. They made room for us to sit, and immediately began asking questions. "Where are you from?" "How long are you planning to stay in Japan?" "What kind of work are you looking for?"

It was like a job interview. And then it was our turn to ask questions. Most of them worked as English teachers in private schools and earned a lot of money. Sharon saw my interest in the amount of their salaries, and she smiled and asked me if I wanted to replace her working at a club the following evening. She had to fly to England and wouldn't get paid for two weeks if she left without giving notice. She seemed really eager to have me stand in for her.

"I don't know a word of Japanese," I warned her, "we just got here, and I don't know how to get along alone yet. I don't even have the right kind of clothes. I'll need at least a couple of days to get acquainted before I start looking for work."

She said she had a lot of clothes she could give us both, "and you, Suzy, I can tell you how to get from here to the club and back." She could see how confused I was and said, "Don't stress out, we all felt like that in the beginning, and everyone helped us."

It was three in the morning when she took us to her room and showed us blouses and slacks, shoes, tights and even makeup, all things she would have no use for in England. We tried to follow, but we were really too tired to make sense of what she was saying. She smiled and said, "Go to sleep. Tomorrow afternoon I'll go with you to the train station and take you to the places you'll need most if you decide to stay." I went to sleep feeling wonderful. We had a clean, neat room, the bedclothes smelled nice, and that was my last thought before I fell asleep.

Sherry and I woke up around noon. I stretched and got out of bed, surprised by the sudden difference in temperature between steamy Thailand and cold Japan. We unpacked, divided the shelves in the closet between us, and as we put things away, I was certain Sherry and I would get along fine. She had a terrific sense of humor and I was glad I had decided to continue my trip with her.

When we finished we went outside to look at our surroundings in daylight. There was an enormous indoor shopping center near the train station and the cold air drove us inside. Holiday decorations were everywhere and colored lights decorated the Christmas tree. At the supermarket we bought the basics for a late breakfast: milk, coffee, sugar, bread and cheese. There were enough American products on the shelves to make us think we were in an Israeli supermarket. The produce section was a surprise, however, because every vegetable and every piece of fruit was individually wrapped in cling film and sold separately. Some of the items in the baked goods section were a mystery, apparently having been flavored with green tea. Little white balls filled with something red turned out to be rice cakes filled with sweetened red beans. We didn't find them particularly tempting, we were more used to the pastries of the Middle East. We did, however, find something that looked familiar: the white bricks in tubs of water, we were certain, were the salty white cheese we knew from home. Our interest brought an employee over, and he pointed and said, "Tofu." We had no idea what tofu was because it wasn't being sold in Israel yet, and not understanding, we continued shopping.

Fish and seafood were arranged separately, according to species, in Styrofoam containers. We saw clams and calamari, eel and shrimp and all kinds of fish we had never seen before, most of them still alive. I had never liked the seafood we had in Israel and the smell made me nauseous. In the end we wound up buying junk food with familiar names that cost a small fortune.

From the supermarket we went to the clothing outlets where they were selling standard clothes, conservative clothes, nothing like what people wore in Israel, and quite unlike what we had seen at the train station, where people were dressed elegantly, according the latest fashion. However, there was nothing in any size larger than Medium or 6½ in shoes. We couldn't find a single shoe store with larger sizes. I was astounded to find I was considered large by Japanese standards. Everything in life is really relative.

In the undergarment stores we were also in for a surprise. They had tiny padded bras and underpants that looked like preteen wear. I asked if they had anything larger and was politely told that they didn't.

We went back to the guesthouse to make lunch. Sharon came into the kitchen and suggested the tour of the city she had promised. It was clear to me that our cloths were unsuitable for the Japanese winter and she offered us two jackets, for which we were very grateful.

So for the second time that day we walked to the train station, but this time with a guide. Sharon pointed out a couple of side streets which had cheaper produce and butcher shops. She also took us to a local restaurant where the food was cheap but good, and told us she and her friends often ate there. In front of each restaurant there were samples of the food they served, but made out of plastic, so we could point at the plastic model and show the waiter what we wanted to order. From there she took us to the post office, a laundromat, and a gym which she said had low membership fees. We didn't understand why we would want to join a gym, but she said all the girls in the guesthouse were members because it meant they could use the gym's showers and saunas – the shower in the guesthouse, she said, was always in great demand. And as soon as Sherry and I received out first paychecks we joined the gym and forgot about the guesthouse's narrow shower. Sharon was a gold mine of information. She took us to the local city cultural center where we signed up for free Japanese lessons taught by local volunteers. Then we went to eat at a Western restaurant. While we were eating our pasta with tomato sauce, Sharon said:

"I've lived here for many years. I worked in the hospitality industry and taught English and managed to save a lot of money. Now I'm planning to leave, return to

England and do something else with my life. I'll come back, but only to visit. I think you'll like Japan. It's easy to have a high standard of living here."

Working as a Hostess

"Dress up and put on makeup," Sharon said to me before I went to meet her employer. I wore a black miniskirt, a close-fitting white blouse, black tights and high-heeled shoes. I wore makeup and wrapped myself in a long, warm woolen coat. Everything I was wearing was borrowed from her. In Israel it was what I would have worn to a fancy wedding, but here it was just basic work clothes. No one I knew back at home would believe I was wearing high-heels, and in fact I had never worn them before and didn't know exactly how to walk without tottering. It was bitterly cold outside and I found it difficult to walk in a hurry. We made it to the train station and I was glad the nightmare was over, at least for the time being. We took the train to the Shinjuku station, and despite the late hour the station was hustling and bustling as though it were rush hour. I felt uneasy during the train ride as there were so many people around me, and I couldn't even reach a strap to grab onto to keep from falling each time the train stopped and departed. There was nothing I could do other than lean on other passengers, and they looked at Sharon and me suspiciously until we got off the train a few minutes later, although it felt much longer to me. I saw a few exit signs, each one numbered.

"Write down the exit number," said Sharon, "Tomorrow you will have to go to work by yourself." As Sharon and I lined up with the people waiting to exit the station, for the first time in my life I got the physical sense of the word *crowd*. Each and every person was dressed like a model, and everyone waited in complete silence as the line moved forward. One after the other they inserted their tickets into the appropriate slot and went on their way. Outside the station we entered a well-lit area of bars and restaurants. I couldn't stop looking around, and I saw groups of men entering alleys leading to small doors to buildings.

"All these buildings are bars and night clubs," Sharon explained when she saw how confused I was. "Every day after work men leave their jobs with their co- workers and go out to relax. Only afterwards they go home to their wives and children."

She said the club she worked in was relatively small for the area. "When you address your boss, you call him 'Master'. He stands behind the bar and mixes cocktails, prepares light meals for the customers, and your job is to bring them their food and drinks. Each time, the Master will decide who you will host. Your job is to have them order as much alcohol as possible. They usually drink scotch or bourbon. Every patron has his own bottle with his name on it behind the bar, and you have to encourage them to order a new bottle."

I met the Master in the bar on the fourth floor. He was a short man with thick, hairy eyebrows. He was wearing a black suit jacket, a white shirt and a bow tie, and to my eyes he resembled a clown. He hadn't been expecting me and he looked surprised to see me walk in with Sharon. She went over to talk to him, gesticulating with her hands, explaining the situation and that she had managed to find someone to replace her immediately. He looked at me, examining me up and down, and finally nodded his approval.

She came back to me and explained my working conditions, mentioning that among other things, the Master knew no English. "Don't worry about it, all the customers speak it and will translate for you. He relies on their help and they're always glad for the opportunity to use their English."

My hours were from eight in the evening until midnight, and I would have no trouble catching the last train. "It's your responsibility not to miss it, but if there are a lot of customers and he wants you to work overtime he will pay for a cab to take you home." My pay would be $25 an hour, paid weekly every Friday. Sometimes I would have to work on Saturdays, but for extra pay, obviously.

I did the math and realized that if I worked only four hours a day I would be making $500 a week. Of that, $125 would go for rent and I would have $375 to live on, a lot of which I could save, and that was without counting overtime. I tried not to show how overjoyed I was. After I accepted the conditions Sharon told me more about what the work entailed, and stressed again and again that after the club's guests had paid the cover charge, I had to make sure their glasses were always full. "Don't worry, the guests are nice people, you're going to love working here." She said goodbye to the Master, received her final salary and wished me good luck. I thanked her for everything, and she winked at me and left.

Just after eight P.M. the bar opened its doors and a group of eight men walked in. They sat at a corner table and the Master gave me hot towels to serve them, which they used to wipe their hands and faces. One of them asked the Master where Sharon was, and was told that she had gone home to England. "Suzy will serve you instead," and he told me to sit with them.

"Where are you from?" one of them asked me, with a thick Japanese accent.

"Israel," I answered.

It wasn't the answer they were expecting and it made them curious. A year ago the First Gulf War had been fought and Iraq attacked Israel. They wanted to know where I was when the Scud missiles were fired. I said that at the time I was working at the Diamond Center in Tel Aviv, at the very heart of the military drama. They wanted to know about gas masks and sealed rooms, and I was happy I had started such a lively discussion. I didn't notice the passing of the time and was surprised to discover it was almost midnight. Throughout the evening, instead of bringing them food and drinks, they were bringing it to me, liquor included. I asked them questions as well, and it turned out they all worked at the same life insurance company and one of them was the head of sales. I liked him a lot and I thought he liked me too. He kept offering me different Japanese dishes as well as liquor. Every now and then the Master came to our table to suggest more refreshments and tropical cocktails. He was apparently a professional bartender because each drink was wonderful, each one decorated with different-colored tropical fruits.

At one moment I stopped listening to the conversation for a couple of minutes and thought about how weird the situation was. I was sitting with them, just hanging out, really, the way I would with a group of friends, laughing and having a good time, but it was a job and I was getting paid for it. The only problem was their heavy Japanese accents which at times was difficult for me to comprehend, even though they were speaking in English. It took me a while to understand that they pronounced the "L" like "R", but when communication failed we resorted to talking with our hands and it always worked. Despite all the difficulties, they said it would be easy to remember my name because in their elementary school English textbooks the dialogues were always between Suzy and Tom. I smiled to myself, because for them my name was "Suji," no matter how hard they tried to pronounce it differently, "Z" was impossible. When they had finished eating and drinking, Okubo-San, the head of sales, asked if I wanted to join them for the rest of the evening. They promised they would send me home by taxi, and the Master nodded his consent. He had one of them explain to me in English they were long-time club customers and that I had nothing to worry about. In reality, I didn't need the Master's reassurance, because Okubo-San was sufficiently the motivation for me to continue the evening with them.

We left the club and walked for a bit past a couple of buildings, then entered another club, this one down a flight of stairs into a basement. I was shocked to find it full of drag queens. They looked feminine but their voices were low and masculine. They had heavy makeup on and were dressed like Playboy bunnies. They greeted us with applause and cries of *konichiwa*, which means "Hello."

I could tell Okubo-San and his friends came to the club often. "Hostesses" led us to a table in front of the stage and brought us hot towels, exactly as I had done just a couple of hours earlier. I was relieved the walk to the club had been short as it was very cold outside. We had to order quickly because the show was about to start. I had already drunk all the alcohol I could so I asked for a soft drink, while my new friends kept drinking scotch on the rocks.

The lights went out and when the cabaret dancers came on stage I recognized them as the bunnies who had greeted us. They sang and danced to cheers and applauses from the men in the audience, who threw money at them, especially when they stripped and showed their newly acquired breasts. I was stunned. One of the hostesses sat next to me and said in broken English, "You look like Brooke Shields." I laughed, not only because she thought I looked like a famous actress to whom I bore no resemblance whatsoever, but because she was making such an effort to sound feminine.

It was already three in the morning and I was exhausted. The day had been full of new experiences and the only thing I wanted was to put my head on the pillow and fall asleep. Luckily, once the show was over everyone stood up, paid the tab and left the club. They stopped a couple of taxis on the main street and before getting in they bowed to Okubo-San, who bowed back to them in return. Their formal leave-taking manner seemed odd to me, especially since despite their apparent friendship throughout the evening they behaved like strangers.

I shared a cab with Okubo-San, who lived in Tokyo's nearby Nakano neighborhood. I sat in the back and gave him a note with the address of the guesthouse. He told the driver where to go and we set off. Both of us dozed off until the taxi stopped. I thanked him for his kindness and asked him to thank his friends for me. We said goodbye and I waved. Drunk and tired, he could barely wave back.

I was cold and ran into the guesthouse. Everyone was asleep and I tiptoed into the room not to wake Sherry up. Without taking off my clothes or even my makeup I lay down on my futon and fell asleep.

It was late in the afternoon when I woke up. I found Sherry downstairs in the kitchen talking to the girls we met the previous evening. Sophie and Louis were also there, and it turned out Sophie was Claude's cousin. They said they had both a scholarship to study Japanese, which was why they were able to serve as translators for the guesthouse residents.

Everyone stopped talking when I came into the kitchen and looked at me. "So, how was your first day at work?" I told them about Okubo-San and that I liked him a lot, and about going to the club afterwards. They wanted to know every detail and I had fun telling them all about it, and in retrospect all the events took on a special glow. I excused myself but I had to go back upstairs to prepare for work. For the second time I wore the short skirt Sharon had given me, but this time I wore trainers, deciding to take my high heels with me in a bag and only put them on once I got to the club. This was a good thing too, because I could navigate the train more comfortably.

A Romantic Date

When I entered the club I was happy to see that Okubo-San and his entourage were already there. I sat with them and was eager to know a little more about them, at which point they took out their wallets and showed me pictures of their families, wives and children. Okubo-San did not, however, nor did he join the conversation. He said, "I'm divorced and I'm a single parent, bringing up my two sons alone." All I did was nod; I didn't say anything. I was surprised to discover, even then, that he wasn't married. In the meantime, the Master had prepared their cocktails and a plate with cheese and other snacks, and I got up to bring it to the table.

"Suji," they said, "we want to hear more about the army and life in Israel." I told them about my family, about my military service and about my trip to Thailand, which had led me to Japan. They found it hard to believe that I had arrived in Japan only the day before yesterday and had already found work. The evening progressed pleasantly, and at midnight they said they were leaving and again asked me if I wanted to accompany them, this time to a different bar. I agreed immediately, glad to be able to return with them by taxi rather than have to walk from the train station to the guesthouse in the cold.

We went to a karaoke bar, where the hostess ushered us to a pre-booked private room, where food and drink were already waiting for us on the table. We sat facing a large monitor and received a folder with a list of songs in English. Everyone chose a song, and they wanted me to choose one too. The words to the songs appeared on the monitor, and taking turns, each one got up on stage to sing their chosen song, using professional microphone. This was no laughing matter for them, as they sang to the best of their ability and were applauded by the audience. The closer we got to my song the louder my heart pounded, and when it was finally my turn. I hoped the earth would swallow me up. As I made my way to the stage to sing Elton John's "Crocodile Rock," I felt my cheeks burning. I tried not to sing out of tune but unfortunately it was not to be. People realized it immediately and tried to help me at least keep the beat. I felt mortified and was relieved when the song finally came to an end. Still, the audience was very polite and clapped for me as I made my way back to the table. That was the last time I agreed to sing and no one has ever tried to pressure me since. People kept singing and drinking, and I noticed that the more they drank the better they sang. They couldn't believe there was no karaoke in Israel.

The evening ended at three in the morning with the ceremonial farewell of bowing to each other that I had witnessed the previous night. Again I found myself sharing a taxi to the guesthouse with Okubo-San. This time we were less tired, and he turned to me and said, "Can we meet again, alone this time?" My heart went into overdrive. It was the last thing I thought he would say and it caught me unprepared. I looked him in the eye and simply said, "Yes." I hoped that by answering so quickly I hadn't revealed the emotions raging inside. Okubo-San said he would come to the club the following evening before my shift ended and then the two of us would go somewhere together.

He was quite tall and his eyes were very kind. I had been impressed by his appearance from the very first time I laid eyes on him. He was wearing a suit and I could smell his aftershave, which had a pleasant scent. "OK," I said, with no further comment. I was afraid if I said anything else I would reveal just how attracted I was to him. This was love at first sight. I told Sherry and Sophie how I felt about him. They asked for all the details and responded to every anecdote with the same enthusiasm I felt.

The next day he walked into the club a few minutes before my shift ended. We sat at the bar and he ordered one of the Master's cocktails for me. He told me his wife had left him the previous year. "She had wanted to leave a long time before, but I wouldn't let her go and take the children, so she stayed with me for a few more years." He was very open about what had happened. They argued back and forth until she agreed to let him take custody of the children, which he explained was unusual in Japan. Usually the mother gets full custody and the husband is left without visitation rights or participation in the children's upbringing.

I asked about the children and he said he had two boys. "Michitaka is 11 and Tomonori is 13. After my wife left I found out how hard it is to do everything alone. I had to learn how to take care of them and of the household as well as to work full time. Today I'm already used to it," he said with a smile.

Okubo-San seemed like a devoted father. Every evening after work he went home to be with the boys and give them dinner. He stayed with them until they went for extra tutoring at the *juku* prep school, where, I was surprised to learn, classes were held between seven and ten at night. He explained that "almost all Japanese children take extra lessons at a *juku*. The teachers prepare them for the entrance exams to good high schools. Children who don't attend *juku* schools have far less chance of being accepted by top universities."

It was easy to talk to him. He told me he was the manager of one hundred life-insurance agents, and as a bonus, every time they exceeded their quota, he treated them by taking them out for drinks. After that night I met him every night and I learned more and more about him. He told me about his children, his own childhood and his life as a divorced man. Three months later I knew him much better, but it occurred to me that we always met at night. I had never seen him during the day. One night he surprised me by asking if I'd like to meet his sons. I worried it might be a little too soon for that. I smiled but didn't give him an answer. I wasn't sure I wanted to take the relationship to the next level and go beyond the late-night entertainment. I was flattered but also embarrassed. The suggestion that I enter his house and meet his children showed how serious he was about our relationship. I liked going to clubs with him and listening to him share his problems as a single parent, but was content to leave it at that.

After that conversation, when my shift ended at midnight, Okubo-San suggested we go to a Korean restaurant. I was happy to accept and to continue the status quo of our relationship. There was a built-in grill called a *gogigui* in the middle of our table and next to it slices of marinated raw meat. He took a slice, put it on the grill, cooked it lightly on both sides and placed it in my plate. He passed me a small plate of hot sauce and told me to dip the meat in it. Next to the meat there was a plate of raw vegetables for the grill. He told me the dish was called *yakiniku*, and was very popular in Japan.

We sat in the restaurant until almost dawn and for the first time I told him about my family. My mother died of cancer when I was a child and my father remarried a woman I didn't like. Okubo-San listened to me attentively and with great patience. On our way home in the cab he asked me if I wanted to spend the weekend with him. I was a little hesitant and asked if I could bring my friend Sherry with me. When he agreed, though still unsure, I agreed. Luckily Sherry jumped at the chance, happy to finally meet the man I was in love with.

I was very fortunate to have found the job at the club. I met many great people who were all very kind to me. I received a lot of offers to spend weekends with them, and politely declined them all. Apparently the Japanese really liked foreigners, and respected anyone seen in their company. Initially I was wary of stalkers, but soon learned my fears were baseless. Japanese men have a great deal of respect for women, and not one of them even hinted at anything that could be interpreted sexually.

Sherry had found work at a large club and told me that most of the customers were Asian. The club also had karaoke rooms, which meant that every evening she had to get up on stage and sing. She loved it, and like me she enjoyed the atmosphere and high remuneration. She was invited out almost every night, but her goal was much simpler. She hadn't come to Japan to fall in love but to make enough money to continue her travels. We exchanged stories in the early hours of the morning, sometimes joined by others who lived in the guesthouse and were also working at night clubs. The club customers used to be so drunk they could not behave themselves, which felt very odd to us. We began to understand that the Japanese businessmen had two sides to them, one for the morning and one for the evening. In the morning they were serious and shy, and in the evening, happy and noisy.

My routine, like the other members of the guesthouse, also included taking Japanese lessons at the local cultural center. The teachers were elderly and could speak English. It seemed to me they enjoyed their weekly meetings with foreigners who had come from all over the world. Within a month I learned to read and write *hiragana*, one of the four Japanese writing systems; it is composed of 46 signs, and Japanese children learn it when they enter the first grade. Most of Japanese writing is based on *kanji* and *hiragana*, and words taken from foreign languages are written in *katakana*. *Romaji* is used to write Japanese using the Latin alphabet, and is used for computing. Sophie had spent four years learning how to read kanji before she came to Japan, and told me there were more than two thousand signs, each one with a different meaning. We didn't learn kanji but we managed to get along because there were many places where hiragana was sufficient for basic communication. In Tokyo the train station names were written in English too, but once you left the city there were fewer English signs, so knowing hiragana meant we could orient ourselves. Within a short period, I learned the words for numbers, colors, and some nouns and verbs. Japanese was an interesting language, and I kept wanting to know more. I met Hidaki-Sensei at the gym and he told me he had one Japanese parent and one English, so he was fluent in both languages. He taught Japanese, and I immediately took the opportunity to ask him for private lessons. He was happy to oblige.

We arranged to meet for lessons twice a week at a local café. He taught me kanji which exposed me to a much larger vocabulary. This new knowledge became a driving force and motivated me to study even harder. The more I learnt, the more I wanted to know.

"Will You Marry Me?"

Of all the club customers I hosted, I enjoyed hosting Okubo-San most. Often he didn't come to the club for several nights, and when that happened it felt as though my shift would never end. I did enjoy the company of other customers, and while they were very pleasant to be with, I still felt I was working. With Okubo-San I was simply having a good time.

Most of my regular customers were married and had children. They were employed by large corporations and liked to come to the club after work. That was their daily routine, and I learned to expect their awkwardness as they walked in. They were very reserved and even embarrassed at the beginning of the evening and needed at least half an hour to relax and feel at ease. I made sure their glasses were full of scotch diluted with water and ice, and added hard liquor to Chinese tea. I had no problem waiting patiently for the effects of the alcohol to act and observe them as they loosened up. It happened every time. They began making jokes and were laughing and no longer self-conscious about their broken English. They used it freely to converse with me. Furthermore, as soon as the barrier between the boss and employer dropped, their English improved and they became a homogenous group. Watching this change every evening was astounding to me. Yet, as soon as the effects of the alcohol wore off, each one returned to their innate inhibitions, and as all signs of the evening's camaraderie were gone, the reserved Japanese conduct took over again. A bit like Cinderella after the ball.

Sometimes on weekends the Master asked me to come to work for a special event and I would offer to bring Sherry with me as backup; he was always glad for the extra hands. She would spend the evening doing things in her own way such as dancing and singing to the customers, and I discovered she was a very talented dancer and singer.

Within a short time both of us had saved quite a lot of money. At the beginning of every month we paid Claude rent and still had a lot left over. We found local cheap places to eat at and inexpensive stores to shop at, and our life was simple and rewarding. When our visas were about to expire the people in the guesthouse told us we had to leave Japan, go to a neighboring country and stay there for a few days. After that we could return and would be given another three-month visa. There was no way to renew our visas while we were still in Japan, and they recommended we get letters from a local resident inviting us to stay in his home. That would ensure quick authorization for a new visa from the Japanese ministry of immigration. One of Sherry's customers agreed to write the letter for her, and Okubo-San was happy to help me out. He didn't want me to leave Japan and said he would wait for us at the airport in case there were problems with the Japanese immigration.

The Master was not pleased I was taking five-day off, but he understood I had no choice. Our plan was to pack most of our belongings and leave them in the guesthouse. We left our addresses with Claude so that if we couldn't return to Japan he would know where to send our luggage to. When we told Sophie we were planning to fly to South Korea, the closest country we could find, she said she would come with us, and we were happy to have her join us.

A week before we were supposed to leave, after I finished working, Okubo-San and I went out to a restaurant. He was very quiet and looked sad. After a long silence he surprised me by saying, "I'm in love with you." I didn't answer immediately, but my expression gave me away. I stopped myself from speaking, because I was still afraid to commit to a relationship which could hurt both of us.

Finally I said, "I don't think I'm going to stay in Japan for much longer and it would be better if we remained just friends. I don't want to hurt you. If our friendship develops into something more, it won't be easy for me to continue in my travels."

I was being perhaps too rational, but in any case he turned to me and said, almost pleading, "It would be a waste if you left Japan having seen only Tokyo. Come with me to the sea this weekend." He needn't say anymore; I was only too happy to agree. I had put the cards on the table and was frank about my dilemma, which was at the center of our relationship. Now, after I had said what I had to say, I could accept the opportunity to see new places and spend time with the man who had captured my heart.

At the end of my shift on Friday night he was waiting

for me, standing next to his car at the corner where we had agreed to meet. It was the first time I had ever seen him wearing jeans, and they looked good on him. We drove on a highway for about four hours, talking and listening to Eric Clapton on the radio.

"Would you like to stay in Japan longer?"

"Yes, definitely." The thought of staying in Japan was very appealing. I loved living in Japan from the very beginning, and in all truth I had no desire to go home. I said, "I would like to apply for a student visa and go to a Japanese language school."

"I can be your sponsor," he surprised me. "I can help you get the documents you need and will apply for the visa myself."

Just before dawn we reached Izu, a mountainous region with a spectacular view of the ocean. We stood on one of the peaks with the sea below us and an astonishing clear sky above. It was breathtaking. Okubo-San hugged me and we kissed for the first time. His lips were soft and sweet, and confirmed what I had known for a long time, I was in love with him.

When we finished kissing he said, "Suzy, marry me. Stay with me here in Japan. I will make you happy. I'm building a new house and I want you to come and live with me and my sons."

I was stunned. I said, "How can you propose marriage when you don't really know me? I have to get to know you and your children before I can consider marrying you." I stopped for a second to catch my breath, and said, "Think of what's best for your children. My own experience with a step-mother wasn't very positive. It taught me how difficult it is for children to get used to another woman who is not their mother in their home."

He smiled and said confidently, "I know what I feel and I know what I want, and what I want is you." His assurance made my heart pound so loudly I could no longer hear him. However, I managed to keep cool and smiled shyly. I asked him for some time to think about it and to get to know him and his family better.

It was five in the morning but was warm and pleasant. We drove down the mountain to the beachside. We lay on two of the tanning beds already placed on the shore and slept for an hour.

From there we drove along the coast, inhaling the salty air. Okubo-San drove but kept looking at me, and as he stroked my hair he said again, "I will make you happy. I like being with you." He promised that when I returned from South Korea we would go on trips again.

"The parents of one of my employees own a traditional Japanese hotel," he said, and that was where we were heading to. We were received by the owners themselves, who bowed their heads so low they almost touched the floor. I was embarrassed, and generally speaking found it hard to get used to this Japanese ceremonial behavior, which seemed humiliating. They gave us robes, towels and toiletries, and led us to a traditional Japanese room. The windows were made of rice paper, and two futons were set on a tatami mat on the floor. The window faced a garden with an artificial waterfall.

There was a hot water dispenser for the preparation

of tea, and rice cookies. Okubo-San suggested I take a dip in the hotel's hot water bath, which he said was especially relaxing. He accompanied me to the women's bath and then proceeded to the men's.

Apparently the bath house was in great demand. Dozens of naked women sat on low plastic stools, scrubbing their bodies with washcloths dipped in soap. Then they shampooed their hair, wrapped it in a towel and entered a large public bath lined with stones. The water was a very hot, 43 degrees Celsius. I tried following the women's actions but I couldn't stay in the water for more than a few seconds. It was so hot I felt I would faint. I left the pool and rinsed myself with cold water. I looked around and could see no one else found the water too hot. The women in the bath were chatting away and looked truly relaxed.

While we were together, resting and eating, we spent the time getting to know each other better. We discussed such issues as food, songs, culture, and then we spoke about his children. He said they were spending the weekend with his mother. "When you return from South Korea," he said, "I want you to meet my family, my parents and my children."

"At some stage in the future," he said emotionally, "I would like to go to Israel with you and meet your family, in order to ask your father for his permission to marry you. I'll promise him I'll take good care of you." His plans held no bearing with me. As far as I was concerned, it was all utterly unrealistic. He had no idea of the extent of the gap between the Japanese and the Israeli cultures. Furthermore, I had no idea how I was going to tell my father that I was in love with a divorced man, who was 14 years older than I, had two children and was Japanese and not Jewish. I could not fathom how to explain to Okubo-San my father's expected anger, and how he would oppose the relationship. My father was conservative and traditional and his ideas were outdated, and I knew nothing would ever change him. I kept that to myself and told Okubo-San that I needed time. He didn't say anything and we went back to listening to sad music.

The sexual tension between us was building throughout the evening, and peaked when we entered our room. Any pretense of restraint was dropped to the floor along with our robes as we fell into each other's arms under the blankets. His kisses were gentle and my entire body responded. I surrendered myself to his smooth, sweet fragrant body. We kissed for a long time, and he whispered that he had been waiting for this day from the moment we met. Making love with him was magical, and he kept telling me how much he loved me. For the first time I felt secure and calm, a feeling which had been lacking in my life for a long time.

Afterwards I curled up in his arms and it felt completely natural and right. However, I was still bothered by what I knew my father's response would be.

The following morning, we returned to Tokyo via Yokohama, where we stopped to eat dinner at a gourmet French restaurant on the top floor of the InterContinental Hotel. We drank wine to toast the new stage of our relationship. We sat at a window table and had a bird's eye view of the entire city, its port and the bridge connecting it to Tokyo. I was happy. I was in love with Okubo-San and I felt blessed.

We ended the evening with a walk around Yokohama's China Town, which was full of colorful stores and restaurants that served mostly pork and seafood. I knew what ordinary Israeli seafood looked like but had never tasted any. The menus were vastly different from those of Israel's Chinese restaurants. We went from stall to stall, drank coconut milk and bought desserts for Sherry and for his children. It was already late but we didn't want the evening to come to an end. In an hour and a half's drive in the car the weekend would be over, and we would be back in Tokyo, facing the unpleasant reality of our imminent separation. I had to leave for South Korea, and who knew if I would be able to come back?

At the guesthouse, everyone was waiting for me in the kitchen, eager to hear how my weekend had been, but this time I was still inside my own bubble and apologized for not answering right there and then, and promised I would tell them at another time. I went to my room, with Sherry and Sophie at my tail. I had to pack and get ready for the flight to South Korea. They waited patiently for me to tell them about my weekend, and when I had finished packing and everything was ready, I started recounting my adventures, and when I told them about Okubo-San's marriage proposal they both applauded. Sophie had a Japanese boyfriend and Sherry was friends with many of the locals, but marriage was something else entirely.

The next morning we waited downstairs for Okubo-San to take us to the airport. He arrived exactly on time and I introduced him to Sophie. He had already met Sherry, and she spent the entire car ride speaking Japanese with him. He asked her about the school where she learned Japanese, and if I could enroll when I returned from South Korea. She gave him the school's telephone number and he promised that while I was away he would try and arrange for me a student visa.

He walked me as far as the boarding gate, and every minute in his company was sheer joy. I had known him for exactly three months, but I felt as though I had known him my whole life. We hugged and kissed goodbye, and I promised to let him know the second I landed back in Tokyo.

Test Drive

I thought Tokyo was cold but Seoul was much, much colder and drier. Just walking around the streets was difficult, the cold was relentless and bone-chilling. There were stores under the hotel and the first thing Sophie, Sherry and I did was buy gloves, woolen hats and warm jackets. The club customers in Tokyo recommended Korean food and I could understand why: it was mostly various kinds of meat grilled over hot coals with spicy barbecue sauce, which was exactly what the Japanese liked. Japanese food was less spicy than the Korean, which I found to be way too spicy to my liking. Every time I ordered something I had to tell the waiter not to add the hot sauce to the dish and still it was too spicy and left my mouth feeling like it was on fire. I couldn't enjoy my meals. It was strange because in Tokyo we had occasionally gone to Korean restaurants but the dishes had apparently been tailored to the Japanese palate. Several times I left most of the food on the plate and so decided to refrain from Korean food. Instead, I opted to eat the American fast food at McDonalds, KFC and Pizza Hut.

We spent the first days in Seoul, South Korea's capital, walking around the city. shopping for shoes, clothes in our sizes and new leather jackets, all with fairly reasonable price tags. In Japan everything was so expensive I could barely buy anything and finding clothing in my size was a problem.

The time we spent in Seoul reminded me of the crowded streets in Thailand, the peddlers on every street corner offering tourists worthless trinkets. I longed for the politeness and restrain of the Japanese people. In fact, I wanted to return to Japan as soon as possible.

The only comforting thing was our companionship. Living together under the same roof we had gotten to know each other even better. Sophie told us about life in France, and how the French government paid for university education. That was why she had been able to study for so many years without having to worry about tuition fees. She did work during vacations though, to pay for the rent. She also received a grant to study in Japan, along with bimonthly payments for rent and pocket money. To me it sounded like a dream. She received everything from the French government and her life in Tokyo was happy. She said she planned to stay in Japan for a long time and hoped that once she had finished her studies she would find an interesting job.

I kept thinking about Okubo-San, and as I was going over in my head what had been said during our last weekend together, the idea of staying in Japan became more and more attractive. I loved Japan and I loved him, and returning to Israel was out of the question.

I was surprised to find that being far away from my father brought us closer. He called the guesthouse every weekend and the distance enabled me, for the first time, to express the feelings I had kept bottled up since his remarriage. I admitted I had never liked his new wife and he listened and didn't respond to my angry tone of voice. All he said was that he wanted me to find my direction in life and be happy, no matter where. He didn't understand why I was staying in Japan for such a long time and asked me why I had changed my plans of traveling all over the Far East. I believed he sensed I was hiding something, but he never asked, until one day he said, "What have you found in Japan that's keeping you from travelling the way you had planned?"

I said, "I like it here," which was a partial answer, but true. "I have a job, I'm having a good time and I'm saving money." I was afraid to tell him the truth, which was that meeting Okubo-San had completely changed my plans. It was clear, as far as I was concerned, that I would stay in Japan far beyond the expiration of a tourist visa.

When we landed back in Tokyo what I had been afraid of came to pass. Sophie and Sherry passed through passport control with no problems, but when my turn came, the immigration officer stopped me, looked at me suspiciously for a long time, and ordered me into a nearby interrogation room. My heart pounded and I was afraid I would be expelled from Japan. I had feared this all along and now the danger was more real than ever.

I sat across from two English-speaking investigators. They examined my passport cover to cover and asked, "Why did you return to Japan? You were already here for three months!"

"I want to travel outside Tokyo," I answered, as I had been told to say. "I haven't been to any of the islands yet."

"Where did you get the money to continue your trip? Did you work in Japan?"

"No," I said, following the script, "I'm staying with a Japanese family, I have a credit card and some cash too, and my parents send me money from Israel."

One of them wanted proof. With trembling hands, I gave him my international credit card, the letter from Okubo-San, and all the cash I had saved over the past three months from the salary the Master had paid me.

He called Okubo-San's office and luckily he was there. I couldn't understand what they were saying, but it was a short conversation and when it was over the investigator became less stern. He returned the letter, my credit card and money, stamped my passport, and sent me on my way.

Sherry and Sophie who were anxiously waiting for me by the baggage carousel, breathed a sigh of relief when I finally joined them. They hugged me and said they had been afraid I would be deported. Once we all calmed down I asked them to wait for me while I called Okubo-San to thank him for his help. He was happy to hear my voice and told me they asked him why I was living in his house. He told them I was waiting for my student visa and in the meantime learning Japanese at a school in the city. He said he had met me several years ago while traveling in Europe, and I had become a family friend. He also promised to be responsible for me and said they had no reason to be concerned. I thanked him again and again for helping me, and we made a date to meet at the club the following night. It was clear that without him they wouldn't have let me back into Japan. We took a taxi to the guesthouse, unpacked our suitcases, and since we weren't planning to work that evening, decided to celebrate our return to Tokyo.

I was impatient to see Okubo-San again. When we met the next day, to thank him for his help I gave him a particularly nice Zippo lighter I bought in South Korea. He was so happy to see me, and promised the next time I returned to Japan he would be waiting for me at the airport, so that if there were any problems they could summon him over the PA system and he could take care of everything immediately. I told him there wouldn't be a next time, the Japanese didn't want foreigners in Tokyo, I wasn't welcome, and maybe it would be a better idea if I simply left Japan.

"No, don't worry," he said, "I called Sophie's school and if I am willing to sponsor you there is a chance you can get a two-year student visa. I've already made an appointment to meet with the director." He smiled and added, "I won't let you go so easily. You're going to stay here with me."

A week later we had a meeting with the director of the language school. She was a middle-aged woman and when she spoke it was as if she had examined each and every word carefully before talking. She explained the long, complicated procedure of applying for a student visa. Okubo-San had to provide pay slips, documents showing proof of his position in the company and a list of his assets. I had to show proof of my marital status, transcripts from my schools in Israel, a copy of my passport and a letter explaining, in detail, why I wanted to learn Japanese.

She said once I had a student visa I could begin my

studies, which would cost $500 a month, and went on to list the school's strict rules. Five hours of study a day, and anyone who cut classes or didn't study seriously all the time would be reported to the immigration officials and their visa would be revoked. Okubo-San set another appointment with her for the following month, promising we would come with all the necessary documents.

I hoped I could get help from the Israeli embassy in Tokyo, but alas no, I was told in no uncertain terms, and quite coldly, that only the Israeli Ministry of Interior could provide me with what I needed. I called my older sister Haya, who had been like a mother to me since our mother died.

She promised she would send me all the documents I needed from Israel, and in the meantime Okubo-San helped me to write a letter to the Immigration Department applying for a student visa. He had me write that I wanted to learn Japanese to be able, in the future, to develop commercial relations between Israeli and Japanese companies and to act as the mediator. I praised Japan's culture and language, and emphasized my enormous curiosity about everything Japanese.

The month passed by and once again we found ourselves in the office of the stern school director. We gave her all the necessary documents she had asked for and she promised Okubo-San she would contact him as soon as she received an answer from the department of immigration.

Waiting was nerve-wracking, but in the meantime I went back to the familiar routine of working at the club and living at the guesthouse. I met Okubo-San every weekend and we went to "love hotels" that rented rooms by the hour. I told him that for the time being it was better to leave things as they were. I still didn't feel ready to take our relationship to the next level, which meant meeting his children. I didn't want to confuse them, especially since it was uncertain if I would be able to remain in the country.

The love hotels had rooms that were designed with special gimmicks. Some had revolving beds, or heart-shaped beds, mirrors on the ceiling, suites with a separate room with karaoke equipment and a Jacuzzi, so you could sing in the shower with style. The reception desk of every love hotel had a catalogue with pictures and descriptions of the different rooms, which Okubo-San and I looked at carefully to choose the room that most suited our mood. He explained that houses in Japan were very small and crowded and offered very little privacy, and therefore it was perfectly acceptable for couples to take rooms in hotels when they wanted to be alone. The hotels were also venues for couples conducting secret love affairs or single men who lived with their parents and needed a little privacy; prices dropped between midnight and morning. Every Friday night we went to a different luxurious hotel and pampered ourselves.

Those meetings completely altered my life, and I came to realize that I was living from one Friday to the next. Okubo-San came to the club in the middle of the week quite seldomly and most of our meetings were on weekends, far from the eyes of his employees. He said he didn't want them to gossip about him. To keep from accidentally revealing the nature of our relationship he usually took them to other clubs or bars. Not seeing him every night made my work far less enjoyable. I was tired of telling and retelling the same stories about Israel and got sick of watching Japanese men get drunk and telling me about their troubles. I no longer knew which I preferred, their reserved manner when they entered, or their drunken state when they lost their inhibitions and couldn't stop talking.

Sherry told me she was also tired of her job but both of us knew that the work was easy and paid more than anything else we could find. Where else could you sit with a group of Japanese men who were not only extraordinarily polite but who brought you presents as well, earning more than $100 for a four-hour shift, plus tips.

The Japanese idea of entertainment was foreign to us Israelis. Japanese men, especially in groups, were so different from Israeli men, who would sit in a bar in Tel Aviv and tell jokes they had heard during their last army reserve duty and were very friendly with each other. The Japanese who went to the clubs and bars went as a group, all of them from the same company or department, and that was the only thing they had in common. The reason they went out together was to get very drunk, sometimes to the point of passing out. Every evening a group of men would come in, drink beyond control and embarrass themselves. At the end of the evening they could barely remember their own names or where they lived. The tab for the small fortunes they spent on drinks was picked up by the company they worked for. It was the favorite form of entertainment for millions of Japanese, and like a herd of sheep their bosses gave them whatever they wanted. What was really absurd, as far as I could see, was that those nightly outings were considered part of their job, and when the boss issued an invitation no one could refuse on accounts of needing to be home early.

Sherry and I had had enough of seeing drunk Japanese men and decided we would quit before long. She also decided that when her second visa expired she would return to Israel and go back to studying and having a regular job. We decided that when the time came we would both quit and visit the Philippines, and then split up. In the meantime, my application for the student visa had been approved but I had to go back to Israel to pick it up from the Japanese embassy in Tel Aviv.

Before I left, Okubo-San again asked me to meet his children. He wanted me to live with him in his new house and promised he would help to pay my tuition. I agreed but asked Sherry to accompany me. I didn't know what to expect. Okubo-San had told me about them and I felt I knew them a little, but I was nervous about what they would think of the woman their father had been meeting for the past six months.

They shook my hand formally and said in English with a heavy Japanese accent, "We don't speak English". Sherry and I chuckled and tried to communicate with them with our minimal Japanese vocabulary. Both boys looked older than their age and were tall and broad-shouldered. Okubo-San suddenly looked thin next to them. We went to Nerima, the neighborhood they lived in, to the bowling club in a large shopping mall near their house. Both boys were accomplished bowlers and it was obvious they had a lot of practice. Sherry had already met Okubo-San several times and felt comfortable with him. He told us he was planning to cook *shabu-shabu*, a Japanese dish of thinly sliced meat and vegetables boiled in water in a hotpot and served with dipping sauce. He chose trays of thinly-sliced beef and vegetables, and bought beverages as well. We drove to his house, which was only a few minutes' drive away from the mall. The house was three stories high and he told us he had moved in only a few weeks before, apologizing for not having time to tidy up. The living room and the kitchen were on the first floor and had wooden floors. There were black leather sofas in the living room, and one quick glance proved he had nothing to apologize for, because everything was in perfect order. The children went to watch TV and Okubo-San asked us to come into the kitchen with him while he prepared the meal. The children were watching a comedy and laughed all the time, but I could understand nothing of what was being said. Sherry was impressed by the house and the children, and I was also relatively relaxed. I had been certain Okubo-San lived in a traditional Japanese house, but nothing I saw was traditional about it.

Okubo-San invited us to eat. A gas burner had been lit in the middle of the table and he put a kind of copper pot on top of it with a hollow tube in the center, like a Bundt pan, full of boiling water. There were plates of sliced meat and vegetables on the table, mushrooms, okra and Chinese cabbage, and each of us had two little bowls and a pair of chopsticks. He poured sesame sauce and ponzu sauce, which was a mixture of soy sauce and vinegar, into the bowls, and then we each received a dish of boiled white rice. He sat down and dipped a piece of meat into the boiling water, and when it had changed color he fished it out and dipped it into the bowls of sauce, asking us to do the same. He suggested we try a different sauce each time. The children ate the same way their father did, and we followed their lead. The food was wonderful. I still wasn't used to the taste of sticky rice, but eventually came to like it. Okubo-San showed us how to cook the vegetables the same way, and once they were done dipped them quickly in sauce. He also gave us tofu, which we had mistaken for feta cheese on our first day in Tokyo. It was the first time I tried it, and one small bite was enough for me to know that I didn't like it. When we finished eating Okubo-San suggested we go to the neighborhood karaoke club, where we could have a room for two hours. We accepted his offer, but politely declined to sing. Public singing was not for us, especially after we saw how well Okubo-San and his children could sing. Eventually we agreed and got up on stage. Sherry could carry a tune with no problem, and I joined her in a whisper.

We stayed there until late, and Okubo-San suggested we sleep over. We were happy to accept the invitation. Sherry slept in a large guest room, and I slept with Okubo-San in his bedroom, but only after we had made sure he had told his children about me and prepared them for the fact that Sherry and I would stay the night.

"So," he said once we were alone, "what do you think of my children?"

"They look a lot bigger than most of the people I've seen so far," I said.

He smiled and said, "They only look big. In many respects they're still little boys."

His bedroom reminded me of the room of a typical

single man. He had a double bed, a dresser and a clothes closet and a TV with a video cassette player. It was a special night for us, because we had been to bed before but this was the first time in his kingdom. I caressed his smooth body lovingly and his touch and kisses were most pleasing to me. We fell asleep in each other's arms and I felt safe and warm. In the morning he got out of bed to prepare breakfast.

After that weekend we no longer went to hotels, but rather met in his house and spent the time with his children. We began acting like a family, and after several weekends where we went to the Tokyo Disneyland or visited cities along the coast I began to enjoy their company. Tomonori was shy and formal, while Michitaka liked to fool around. They were only three years apart, but their behavior made each year obvious. Okubo-San told me they liked me and agreed that I could move in with them. On the one hand, I really wanted to live with the man I loved, but on the other hand, I was concerned by the challenge of living with his children, whom I had just met. In addition, I liked the freedom I had in the guesthouse, where my friends lived and where the atmosphere was young and informal. I shared my dilemma with Sophie and Sherry. Freedom was top priority to Sophie, and no amount of money or comfort or convenience would convince her to give it up. Her mantra was that a woman should progress and succeed in life by herself, and occasionally mentioned that one day she might become a single parent. Sherry also had concerns about Okubo-San's children. "It's not so simple," she kept telling me, shaking her head to emphasize the seriousness of the matter.

Out of the storm of conflicting emotions and considerations, I decided to go with Sherry to the Philippines for two weeks, to gain momentum in quiet, neutral surrounding. I told Okubo-San we were going, and he and I talked over my exiting and reentering Japan. I said I would show the immigration officers my temporary confirmation of the student visa, promising that in the very near future I would go to Israel for the necessary documents. He understood my need to go and asked me to promise that when I returned from the Philippines I would stop working nights. He didn't want the children to know I worked as a hostess. As long as I was a foreigner in Tokyo wanting to earn money to continue my travels, working as a hostess was considered legitimate. However, when our relationship changed and my circumstances in Japan changed that kind of work was no longer considered appropriate.

In June, before I flew to the Philippines, I told the Master I was quitting. I suggested he hired Mika to replace me. She was an Israeli girl who was living in the guesthouse and was looking for work. In the meantime, Sophie had left the guesthouse and rented an apartment in the city with a roommate, and was going to start her studies at the university. I was happy we had met and spent the time together. I admired her strength and independence, and her ability to learn Japanese, which was such a complex language, not to mention her decision to study in a foreign university.

Given the changes, we decided to hold a going-away party at the guesthouse. We invited Claude and thanked him for how kind he had been to us, and for providing us with such pleasant surroundings. We saw him as a kind of father figure to us in Japan.

Before we went to the Philippines I stored most of my belongings in Okubo-San's house and took only a backpack with my summer clothes. By that time I had been in Tokyo for six months, had a well-paying job and enjoyed the affluence, the order and cleanliness Japan so generously offered, something I never saw in any other country. I was very fond of the local residents and found I enjoyed their company a great deal.

I Say Goodbye to the Master

Before I left for the Philippines I called my father. I told him I was planning to stay in Japan and study, not saying a word about Okubo-San. Actually I didn't know how to tell him. I said I was going to visit Israel in the summer and then come back, and he was happy we would meet again. He seemed genuinely interested in what I was planning to do.

The Master held a farewell party for me at the club. Everyone came, Sophie and Sherry, and of course, Okubo-San, and all the customers I had served for the past six months, and even three of Okubo-San's employees, who had often accompanied him. It was an emotional evening. The club had been a large part of my life for half a year, it was small and intimate with enough room for only about 20 customers when full. There were upholstered sofas around the tables for people who came either in groups or by themselves but wanted to sit with me, and ten more seats around the central bar where the Master tended the bar, served food to regular customers and chatted with them.

The bar was on the tenth floor and the lighting was

dim. I liked to look out at the lights of Shinjuku, which was one of the largest neighborhoods of Tokyo, watching crowds of people on their way home, lit by the flashing neon signs on the buildings. Tokyo was a city of perpetual motion, and I knew there was no other place like it.

The following morning Sherry and I flew to Manila. Vacationing in the Philippines was a watershed event in my life. It marked the end of the time I has spent with Sherry, and together and individually we had changed our concepts and grown and matured. We discussed our plans during our last night at the hotel in Manila. Sherry was going to return to Israel and then to the United States and I wanted to return to Japan, of which I spoke enthusiastically. I wanted to learn Japanese to break through the language barrier and open the door to life in Tokyo. Even before our vacation I had decided to remain in Japan but now I had definitely made up my mind. My life was going in a new and exciting direction.

Back to School

This time I entered Japan without waiting and being interrogated at all. Along with my passport I had a letter from Okubo-San stating he is my sponsor and I was thus cleared by immigration without a fuss. Okubo-San and Michitaka were waiting for me in the arrival hall. I wanted to rush into his arms and kiss him, but both of us acted with restraint. Michitaka was obviously embarrassed and I understood his feelings perfectly. Once we got home I unpacked and gave them the shirts I bought for them in Manila. We spent the evening as a family eating dinner together and then the children went to play video games in their room. Okubo-San and I watched a movie with English subtitles and talked about my studies, which would begin the following week. He spread a map on the table and marked the route from the house to the school. I felt a great sense of relaxation and security, as he was a person I fully trusted.

The following morning, we went to make final arrangements for me starting school. I was very excited. Okubo-San left me at the school and after I paid tuition for the first three months I received my schedule and a list of textbooks. I had an easy, convenient schedule, two hours in the morning, a long midday break and more classes in the afternoon. The school director said that at the end of the first three months, students were tested in writing, speaking and comprehension, and those who pass the exams move up to the next level. Those who failed would have to repeat the first three months, tuition fees included. I registered for the beginners' course and was told to return the following week, when school began.

When I had finished registering I met Okubo-San at a restaurant. Once I realized the implications of what I had just done and the consequences, I began to feel skittish. I was familiar with Okubo-San from our nights together, but being with him during the day, when he was quiet and serious, was strange and embarrassed me. He said almost nothing during the meal, looked at his watch a couple of times and finally said, "I have to go back to the office. Do you think you can find your way back home alone?" I said I could.

We parted on the street and I felt completely alone. I decided to take a walk and enjoy a little window shopping for a while before taking the train home. Everything I saw was expensive, too expensive for me to waste my hard-earned money on. I would spend it only on one thing, learning Japanese. I bought my textbooks and hurried to the train station.

I didn't really like taking the subway. It was always crowded and there was no way I could find a seat. In addition, the aisles were so crowded I was afraid I would miss my stop. Changing trains meant trying to find the right line and I felt lost and confused. In the end I always found my way, but it was like finding your way through a maze, and it was very depressing. I realized that studying would mean spending one hour on the trains in each direction, so I looked for an alternative, such as buying a scooter.

The house was empty when I arrived home; Okubo-San was at work and the boys were at school. I went from one room to another, picking up and tiding things in what I felt was a logical way. Tomonori's possessions were scattered around the whole house and his room was a mess. There were half-eaten candy bars on the floor, empty glasses, CDs and clothes scattered all over. Michitaka's room was more orderly and took less time to tidy. I had tried to find a way to communicate with the boys. I still really had no way of getting through to them, and it was a real challenge, not just verbally but culturally as well. I knew the new situation was complicated and confusing for them.

After I tidied their rooms I went into the living room and kitchen and tried to organize the cupboards. There was no order anywhere. I took all the children's personal belongings that were scattered all over the kitchen and living room including their comic books, a guitar, clothes etc. and took them to their rooms.

Then I moved the furniture around a little to make the room seem more spacious. I thought perhaps I could do the same thing in the children's rooms, and decided to talk to Okubo-San about it when he came home from work. I wanted to suggest we do it together over the weekend. I obviously wouldn't invade their privacy without permission. Finally, I went into the bedroom. Okubo-San's closet was full of suits, ties and white button-down shirts. I divided the closet in half, rearranged his clothes on one side and hung up my own on the other. I moved the furniture around a little as well so it would be easier to get around.

Finally, I had to prepare dinner for them but I didn't know how to cook. In Israel I had never actually cooked a meal, I just put together the odd bits and pieces. A full meal for a family, however, I had never prepared. Okubo-San came home in the early afternoon with a bag of groceries for the evening meal. I could tell he noticed the changes I had made around the house, but I couldn't tell if he was pleased or not. He didn't say anything, and I sat and watched while he made dinner, writing down everything he did. He obviously knew his way around the kitchen. He took out a large rice sieve, put in five cups of rice and rinsed until the water ran clear. Then he showed me how to measure the water for cooking the rice, according to the markings on the side of the rice cooker. "For five cups of rice you fill it up to here," he said, pointing to the number 5. "Then you press this button and forty-five minutes later the rice will be ready." Rice could be made in the morning; the pot would keep it hot all day long.

In the meantime he filled another pot with water and once it had boiled added a powder that smelled like fish. He cut green onions into thin slices and tofu into cubes, and added them to the boiling water. Ten minutes later he turned off the flame and added a tablespoon of miso, dissolving it by stirring it with chopsticks. He took a wire grill out of a drawer and put it over the gas to cook strips of fresh salmon. Ten minutes later he turned the fish over and cooked the other side. The rice cooker beeped and he called Tomonori and Michitaka into the kitchen and served them soup, rice and salmon. There were various kinds of Japanese pickled vegetables on the table; they always accompanied meals.

He said he made fresh rice every day and it was eaten with every meal, just the way bread was eaten in the West. The miso soup had no fixed recipe, it depended on what the cook felt like making. Spinach, eggplant or potatoes could replace the green onions. He said his children particularly liked fish, but sometimes he made roast meat or hamburgers. The children had never eaten Mediterranean food and asked me to make them an Israeli meal. I was thrilled because I saw it as a way of getting closer to them, and got thinking of what I could prepare for them.

That evening, when we were alone, I asked Okubo-San to ask the boys, in a way that wouldn't be offensive, to be tidier. I raised the idea of rearranging the rooms and he agreed and suggested we would all do it together the following weekend.

Two nights later I served an Israeli meal. We had chicken schnitzel, mashed potatoes, salad, avocados and chicken soup. I could tell by the way they looked at the avocado they had never seen any before, let alone tasted it. They were very expensive in Japan and not very popular; I had bought three. I promised I would cook other Israeli dishes too.

Despite the apparent smooth transition into Okubo-San's home, I still didn't feel I belonged there, and I felt even more foreign when Okubo-San left in the evenings to entertain clients. Tomonori and Michitaka were in their rooms and I was left alone in the living room to think and reflect on the step I had taken, and it seemed more and more insane. More than once I considered escaping this new reality I was living in, and to return to the life I had known when I worked for the Master.

My language studies were particularly grueling despite the midday break, and I was under a lot of pressure. Every day we learned new kanji symbols and had vocabulary tests at the end of each week. Beyond recognizing the characters, we also had to learn how the words changed in different contexts. They could be read in Japanese or Chinese and there were of course exceptions. It was all a matter of memorization and I couldn't always find a mnemonic device or other ways to memorize them, so I spent endless days and hours writing them over and over again. Tomonori and Michitaka happily helped me with my homework. They corrected my spelling and taught me the strict kanji rules. Every letter had to be written in a certain direction and they said it was the foundation for learning kanji. Japanese is written vertically from left to right, and it was difficult for me because I was used to writing from right to left. They had a Japanese-English dictionary and they used it to help me when I searched for a word. Tomonori spoke to me with the little English he knew and that helped, especially when our communication got stuck. It also helped me a lot in getting closer to him. Michitaka, on the other hand, kept his distance unless his brother was present.

After a month I started to speak basic Japanese. I felt the language barrier was slowly beginning to lift and the children and I were closer to each other. Most of the time we either talked about my Japanese lessons or their English lessons, but our lives continued pleasantly. They invited their friends over, all of whom were very interested in the foreign woman living in their home. Almost every day when I returned home they were waiting for me with a group of friends. They would rise and bow, their expressions both shy and curious. Their attempts to greet me in English always put a smile on my face. Their friends called them Okubo-Kun. When I asked why, I was told that the suffix *San* was for adults and *Kun* for children, and always followed the family name. His employees always called him Okubo-San, but at home they used first names. I asked him that evening if what the children told me was correct, and he confirmed it indeed was, and added I could call him by his first name, Makoto.

I was embarrassed, because I understood that for the past months I had been calling him by a formal name that was inappropriate for our relationship. I couldn't understand why no one, including him, hadn't bothered to correct me. I decided it wasn't worth the fuss and from then on called him by his first name, Makoto. I called Tomonori Tomo, which is what his father called him, but continued calling Michitaka by his full name, because he didn't have a nickname.

At the end of the second week we went to visit Makoto's parents, who lived in Tsukuba, a city about 60 miles from Tokyo. On the way he told me Shizuka, his father, had been in a traffic accident ten years previously and had sustained a serious head injury. Before the accident he had participated in regional marathons and for years had run six miles every evening. One evening he was hit by a young man riding a motorcycle and was tossed into the air, hitting his head on the road as he landed. He had surgery and spent six months recuperating in the hospital. Unfortunately, he was finally diagnosed as having suffered irreparable brain damage. He was confined to a wheelchair and spent his days watching TV, unaware of how serious his condition was or what was going on around him.

Kurako, Makoto's mother, has been taking care of him since he got home from the hospital. Fortunately, his father had been thrifty and saved enough money during the years prior to the accident, so the situation was not compounded by economic worries, and she could remain at his side.

From the outside his parents' house looked like a giant pagoda. Japanese tradition was evident everywhere, both inside the house and outside. It was surrounded by a large, well-maintained garden, every plant standing in its place and every hedge perfectly trimmed. There was a bamboo forest behind the house on land that belonged to the family. Makoto told me they had a gardener who came regularly.

The house was extremely impressive and entering it was like walking onto a movie set about ancient Japan. There were many sliding doors, each one leading to a room in which either clothes or food were stored. Some of the doors could be moved or dismantled to change the interior of the house according to need. The floor was covered with tatami mats and the entire first floor was surrounded by a closed porch with glass doors overlooking the garden.

Makoto's mother came from a wealthy landowning family, all of whom lived in the same area, and whose assets had been passed down from generation to generation. After the accident Kurako had rented out a lot of the land to local farmers, bringing in a monthly income.

She was waiting for us and received us with a smile.

She was a small woman whose looks belied her age. She asked Makoto to translate for her and said she was happy to meet me and apologized for not speaking English. She said, "If my son loves you, I love you too." That meant so much to me and I was quite moved..

Norio, Makoto's older brother, had come especially to meet me, and I felt embarrassed. He was seven years older than Makoto and spoke English fluently, having lived in New York for three years in his youth. In appearance he was very different from his brother, short and not very handsome. His first words were, "Do you love my brother? I hope your intentions are serious. I am worried you will hurt him. He is a little naïve and tends to trust people."

He was honest with me so I was honest with him in return. I said, "I love Makoto very much but I'm still not certain if I will remain in Japan." He looked at me suspiciously and I explained I had to get to know his children and see if we could get along, and if we could I would remain. It was evident from his expression that what I said had displeased him. However, I rather liked him, and as dinner progressed and we kept talking he seemed to warm up to me more and was less suspicious. I thought it was probably because we were speaking in English, which made for much better communication.

Regular biweekly visits to his parents followed my initial encounter with his family and Kurako and I formed a bond that transcended language. I loved visiting the house and neighborhood. It was impossible not to love them and the vast space which simply didn't exist in Tokyo. The entire region was carpeted with rice fields, and it was always pleasant to replace Tokyo's grayness with the green fresh lush stretching around us for miles.

Eventually I knew I couldn't procrastinate any longer and I had to tell my father, especially since I had decided to stay in Tokyo. We talked about it the first time when I returned from the Philippines. Now I told him about Makoto and he said, "I had the feeling you had fallen in love in Japan and that's what was keeping you from coming back to Israel." He said he was happy for me, which surprised me, and added that before my mother had died he promised her he would let me choose my own path in life, including my love life. He was happy I would soon be coming to visit and admitted it was difficult for him to accept that I would be living so far away from home. It was one of the most open conversations we had ever had. He said sometimes he felt guilty about how I had grown up and how sad my early years had been, and repeated he was glad I had found happiness.

I told Makoto about the conversation with my father and he suggested he accompany me to Israel to ask my father for permission to marry me. That added a new dimension to the trip and I was happy I had only one month left of language school.

The first three months had passed quickly. I was completely dedicated to my studies because my goal was to break through the language barrier and have fluent conversations with Michitaka, Tomonori and Kurako. After school I continued studying at home, looking up words in the dictionary and practicing writing kanji. I had to narrow the gap between me and the other Asian students in the class who came from Hong Kong, Taiwan, South Korea and China, who had the advantage of knowing the Chinese characters. Although they had to learn how to pronounce the words in Japanese they already knew the meaning, which was vastly different from my situation. However, I had the advantage of living with a Japanese man and spending time with his family so I could practice almost non-stop. At the end of the first three months I passed all the exams and moved up to the next level.

The students in my class kept to themselves and showed no interest in conversing with foreigners. The only exception and the only one I felt comfortable with was a girl named Cai. Initially I thought she was Asian but it turned out she was Australian. Her mother was Japanese and her father was Vietnamese, and they had lived in Australia for many years. Since she spoke English we could communicate easily. She was stunningly beautiful and dressed in the latest fashion.

Our friendship grew and after class we would go to coffee shops and talk about almost everything. She had a Japanese boyfriend who was also called Makoto, which we both found very funny. She said her Makoto was older and married and had told her quite frankly that he had no intention of divorcing his wife. However, he loved Cai and had promised to sponsor her in Japan, and was also paying for her language studies.

I told her about my Makoto, who had no wife but two children. When I told her he had proposed marriage she warned me not to marry a Japanese man. Actually, she wasn't the only one; practically everyone I spoke with pulled a face and warned me against it. The main reason was that Japanese men were difficult to get along with and inattentive to their wives. I was confused. I was head over heels in love but kept hearing about cultural differences and the language barrier, things I would never be able to overcome.

I had conflicting thoughts and emotions which fluctuated almost daily. Nationality aside, just looking at him the way he was, I knew he was the man I wanted to spend the rest of my life with. His love for his children was captivating. He was a devoted father and invested everything he could into raising them. As my command of the language improved I conversed better with Michitaka and Tomonori, and we began to develop a warm relationship. I got to know them and enjoyed their company. They taught me about the music and fashion of Japanese youth. They enriched my vocabulary with slang that no school teacher would ever teach. When I tried to impress my teacher by talking like a street punk she was horrified. "You're a girl, you must never say such things," she said in a very stern voice. There was no way I could ask her why, so later I asked Makoto. He said, "In Japan men and women speak differently. Women must not use the same words as men use, especially young men and boys."

Nevertheless, I couldn't internalize the significance of the difference between men and women in Japan. It took years before I learned, the hard way, the differences in the Japanese language and in other aspects, between men and women.

Israel: First Visit

A year had passed since I left Israel with a one-way ticket. It was summer vacation and I decided the time had come to go home for a visit. Makoto would come two weeks after me because first I had to talk to my father about my plan to stay in Tokyo. We had spoken about it on the phone but I wanted to talk to him again, this time in person, so that everything was clear and no question went unanswered.

My family was waiting for me at the airport in Tel Aviv. Seeing them, especially my father, was a very emotional moment. What made me even happier than a family reunion was knowing I had a return ticket to Tokyo. Staying a month in the place I had fled from was going to be one very long haul, especially since it meant daily friction with my father and his wife, Charlette. I really didn't want to buy the plane ticket and I was frustrated. It wasn't going to be easy to return to a place with so many bad memories, especially when I was dreading having to meet Charlette again. She was one of the main reasons I became alienated from my father and fled from Israel. I didn't like the way she treated him, and I had watched them bicker and argue for years.

But I was coming to the meeting as a completely

different person, different and much stronger. Instead of the angry, accusing Suzy I used to be, I was now a calm, happy Suzy. Actually, I was surprised by my ability to remain objective and restrained. I had no need to react to what was going on around me, I didn't hate anyone, and just kept my distance. I believe that knowing I would be there for a short period helped me keep control of my emotions.

My room was exactly as I had left it and all my possessions were still there. As soon as I saw nothing had been changed I went to the window to look out at the beach. The sea and an Israeli summer were the two things I missed most. Summer in Tokyo was even hotter and more humid than in Tel Aviv. During the summer all the Japanese stay at home or escape to air-conditioned shopping centers or offices. It is almost impossible to stay outdoors. We only went out into the street during the summer if we had no other choice, and walking was a nightmare. On the other hand, the air conditioning was very strong and if everything was closed it was freezing inside. Going out to the scorching heat then in to the freezing cold back and forth all day made us all get sick.

I was looking at the scenery of my childhood when my father peeked in and asked me if I wanted to eat something. He had gone to the local supermarket and returned with bags full of things I could not find in Japanese supermarkets. There were pitas and whole wheat bread, eggplant salad, a Romanian fish roe salad called *ikra*, red cabbage and mayonnaise salad, hummus, tahini, pastrami and salami, even cottage cheese, hard salty white cheese, and semi-soft bland white cheese, all the foods I loved, I was ecstatic. The

Japanese bread was white, soft and sweet, and tasted more like cake than bread. I missed eating bread and pitas and Israeli cheeses. I sat at the table and enjoyed the food more than I would have enjoyed a meal at a gourmet restaurant.

The date of Makoto's arrival was approaching and it was imperative that I speak to my father before, especially to deal with all of his expected opposition to my plans. I told him Makoto was divorced and had two children. At that point my father asked to postpone the discussion until after he had met Makoto and seen what he was like. One thing he did say, very sternly, was, "You had better know right now that the day will come when you find out for yourself why she left him. Don't forget that there are always two sides to every divorce." There was nothing I could say to that and it took me years to discover the reason. My father again told me what he had promised my mother that he would never interfere in my life or my choice of a partner. "I'm sorry you've chosen to live so far away, but it's your decision. Just remember, no matter what happens, you can always come home. Don't be embarrassed. I want your Japanese man to know that you have a home and that you have a father who loves you and cares about you."

His words touched my very core. I always knew, deep inside, that I had a place to return to, and that no matter what happened, no matter where I was, my father would always bring me home, but I was still happy to hear him say it. It was important for me to know he respected my decisions even if they were contrary to his expectations, and to know he wouldn't close the door on me because of the path I had chosen.

Charlette was no longer a threat. Knowing I had a life waiting for me in Japan eased the feelings of resentment and opposition I had harbored for so long. I had also managed to put aside all the history between us, secure in the knowledge that in a month she would be out of my life again. Our mutual ceasefire changed the atmosphere at home and I enjoyed myself far more than I thought I would.

Makoto's plane landed at night. When I picked him up from the airport I could see he was tired from the flight and nervous, probably about meeting my family. I didn't want to make life harder for him so I kept quiet. Even though it was late my father waited for us. He shook Makoto's hand and said, "I want you to feel at home here." He told Makoto to use the home phone to call his sons whenever he liked and wished him a pleasant stay. It was a very nice gesture which warmed my heart, and I hoped it would make Makoto loosen up. He thanked my father and said his children, Tomonori and Michitaka, were with their mother in Okinawa and had given her our phone number in case of emergencies.

Despite the late hour I suggested we go to the beach in Herzliya, which wasn't far from our house. After having seen the Japanese coast, I knew I had nothing to be ashamed of. We found vacant beach chairs and watched as people walked by. It was quiet and all we could hear was the waves. We had a week of vacation at our disposal; that was all the time Makoto could take off work. I told him what I had planned, and the next morning we were on a plane from Tel Aviv's airport on our way to Eilat. I had reserved two nights at the Princess Hotel, which was new and recently opened.

Everything was shiny and clean, which was a relief for me because Makoto wasn't so sure about staying there.

He loved Eilat and the desert. The scenery was unlike anything he had ever seen because outside the cities in Japan, everything was mostly forests and green. I pointed in different directions like an excited tour guide, here we are in Israel, that's the Red Sea, over there is Egypt and that side is Jordan.

We spent most of the day in the hotel pool and in the afternoon walked along the Eilat promenade. It was my chance to buy clothing and books in Hebrew, because in Eilat there was no VAT. Makoto was very quiet but I knew he was trying to get acclimatized. He kept looking around, and I caught glimpses of him looking displeased and even disgusted. I knew it was hard for him to come to terms with Israel's informality, and it worried me, but on the other hand I knew an Israeli-Japanese couple arouse curiosity, and people stared at us shamelessly. When Makoto mentioned it I laughed and said, "That's exactly how I feel in Japan, that people are staring at me all the time. Now you know how uncomfortable it feels."

We flew back to Tel Aviv and my sister Haya picked us up at the airport. We arrived exactly in time for Friday dinner, the biggest meal of the week in Israel, often with the whole family present. The meal was indeed festive, my father blessed the wine in Makoto's honor. We ate and drank and it was a wonderful way for Makoto to meet my extended family.

After dinner we sat in the garden and my father wanted to know Makoto's full name. He asked how he should address him. I explained how people addressed one another in Japan. From that day he called him Okubo-San.

The relaxed atmosphere was the perfect opportunity for Makoto. He took out the "Hebrew" text we had written in katakana in Tokyo and read, "I want to marry Suzy, she will be happy with me in Japan." It sounded pretty much like Hebrew. It struck a chord with my father, who said, "I hope she really will be. Take care of her, she's my youngest and very dear to me." Makoto smiled because he knew that he had just received permission from my father to marry me.

After a Saturday of visiting Caesarea, Haifa and the port of Acre, I felt my family was beginning to get used to the idea that Makoto and I were a couple. When I was in the army, my brother and his wife had lived in Japan for a year, and Makoto's visit was an opportunity for my brother to practice the few words of Japanese he remembered from working at a street stall. Makoto also made an effort and successfully initiated conversations with my family in English.

On Sunday we went to the Dead Sea. In geography lessons Makoto had learned it was the lowest place on Earth, but never expected to see it. He was impressed by its beauty and asked me to take pictures. Enjoying ourselves as a couple was good for both of us. Late that night, lying next to him in the hotel, I thought how wonderful it was that he had come into my life. We weren't emotionally extravagant but the look in his eyes, his gestures and the things he said showed he was happy being with me, enjoying himself and glad of the opportunity to become acquainted with my home and family.

The next morning, he was a little less restrained and

before we left the Dead Sea on our way to Jerusalem, he decided he would drive instead of me. He admired the colored strata of the rocks in the Negev, Israel's desert, which were unlike anything he had ever seen before. In Jerusalem we went to the Old City and the local market, where he bought typical Israeli sandals and souvenirs for his children, his family and his employees, since after every trip, even inside Japan, it was customary to bring presents. The vendors immediately realized they had a tourist with full pockets and were only too happy to suggest things for him to buy. We stopped for lunch in one of the market restaurants and I said we should have grilled meat, which he liked very much. I teased him by saying, "Now you're a real Israeli."

We went to the Western Wall, which he had read about and it filled him with awe. I showed him the Jewish side of Jerusalem and the Muslim side, and his surprise grew when he saw the crowd of black-clothed men, the ultra-Orthodox Jews, at the Wall and in the alleys. Until then he had only seen them in pictures.

We spent his last day in Israel with my father on the beach in Herzliya. We swam in the Mediterranean Sea, drank beer and enjoyed everything the beach had to offer. It was in this relaxed setting that my father surprised me by saying to Makoto, "The next time you come, bring the children." No other words were needed, it summed up my father's conclusion. Makoto smiled and nodded, and promised he would bring them the following summer.

There was only one thing I still had to do before Makoto went back to Tokyo. On the last night we were in

Israel, I invited all my best friends to meet him. I had written to them regularly during the past year about life in Tokyo and meeting Makoto. They knew how I felt about him and the doubts that were plaguing me, and their opinion was important to me. They agreed he met their expectations and were surprised how handsome he was. Even my father said he "didn't look like a typical Japanese." In Israel people thought all Japanese looked the same: short with glasses. Makoto was tall and the only glasses he wore were sun glasses. I kept saying there were a lot of tall Japanese men who didn't wear glasses, but no one believed me. My friends checked him over, top to bottom, and said he not only looked good, he looked young for his age.

The next morning I took him to the airport, and before he could check his bags, he underwent a rigorous security interrogation. He was surprised by how many questions he was asked and how nervous it made him. Finally, in order to reassure him, I had to intervene. I said he was my guest, that he had been with me throughout his visit to Israel, and that since he had no Hebrew and very little English, I would answer instead of him. Fifteen minutes later he was allowed to go on to the check-in counters. I explained that Israel was often the victim of terrorist attacks and there were security alerts every day, which meant more questions for people entering and leaving the country. Makoto knew nothing about international terrorism; there were no terrorist attacks in Japan and the concept was hard for him to grasp. We parted promising to meet again very soon.

After he left I had two weeks in Israel before I returned to Japan. My two-year visa had been approved and I went to pick it up at the Japanese embassy. I wanted to spend the remaining time with my high school and army friends, but especially with my three best friends. I wanted to hear their honest opinion of Makoto and my plans to marry him. They weren't enthusiastic about the marriage to say the least and told me so. They admitted that they only knew about Japanese culture what they'd seen in the movies, and based on that, women clearly had an inferior position so they were afraid I would be miserable. I told them movies didn't reflect reality, especially not regarding what life was like in Tokyo today.

"Japan," I said, "is very modern, and the status of women is about that of women in Israel." That was how it seemed to me over the past year, but to be honest with myself I knew I really had no idea of what it was like for an insider. It was years before I came to understand how different the status of Japanese women was to that of Western women. They wanted to know if I loved him that much I'd be willing to give up on Israel. They failed to understand that it was thanks to him I could escape a life I hated from the depths of my heart.

The final two weeks passed quickly. I packed a couple of things from my old room, to remind me of the place that would always be waiting for me if I wanted to go back home. My father was upset because he didn't know when he would see me again. He said he would buy a fax machine so we could communicate quickly and more cheaply than by phone. I was happy when the day arrived and I could take a plane back to Makoto and the children and begin a new chapter in my life. My heart had left Israel.

Days of Prosperity

When I returned to Tokyo I found the house in complete disarray. The children had come home from their mother only the week before but it was enough. The living room was full of things that didn't belong and plates and bowls from the kitchen were all lying around with bits of food stuck to them. It took me an entire week to restore the house to its previous condition. As order returned, so did routine. I went back to learning Japanese and Makoto worked late every night. The children also had classes until late so I came home from school every day to an empty house. I used the quiet to study and memorize new kanji characters, and sometimes I went out with my girlfriends. When Sophie returned from a visit to France I was happy to include her in my circle and I introduced her to Cai-San, my friend from school. What we liked best was to go to the clubs in Roppongi, which were mostly frequented by foreigners.

From time to time I invited them to my home, and Sophie slept in the guest room. Her fluent Japanese made her popular with Tomonori and Michitaka, who didn't miss any opportunity to talk to her. I had the feeling she represented Tokyo's young popular crowd to them, and they adored her. I was still miles away from being able to converse freely with them. They had very little command of English and they didn't seem to be making much of an effort to improve. That was one of the things that prompted me to try as hard as I could to improve my Japanese, and it took me half a year of intensive studies before I could break through the language barrier. At that point I felt they lost their reticence and they seemed to feel more comfortable with me. They got used to the food I prepared and they also stopped trying to avoid me and find ways not to answer me when I spoke to them. When Makoto came home late from work we watched movies together and prepared their favorite desserts.

Makoto did everything he could to strengthen our relationship, which made me happy. Every couple of days he would call me from work and suggest we go out, just the two of us, for some form of entertainment. Most of the time we went to clubs, and after a couple of drinks he was more relaxed and spoke more freely. A certain amount of alcohol made him a joy to be with. But when he drank too much I was disgusted. He would stagger out of the club into a cab and once he even forgot the address, which was embarrassing as we had to walk around the neighborhood until we found the house. In the morning he would wake up with no memory of it at all.

Those years Japan enjoyed economic prosperity. Salaries were very high and people had a lot of money. Employment conditions were excellent and employees received all kinds of benefits. There was a covert competition to see whose employees received the most benefits, at the very least an overseas vacation at a five-star hotel. However, the bonuses were for the employees, not their wives.

Wives were not included in the company's environment and that was an utter surprise to me. I found out about it two months after I had moved in with Makoto. He said that one of his employees was getting married the following weekend, and I asked the obvious question: "What should I wear? I don't have anything suitable for a wedding." He looked at me in amazement and said, "You aren't invited." I said, "What?" He explained weddings were expensive and very few people were invited, only family and people the bride and groom knew personally.

The usual present was $300 per guest, money which went to help pay for the wedding. If I had gone with him he would have had to pay $600, which at the time was unreasonable to expect from any guest at an Israeli wedding. Obviously, I realized I wouldn't be going with him but my curiosity got the better of me. I wanted to know what the ceremony was like because one day it would be my wedding. Makoto said it began at ten in the morning and ended at noon. I wanted to know why it ended so early, and with his patience having run out he uttered, "Because that's the way it's done." I managed to extract a little more information from him. Apparently, weddings in Japan are not that different from Westerns weddings. They are usually divided in two parts: the ceremony and the party, followed by an after-party. The reception usually begins with formal introduction speeches from the bride and groom. After the banquet, guests can make speeches as well. The couple swaps rings, cuts a cake at the reception, and at the end, the bride throws a bouquet to the next lucky girl. A few hours later, the after-party takes place. While the reception has a more formal feel, the after-party is quite casual, as it is a gathering of close friends. There was no meal included, only snacks and a giant wedding cake and a lot of alcohol. They played a video of the ceremony and if the family held a religious ceremony in a Shinto shrine, a video of that would also be shown.

That morning Makoto wore a fancy black suit with a white tie. He put some new bills into a *noshi-bukuro*, a type of envelope used specifically for giving gifts of money. It was decorated with a bow made of several strands of thin red metal thread, and he wrote his name on it with black ink. He said goodbye, leaving me depressed for being excluded from the wedding. A local woman would have accepted it without question, but I wasn't a local woman, and it made me consider the miserable status of the Japanese wife, who waits at home for her husband and is never invited to join him at weddings or on the vacations provided by his company. The more I thought about it the more uneasy I felt.

He came back in the afternoon with a bag full of presents. "What's that?" I asked. He said it was customary to give wedding guests presents worth about $50. "It's a way of thanking the guest for coming to the wedding and for his gift." I opened the bag and found three boxes inside. One held a tea set, cups and saucers, another, a bath towel, and the third, cookies. This made me laugh. Makoto asked me to remove the presents from the boxes and use them. Over the years he attended many weddings because his employees were young, and since I didn't want to stay at home feeling sorry for myself we agreed he would tell me about upcoming weddings and I would make arrangements to go to a movie or a restaurant in Tokyo with Cai and Sophie. Even at the beginning of our relationship I understood there were essential differences between the behavior of Japanese and Israeli couples. In retrospect I think I initially ignored it in the hope we would be different because I was a foreigner. I honestly believed he would spend more time with me than men usually spent with their wives if both were Japanese.

On the weekends we were a family. I liked the children's company and during the week I spent time together with them at home. Makoto came home from work at eight and on nights he went out drinking he returned before midnight. Initially it didn't bother me because I needed the time for my language studies, and I spent hours working hard to speak it fluently.

Every now and then Makoto would raise the issue of marriage. He told me how important it was for him, and especially for his parents and children, and said we should set a date soon. He kept telling me that in Japan it was unacceptable for men and women to live together before marriage, and it was important for us to formalize our relationship because of the children.

I, on the other hand, wanted to put the wedding off for as long as possible. I still hadn't come to terms with my new life and I wanted an escape route in case I changed my mind. But Makoto wouldn't leave the subject alone, and eventually it became the main topic of our conversations.

He promised me I would have a good life with him, he would take care of me and would make me happy. He wanted me to have a child and to know the joys of motherhood. Despite the fact I wanted to postpone it, I agreed to marry him and we set the date for November 1994, exactly two years to the month after I arrived in Japan.

I called my sister to tell her the news. "I'm coming to Tokyo to be with you," she said joyously, "I won't let you get married alone." I knew she had felt responsible for me since our mother had died, and she still felt and acted that way. I was happy to know she still had my back.

The idea of a wedding confused my father but he decided to keep his opinion to himself. "I wish you all the best," was all he said; it was a very short phone call. He said he wouldn't come for the wedding but wished me success on the path I had chosen. "Just remember," he said, "I miss you terribly and I'm here for whatever you need." I promised him Makoto and I would visit Israel to celebrate our wedding and also promised I would come for a visit every year; that was the agreement I had with Makoto.

My sister Haya came to Japan and Makoto admired her for the efforts she had made, aware of the depth of our feelings for each other. He had arranged for us to spend a week at the best hotels in Kyoto, Nara and Ise-Shima.

We spent three days in Kyoto, most of the time walking around, sightseeing, and Haya called it "the Jerusalem of Japan." I could understand why, because it was the historical and cultural heart of Japan. It is home to numerous Buddhist temples, Shinto shrines, palaces and gardens, so it looked like a Japanese movie set.

We visited the Kiyomizu-dera Buddhist temple, built into the side of a hill and to reach it we walked through narrow alleys with stores selling souvenirs, Japanese art and traditional Japanese food. We were amazed by the Kinkaku-ji, also called the Golden Pavilion, mostly because of its golden color reflected in the pond surrounding it. We also visited the famous bamboo grove located in Arashiyama.

It was very important for me to let Haya participate in a traditional Japanese tea ceremony in one of the temples. As I expected, she enjoyed it very much. On one night, we were lucky to see two Geishas walking to work in Gion quarter. They wore colorful kimonos and carried paper parasols, and looked like porcelain dolls.

From Kyoto we took the train to Nara, once the ancient capital of Japan; the trip took about an hour. We visited the Todai-ji Buddhist temple, the largest wooden structure, housing a bronze statue of Buddha, the largest Buddha in world. The temple is surrounded by a large, beautiful park with deer. Very tame, they came up to us and we fed them the crackers we had bought at the entrance of the park. The deer are considered to be the messenger of god by the Buddhists.

In the afternoon we took the train and travelled to Ise-Shima, where a pleasant surprise was waiting for us. The hotel Makoto had booked for us had a spa and was situated on an island. We checked in, took our clothes off, put on the hotel robes and went to a doctor who examined our eyes, throats, fingernails and stomachs and arranged for a series of treatments which would be carried out over the next two days of our stay. We spent the entire day, from dawn to dusk, with massages and hot tubs and various treatments. We ate three meals a day in the hotel's French restaurant and were treated like royalty.

I was so happy to be able to spend a week with my sister and greatly appreciated the effort she had made to come for my wedding. If she hadn't, I would have been in the embarrassing position of being in the center of my event surrounded only by people who didn't speak my language. A foreigner, eyed with curiosity and suspicion. The thought of sitting alone at my own wedding and not knowing anyone scared me, so I felt very grateful that Haya would be with me. Both wedding events; the one for the family and the one for the friends were quickly approaching.

The event for the family began at noon, guests slowly arriving at the hotel, the only one with a hall near Makoto's parents' house. Kurako had one sister, who came with her husband and daughter, but his father had seven brothers and sisters, and they basically filled the small hall. The ceremony began in the Japanese fashion, with restraint and in silence. I was familiar with the custom by now and knew it would all change once the alcohol began flowing, which is exactly what happened. After a few drinks everyone lightened up. One after the other the guests took to the stage to sing karaoke. They gave Makoto and me their blessings, and told Makoto how lucky he was to have found a beautiful, young wife from overseas.

The event for friends was to take place the following Saturday evening in the bar where I used to work and where Makoto and I first met. The Master was happy to host the party and closed the bar to outsiders. Makoto surprised me by telling me he wanted the event for friends to be "Israeli style". He remembered I had told him that couples came together to Israeli weddings, and that's what we decided to do for our party. I invited all my friends, some of them still living in the guesthouse, and some of the students and teachers from the language school, and of course my sister and my close friends Sophie and Cai. Makoto invited only a small number of his friends from his university days. He didn't want to invite his employees, given his strict division between work and personal lives. It turned out that most of them didn't even know we had gotten married. This was difficult for me to come to terms with, and deep down I didn't actually believe it. I once confronted him about it and asked if he hadn't told them he was getting married because he was simply ashamed of me. No, he said, he wasn't ashamed, "I simply don't like people talking about me behind my back."

He arranged a day for us for photoshoots at a studio. It involved preparations that took several hours. We wore two kinds of outfits, Western and Japanese. I was glad my sister was still with me because no one else could have laughed so much with me when I saw myself in the mirror wearing a kimono and all the paraphernalia that went with it. Once I was dressed they painted my face, neck and arms a bright white, and finally they placed a traditional bride's wig on my head. Preparations for the Western-style photos were much simpler.

My sister had to return to Israel. She had enjoyed her stay and was happy she could be with me. Before we parted she said, "This visit was unforgettable. Japan is amazing and I promise I will come to visit you often."

We honeymooned in Hawaii and took the children with us. It was a mutual decision. I felt responsible for them because I was now married to their father. I wanted them to trust me and I wanted them to feel secure, proving to them that by entering their home and their life I was by no means a threat to them. They had to feel wanted and know that I wished them to be happy. They had obviously been scarred by their parents' divorce. I couldn't and had no intent to replace their mother but I wanted a good relationship with them and I knew, from my own experience, you only have one mother. I wanted to succeed where my father's second wife had failed.

I was surprised to find Hawaii full of Japanese tourists. They were everywhere, in the streets, on the beach, in the restaurants, and the popular restaurants had menus in Japanese. Even people in stores could hold conversations in basic Japanese. I told Makoto I felt I was still in Japan and we had gone on vacation to one of the islands.

That winter I joined the advanced Japanese language class and could identify about a thousand kanji symbols, which was half of what I needed for my diploma. I took two government exams and passed them both. However, there were two more exams that included the other thousand signs and a lot of new words. I had a long road ahead, and I was at the point where many students gave up and dropped out. There were a lot of reasons that would justify such a decision: tuition fees were high, studies demanded an enormous investment of time and effort, and you ultimately had learned enough to be able to speak with the people around you. Nevertheless, I decided to persevere and pass the final exam in the highest level. I wanted to learn how to read and write, and I wanted, finally, to be able to read the daily newspaper.

As the wife of a Japanese man I got a visa for a year which would then be extended to a permanent residence visa. After several years I could get a Japanese passport but it meant I would have to give up my Israeli passport, which I was unwilling to do. I always felt I was an Israeli and a foreigner in Japan.

Makoto was often absent because of late night meetings with his clients or employees, and I still wasn't used to staying at home without him. Once we were married he became a lot less considerate. His evenings of bar-hopping often lasted until late at night and sometimes into the early hours of the morning, which I wasn't informed about until the last minute. Most of the time I finished preparing dinner and was eagerly waiting for his return, but he would then call and say, "I'm so sorry, but a client just walked into my office and I have to take him out for drinks." That happened at least three times a week, leaving me awake and alone in bed, tossing and turning for hours, unable to fall asleep.

It was a very difficult situation. I couldn't relax until he returned and was in bed next to me, so I cried and was upset all the time, and I kept asking him, "Why did you marry me?" My question was sincere. "Were you looking for a nanny and a housekeeper? I won't stay in Japan just to be your servant. I'm sick and tired of it!" Each time he would hug me and ask for my forgiveness. He blamed work, said it kept him busy all the time, and promised over and over again to make it up to me on the weekend, a promise he always kept. My closet was a silent witness to his promises. Almost every weekend he bought me new clothing and jewelry, but no present could make up for my genuine desire for his presence.

We argued more and more, and he stayed away more often. At one point I began raising my voice and shouting at him, most of the time in English, and he would look at me helplessly. Sometimes he didn't seem to be able to follow what I was saying. It didn't matter to me whether or not he did, what I needed was to let out my anger and frustration. I felt I had been deceived, and that infuriated me. His coming home drunk with a stupid smile on his face enraged me even further. I cried almost every day.

A Visit to the Homeland

Winter ended and the summer vacation arrived. As promised, I told my father we were coming to visit, this time with the children, who were very excited to travel. We planned to visit most of the tourist sites in Israel, many of which Makoto had told the children about.

Once we landed and passed through customs and immigration we went straight to the car rental agency and began a trip of ten days. First we went up north where we stayed with relatives in a kibbutz. It reminded me of scenes from my childhood. I had always liked visiting them. My mother's cousin took us for a tour around the kibbutz showing the children the apple orchard and the kibbutz factory, which were all very new experiences for them.

From there we drove along the Lebanese border and down to the Sea of Galilee. We spent the night in Safed, a city of artists, and Tomonori and Michitaka liked its narrow winding alleys and little souvenir shops. I told them not to buy too much, it would be better to save their money for Jerusalem, where I promised prices would be much cheaper.

During the drive to the Dead Sea Makoto told them about his visit there with me, and they were excited about the idea of floating on the water, which was so salty it would hold them up. We took pictures of them coating themselves with mud, first suspiciously and then with enthusiasm. From the Dead Sea we drove to Eilat, Israel's southernmost city, where other attractions awaited. We rode camels, snorkeled, swam with dolphins and went from one tourist attraction to another.

From Eilat we drove to Jerusalem and the next day my family came to stay with us. Together we toured the walls of Jerusalem and as promised, took the children to the stores in the Old City's market, where they bought souvenirs for their friends. The only unpleasant incident was when a group of children from the Old City approached Makoto, surrounded him and demanded he buy postcards from them. He wasn't impolite like Israelis, and in his own way tried to get away from them, and eventually did. Only after they had disappeared did he discover they had picked his pocket and his wallet was gone, with his money, credit card and driver's license. My father, as the host, felt responsible despite his absolute lack of involvement in the incident. It was a blow to Makoto and left him bitter and with a negative memory of Jerusalem, which unfortunately influenced his general impression of Israel.

We went to the police station with the hope they could get his wallet back. They showed us pictures of children who were known to pickpocket but he couldn't identify any of them because to his eyes, unfamiliar with the local physiognomy, they all looked the same. The police told us the same thing happened almost every day, and most of the pickpockets were children. He warned us not to let it happen again, and let us call the Japanese credit card company from the police station to report the theft.

Fortunately, I had also came with money and a credit card and Jerusalem was the last stop on our trip. We spent the last days of our vacation at my father's house in Herzliya, going to the beach every day. The night before we left we held a party in my father's garden to celebrate our marriage. Only a few people were invited – close family and friends. Everyone wanted to meet Makoto and the children, who were the center of attention; the Japanese family of an Israeli wasn't something they saw every day.

The children were perfectly comfortable in my father's house, and he indulged them with ice cream and all kinds of Middle Eastern desserts. Going to the beach every day was also something new and interesting. After two unforgettable weeks in Israel, Makoto and the children returned to Japan and I stayed for two more weeks. I wanted to spend time with my family and my best friends. We went shopping for the things I couldn't get in Japan – books, spices, clothes in my size and shoes.

We also found time to just talk and I told them about the problems I was having with Makoto. They told me about their problems with their husbands, and I discovered that all couples, regardless of their ethnicities, had complex relations, difficulties and disagreements, that demanded constant efforts to resolve. Knowing I wasn't alone in my martial struggles consoled me a little.

Back Home in Japan

Being in Israel hadn't influenced me alone, Makoto too discovered how much the lack of my presence affected him. When we talked on the phone, and also when I returned to Japan, I could feel a change. He felt alone without me and said he missed me. The children, on the other hand, didn't care one way or the other. When I returned I found the house was in a mess again. I was angry at their negligence and said so, but they didn't react. When I threatened to throw out everything they had left in the living room, they giggled. Despite my anger I organized the house again.

The change in Makoto didn't last long. At first he came home from work early and I could enjoy his company the way I had when I was falling in love with him. If he had to host a client or take his employees clubbing, he would tell me the day before. I felt secure again but to my disappointment the change only lasted a month. He started going out regularly again, sometimes not giving me much of a warning, and sometimes he didn't come home until very late at night. He justified his behavior with various excuses which only made me angrier. "I'm not a Japanese wife who will accept her husband's stories," I stormed. "I know exactly what happens at those clubs, I worked in one, and you can't fool me. I remember how easy it was for managers to get up and leave their employees at ten at night, it's perfectly acceptable if you're married."

He kept insisting it was impossible and tried to soothe me by saying, "I can't just get up and leave. It isn't done, I can't leave until everyone else has." I refused to accept the situation and refused to accept his statements. "I will not sit and wait for you to come home my entire life, it's unacceptable," I said.

Makoto was certain that if we had a child it would work to his advantage and give me a new interest. We wanted to have a child of our own but despite our efforts I didn't become pregnant. After trying for several months I made an appointment for tests at a hospital, and the results showed there was no physiological reason keeping me from becoming pregnant. Makoto decided to take the matter seriously and made an appointment for me at a larger hospital for a comprehensive examination. The tests they administered were thorough, most of them unpleasant, and some that were extremely painful, such as an examination of my Fallopian tubes. They didn't find anything either, but the following month my period was late. Excitedly I rushed to the drugstore to buy a home pregnancy test, which came back positive. My gynecologist explained later that studies had shown that after a Fallopian tube examination woman often become pregnant.

I immediately called my sister to give her the happy news and she was thrilled. Makoto was also excited, but the children didn't really like the idea of having a new baby join the family. That worried me. I spoke with them and tried to reassure them that nothing would change. Tomonori had begun high school and Michitaka was in junior high, and I felt they had both changed a great deal. They had grown taller, both of them topping six feet, taller than their father and schoolmates. Their appetites, which had always been good, became voracious. Every evening I cooked twice as much food as usually and they ate it all in one go. The refrigerator had to be full at all times and Makoto and I often found ourselves in the supermarket filling a shopping cart with food, beverages and snacks to satisfy their endless hunger.

It seemed to me that the larger my belly grew, the more the children changed. Tomonori added an earring, and then another and another until there was no more room to pierce. Then he got his lips and nose pierced. He bleached his hair and dyed it blond, wouldn't come out of his room and played his guitar or listened to heavy rock with the volume turned up to maximum. Makoto and I were clueless as to what to do. Every time he finally put his head out the door Makoto yelled at him angrily and demanded he remove all the piercings covering his face. Michitaka developed tics, blinked his eyes continually and moved his feet around constantly.

This situation was driving me crazy. Without any comprehensible reason I would break out in uncontrollable sobs. I felt guilty for what they were going through. I kept reviewing the drastic changes in their lives over the past year: their father had married a foreigner, in a short time they would have a new sibling, their status at home had been undermined, and Tomonori's relationship with his father were at an all-time low. Makoto was ashamed of the way Tomonori looked and didn't invite him when we went out or on vacations. A few times Michitaka came with us and we could tell he was uneasy without his brother, and he eventually declined our invitations. The tension in the house mounted because Makoto and I were bickering all the time.

The atmosphere at home was very different when Makoto wasn't there. The children helped me prepare meals and we ate together and they watched movies with me just the way they had always done. All that changed the second Makoto came home. The children would race to their rooms and shut their doors. I understood perfectly well why. Makoto was too strict with them. He scolded them all the time and had his set of remarks and threats ready: "What are you doing? Why aren't you in your rooms studying? You had better pass your exams, if you don't I'll cut off your allowance!"

Tomonori and Michitaka never dared to answer back. As soon as he opened his mouth they stood there silently, and when he finished they went to their rooms and slammed the door shut. At the time Tomonori became close to a girl in his school who dressed the way he did, and a lot of times she used to come home with him after school. I welcomed her without reservation but Makoto had a lot to say. He didn't like her appearance and couldn't stand the relationship growing between them. One day Tomonori asked permission for her to come for the weekend and stay in his room. Makoto refused profoundly. "He is only 17," he told me later. "It's too early for him to have sexual relations." Tomonori went behind his father's back and found creative ways to hide his new girlfriend from his father. In Japan every guest takes their shoes off when they come into the house and puts on slippers, which are laid out by the front door. Tomonori hid his girlfriend's shoes in his room and she walked around in her socks. His tricks didn't last for long because Makoto saw them leave through the front gate.

Somewhat later Makoto and Tomonori had a terrible argument, which resulted in Makoto going straight to the girl and saying, "Even if my son asks you to, I forbid you to sleep here."

Tomonori was furious. He lifted the fax machine off the table in the living room and threw it on the floor as hard as he could, shattering it beyond repair. Then he put his hands around Makoto's throat and tried to choke him. I sobbed and begged him to leave his father alone. Eventually he let him go and went to his room still furious, kicking and throwing everything he found in his path. Before he slammed the door of his room he screamed, "You and Suzy sleep together. Why can't I sleep with my girlfriend? You decided to get married and you brought a woman home, why can't I?"

Makoto yelled back, "Because you're 17 and I'm your father! This is my house and I make the rules. This house is not a love hotel, and a 17-year-old girl will not sleep under my roof. We'll talk about it again when you're 20."

The tension at home was unbearable. I didn't know what I was supposed to do and if I was supposed to intervene. I became even more depressed and felt I wasn't strong enough to be pregnant and carry so much emotional baggage around with me.

Talking to a Therapist

That week I started looking for a psychologist to get help for Makoto and myself, one who spoke both English and Japanese. With the help of an Israeli woman I knew from the embassy, I soon found one. Initially Makoto objected. As far as he was concerned, psychologists were for the mentally ill. However, I was so determined that in the end, after endless arguments, he gave in.

We met for the first time when I was sixth month pregnant. The therapist was a young American man who spoke fluent Japanese and had studied at one of the top Japanese universities. Makoto was very anxious before the first meeting and said nothing all the way to the therapist's office. He was unhappy and the situation with his children had pushed him to a breaking point. I took the reins and for two hours I told the psychologist about our family. I gave him as much background as I could and the drastic change in the children between the time we were married and the time I became pregnant.

He asked questions and finally said Tomonori's behavior was primarily influenced by his need for his father's attention, which was why he had gotten all the piercings.

He suggested Makoto ignore Tomonori's appearance, and assured him it would probably lead to a change for the better very quickly. He told Makoto to compliment Tomonori instead of scold and preach to him. Makoto immediately shot back, "I have nothing to compliment him on. I am ashamed of him."

The therapist said "Think of all the good things, all his good qualities. Find something positive to say to him instead of yelling, even something small and simple, and tell him that." He said that until our next meeting Makoto should make time to take Tomonori out of the house so the two of them could spend time together alone and enjoy each other's company. Makoto gave him a disgusted look and said, "How can I walk around the street with someone who looks like that?" He was genuinely upset, and the therapist repeated, "Make the effort, and change your behavior towards the children."

We went home and I didn't know what to expect. We were all pleasantly surprised by the instant change in how Makoto related to the boys, especially Tomonori. He didn't scold or yell at him, and after dinner he asked him if he wanted to walk around the city with him to look at motorcycles. Both of them were interested in anything that had two wheels and Tomonori's greatest desire was to get a driver's license that would let him ride a motorcycle.

Tomonori also liked to cook, and that week he and I prepared Indian food from a recipe he had found. It came out very well and both Makoto and I complimented him on his culinary abilities. He was embarrassed, but at the same time his conduct improved and he became calmer.

At the second meeting with the therapist we talked about Michitaka's tics, which he also said were related to Makoto's relationship with his children. He said Makoto should do the same thing as he had done with Tomonori, find time to be with him alone. The thing they had in common was their love of karaoke and baseball. In the past they had enjoyed doing both together, but that had stopped. The therapist suggested that might have hurt Michitaka.

That being the case, we decided, Makoto and I, to split up on the weekends. Makoto went out with the children and I stayed at home, and given my advanced pregnancy I was fine with the new arrangement. In any case, the weather was hot and I had no desire to be outside.

Once Makoto stopped scolding and lecturing Tomonori's behavior improved. He took out some of his piercings, stopped dying his hair and sat with us in the living room. He got closer and closer to us with time. However, there was no change in Michitaka's tics, and he continued moving his feet in agitation while he was watching TV. I tried to ignore it, but it was difficult for me to see how unhappy he was. We continued seeing the therapist. Makoto kept complaining about how expensive it was, $100 per session, but I ignored it and I asked him to join me every week. The therapist also asked to see me alone sometimes. He asked questions I didn't like answering.

"When you first met Makoto, did he go to bars a lot?" "Yes."

"Did he go home late and drunk a lot?" "Yes."

"Then why are you so angry with him now? You knew

he was like that when you entered into a relationship with him."

He was only telling me what I already knew. Drinking is a big part of the Japanese business culture. "They always drink, he's their boss, and he has to invite them out to bars. It signifies his appreciation of them and is a way of thanking them for their efforts towards the company's success."

The therapist wanted to discuss my complete dependence on Makoto. He asked why everything I did had to do with him. "Once you give birth you have to find something that interests you, and preferably more than one thing." The message was clear.

"You can find a job or a new circle of friends. I want you to stop thinking about how to change Makoto all the time, because you are not going to succeed."

He wanted to see pictures of my friends and family in Israel. After looking at them he wanted to hear about my father and his wife, about my life in Israel before my mother died. It made me nostalgic. My parents were a pair of lovebirds. My father worked from seven in the morning until three in the afternoon, and in the evening he liked spending his time with my mother. They visited friends, went shopping, sat in cafés. That continued with Charlette, whom he married after my mother died.

The therapist kept nodding, as though I had solved the problem for him, and explained how my past influenced my behavior with Makoto. He said I expected to have the same kind of relationship with him that my father had with my mother. He told me I should have an independent life, know how to get along by myself, learn new things and enjoy my leisure hours without being dependent on Makoto. He said I should stop thinking about him and start thinking about myself, and what I was capable of.

"You have an excellent command of Japanese and English; I see no reason keeping you from finding an interesting job once the baby is born." I laughed and laughed. "Who would hire me without a university degree and with my broken Japanese?" Nothing changed his mind. "You'd be amazed," he said, "you're capable of much more than you realize and you shouldn't underestimate yourself." I agreed I would find a job once I became used to being a mother, and think about my future.

In the last months of my pregnancy, I asked Makoto to hire a housekeeper. My belly was so large I couldn't bend over to clean. At first he refused. It came as no surprise, since that was his immediate reaction to whatever I asked for. However, I knew from experience that as soon as I raised my voice, shouted and cried, I would get what I wanted. "You go to bars, you waste thousands of dollars on alcohol, and you aren't willing to pay someone to clean the mess your children make?"

I wasn't exaggerating, the children really did mess up the house, worse than before. Their rooms were full of *things*, food, books, CDs. When I wanted to tidy up the mess I never knew where to start. I spent hours running around the house putting things back where they belonged, then I changed the sheets, dusted the furniture and washed the floors. It was important that they live in a clean, aesthetic environment, like the one I grew up in, but after a couple of days the house was as messy as it had been before.

I found a housekeeper who came once a week and the change was miraculous. Life became more comfortable, and not only for me. The children seemed to breathe easier as well. Apparently they minded less if a stranger went into their rooms and touched their personal belongings, and I could seriously understand them. Just by going into their rooms I exposed their secrets and that was no good for our relationship. The house cleaner's influence extended beyond cleaning and we all relaxed. I knew Makoto had hoped to marry a more independent and more tranquil woman who would manage the house for him without acting spoiled or complaining all the time, someone who would be like his mother. I also had my own unfulfilled hopes. I wanted a man who would come home at a reasonable time, someone who would enjoy my company and be affectionate, the way my father behaved with my mother and then with Charlette. Neither my expectations nor Makoto's expectations were met, and actually we were both somewhat disappointed.

In the meantime, I kept going to the therapist, studied Japanese and spent a lot of time with Sophie and Cai, who often came to visit. I also made new friends, who told me about their lives and their ever-changing boyfriends. I began to feel free and relaxed.

My friend Sandy came from Israel for a visit, bringing books on childbirth and child rearing. They were reassuring and my confidence was somewhat regained. Still, being a mother was going to be a new experience for me and I never felt Makoto was fully involved. I was concerned that soon I would be alone in the house with a newborn. During those frightening times I called my sister a lot and consulted her.

There wasn't much she could do for me in practical terms so she suggested I ask my aunt to come and stay with me for a few weeks, and she was only too happy to agree. I was very relieved, and started making plans. My sister and I agreed that as soon as I gave birth she would arrange to have my aunt's arrival coincide with my release from the hospital. That would be five days after I gave birth, which was the length of time new mothers remained in the hospital.

Despite the advantage of a five-day hospital stay, as opposed to Israel's three days, the bill would be $3,500; in Israel the HMO pays the bill. The only way an ordinary family could afford a hospital birth would be if they had considerable savings, and it made me understand why Japan had a low birthrate. Pregnancy tests and childbirth were not included in the Japanese medical insurance. Every gynecologist's visit cost $50 and the payments mounted up, especially because during the last trimester I had to have a routine checkup every week. Unless the couple had a high income it would be impossible to finance pregnancy and birth, and that was without taking into consideration the costs of raising and educating the child. Nevertheless, not only the rich in Japan were having children. Anyone who wanted a child but couldn't afford the costs could ask for help from the metropolitan government. The couple had to present their tax receipts for the last two years, and then a committee would evaluate their request. If they met the criteria the fees for the pregnancy and birth would be paid by the government and they would receive a small monthly allowance for the first year.

It seemed humiliating, and I was happy that Makoto

was earning enough money to pay for everything, including the therapist, the housekeeping, my aunt's flight to Japan and everything the baby would need, in addition to the everyday expenses. He also paid for everything I asked for to stop the waves of tears I shed all the time, which had become part of our relationship.

Despite my fluctuating moods in the weeks before the birth, he was very considerate and thoughtful. I hoped that maybe the change I wanted would actually occur and that once we had the baby he would stop spending his evenings in bars.

We chose the name Kai for the baby, and I would caress my belly and talk to him. I told him what his new room looked like and how eager I was to meet him. Makoto didn't like the idea that Kai would sleep in a separate room. He couldn't believe I wouldn't sleep in the same room as my newborn baby. He said it would harm the baby, who needed his mother, and said I was being irresponsible. He said that in Japan the baby slept on the futon between the mother and father for several years. In some families the father slept in a separate room to get a good night's sleep and be able to get up fresh for work the next day. I found that funny and I said, "We're going to do it differently. My child will be in his own comfortable bed, we'll install a baby monitor and we'll only get up when he needs us." Our marital bed was important to me and I didn't want a child to come in between us. In the end, however, we compromised. We moved the baby's bed into our room for several months, until he began to sleep through the night without waking up.

Every day I would cross off another item on the list of

things needed to be prepared for the upcoming birth. One day Makoto and I went to visit the hospital where I would be giving birth. I met the gynecologist who had been caring for me since the beginning of my pregnancy and told him I wanted an epidural. I had a smooth pregnancy and I didn't understand why he pulled a face. He said, "We usually don't give epidurals." Makoto stood by me and said, "All of Suzy's friends in Israel give birth with epidurals and they have assured her it would keep her from having labor pains." He then surprised me by saying, "Add the cost of the epidural to the bill." The doctor was not happy but had no choice, saying he would make a note on my file and add it to the bill. I didn't care what the doctor said or thought, as long as I was assured of an epidural that would ease the birth.

My due date was one week away, and in Israel Prime Minister Yitzhak Rabin was assassinated. I was shocked and deeply sorry, and couldn't believe that an Israeli citizen who came from my own city, Herzliya, would kill him due to conflicting political views. Five days later, November 9, 1995, I went into labor.

"It's a Boy!"

Makoto called his workplace and notified them he wasn't coming to work. We got everything ready and went to the hospital. The midwife examined me and said my cervix was not dilated, and the doctor said I should go home and rest. I should come back, he said, when the pains were a few minutes apart. "When that happens, come to the hospital without delay."

The next day, just before dawn, the pains got much worse, worse than anything I had ever experienced. I could barely breathe, and it hurt so much that I cried. I woke Makoto and told him it was time. I was afraid I was going to give birth any minute. All I wanted was to get to the hospital and get my epidural.

It was six in the morning when we arrived, almost 24 hours to the minute since our previous visit. I hadn't slept at all and I was extremely exhausted. Makoto came in with me and filled out the forms. As soon as I was admitted the nurses asked him to leave. They gave me a hospital gown and helped me lie down. As the pain became more intense another nurse joined us and for a minute it seemed as though my pain was shared by all three of us. I begged one of them to get a doctor who would administer the epidural. "This hospital doesn't give epidurals," she told me gently, which made me feel even more helpless. I asked her to call my prenatal doctor who has assured me he would be on call from nine o'clock. One of the nurses gave me a pill to relax me and said I should try to calm down and rest.

The minutes crawled by and it was noon and I still hadn't given birth. There were women on both sides of me, and we all suffered together. I wanted to scream but was embarrassed. I was living through a nightmare. Finally, my doctor appeared. As soon as I saw him I broke into tears and begged him for an epidural. He examined me and said it was too late to administer one because I would soon give birth. I told him I couldn't stand any more pain, and sobbed uncontrollably.

In the meantime, a nurse came in and told me Cai was waiting outside, which was the most encouraging thing I had heard all day. I asked the nurse to help me get out of bed and she helped me to where Cai was waiting. As soon as I saw her I broke into tears again. I kept saying it hurt and I was afraid, and she looked at me helplessly, hugged me and promised she would wait with me until it was all over.

It was already five in the evening and I had been awake for almost 36 hours; I was exhausted and my spirit was defeated. Finally they took me to the delivery room but I expected my doctor to be waiting for me and he was nowhere in sight, only two midwives. I didn't have the strength to protest, all I wanted was to give birth and be done with it. They laid me on my side and through the fog I could hear them say "Push!" From within my pain I pushed as hard as I could until I didn't have the strength to push any more.

At six Kai was born. He weighed 6.4 pounds and was immediately taken to the nursery along with the other newborns. They wrapped me in blankets and told me not to move. I was lying in an empty room, calm and drowsy, happy it was all over. Eventually nurses came in and brought me a hospital gown, a medical hair cover and sterile booties, sat me in a wide upholstered chair and brought Kai to me. I laid him on my lap and looked at him for the first time. He opened his eyes and yawned, and it was as though he had always been there, on my lap. He looked like a little wrinkled ball. I fell in love with him instantly. The nurses looked on with a smile and after a while asked me to try to nurse him. They said mother's milk during the first few days was very important for the child's development. I nursed him and it was one of the happiest moments of my life. They asked me if I wanted to be awakened during the night to nurse him again, and I immediately said I did.

I went back to my room and after two days without sleep I got into bed and fell into a deep dreamless sleep. At two in the morning the light from a flashlight shining on my face woke me and a nurse asked me in a whisper to follow her to the nursery. When I got there I saw I wasn't alone, there were several other mothers there, all of them wearing the same hospital robes and medical hair covers. One of the nurses explained that we first had to weigh our babies, write the weight in a notebook, and then nurse them. We were then to change their diapers, weigh them again, write the weight and return the baby to a nurse.

I nursed Kai every four hours, and between feedings we went to classes for first-time mothers. We saw videos about safety, nursing, and alternatives to mother's milk. We learned how to change diapers and bathe our babies, and how to take care of the umbilical cord before it dropped off and of their navel afterwards. We had no time to rest between feedings. Our schedule for our days in the hospital alternated between nursing our babies and watching instructive videos.

My aunt landed in Japan the same day I took Kai home. Makoto came to the hospital to pick us up, brought us home and then went to get her from the airport. I was anxious to see her and happy to have a close relative with me, at least for the first few days. She brought a suitcase full of presents. My father sent a fancy baby carriage and loads of baby clothes, and he and Haya filled another suitcase with educational toys.

At 27 years of age I was a mother; Tomonori was 18, Michitaka was 16. They were waiting for us when we came home and were excited to meet their new brother. I was surprised by how much affection Tomonori showed Kai, and I realized he liked babies. He asked me if he could hold him and give him his bottle. He wouldn't leave him and wanted to take care of him. Michitaka, on the other hand, kept his distance. He said Kai was too small and he was afraid he would hurt him. Tomonori spent almost all afternoon with Kai, looking at him, and when he opened his eyes Tomonori would smile. He picked him up and put him on his lap. Kai was calm and quiet when Tomonori was around, and that helped me get acclimatized at home. My aunt convinced me not to nurse him so that someone else could give him his bottle, and that would make it easier for me when I had to get up for his nighttime feedings.

Every afternoon when Makoto came home from work my aunt and I went walking around the city. I wanted her to enjoy her trip to Tokyo and not just be busy helping me. Makoto eased into taking care of Kai with no problems, and I could see the advantages of his being a father for the third time. He was experienced, it was natural for him to take care of Kai, and that was very reassuring to me. Kai could sense his experience and was always calm around Makoto. Kai loved being held over his shoulder and being bathed and fed by him, and I could see immediately that as a parent Makoto was far more relaxed than I was. Everything was new for me.

Two days after my aunt arrived, my father called and said that in two days he was planning to come to visit us for a week. I was very surprised and asked him to postpone it for a while, until Kai got a little older and stronger, so we could go on a trip. But my father insisted on coming as soon as possible and refused not to participate in his grandson's circumcision ceremony.

My aunt was much more to me than my mother's sister, she was my best friend. After my mother had died, she remained in close contact with my father. Suddenly, five years after my mother passed away, she was widowed. She was our second mother. That was why I was so happy that my father was coming while she was still in Tokyo, they were the two people I felt most at home with.

I had planned for Kai's circumcision before he was born. I contacted the Israeli embassy in Tokyo and they referred me to the Jewish community, and from there I got a recommendation for a *mohel*.[1] Many of the Israelis I consulted with recommended I hold the ceremony in a hospital with an anesthesiologist. Makoto too was shocked that I wanted to hold the ceremony at home with a *mohel*, he wanted a medical doctor to perform it in a hospital. But I wanted to honor my father even before I knew he was coming, and I was determined to hold the ceremony the way it was held in Israel. After we hung up I was happy I had remained faithful to my gut instinct.

Makoto went to the airport to fetch my father, and again the house was full of excitement. Makoto respected my decision to hold the circumcision at home but conditioned it on his absence. On the day of the ceremony he went to work as usual, and said angrily, "If there are any complications afterwards you will be held responsible. Just bear that in mind." I was under a lot of pressure and didn't answer. I was happy my aunt was there, and I let her take charge of everything. I had invited only a very small number of close friends.

The mohel was a young man who spoke Hebrew and who had lived in Tokyo for several years. He came on time and brought several men from the Jewish community with him. Kai was laid on a large pillow that was placed on my father's lap. Kai cried and I cried with him. Makoto phoned several times to ask how Kai was doing and it was a relief to tell him that everything had gone according to plan and Kai was sleeping. It took only two days for the incision to heal without leaving a mark.

---

1   A Jewish person trained to perform a ritual circumcision

My aunt and I gave Kai a pacifier but when Makoto came home from work and saw it in his son's mouth he removed it. He said Kai had to learn to stop crying on his own, which would be better for him and easier for us later on. The house was full of guests and Kai cried all the time, which was nerve wracking for everyone. I wanted my aunt and my father to enjoy their visit and go home with happy memories. Makoto and the boys took care of Kai in the afternoon so the three of us could walk around Tokyo. My father was impressed by the signs of affluence he saw everywhere, and asked, "Why do you want us to send things from Israel? You have everything here."

I said, "I know, but sometimes I just miss the way things taste in Israel, like junk food and roasted sunflower seeds and pumpkin seeds. There's no way I can find anything like that here."

He told me that before he came he imagined Japan was backwards, old-fashioned and crowded. He imagined the most popular form of transportation was the bicycle and he was surprised by all the modern technology. "No," I said, "that's China, not Japan. Tokyo is like any city in the United States, maybe even more sophisticated and advanced."

My father loved seafood so Japanese cuisine was much to his liking. Every morning we went for a walk, often to the shopping center, to buy presents for Charlette and the grandchildren at home. I was amused by how quickly he acclimatized. Later, while my aunt babysat Kai, we took the train and walked around the city. My aunt was a wonderful cook and Tomonori and Michitaka loved her and grew quite fond of her baked goods, which waited for them on the kitchen counter every morning. On my father's last day in Japan we held a little party for him, my aunt and the birth of Kai.

Makoto's family was also invited, namely his brother Norio and his wife Fumie, and two cousins of whom I was particularly fond. Among the other guests were some couples we were fond of and my best friends Cai, Sandy and Sophie, whom I especially wanted to introduce to my father. Makoto's mother, Kurako, said she couldn't come because she had to stay and take care of her husband. The living room wasn't big enough for all the guests so we had to take all the furniture out. Kai slept through it all; he liked sleeping during the day and being awake at night.

Before my father returned to Israel we went to visit Makoto's parents. My father enjoyed the drive to Tsukuba, especially the green fields and the traditional houses he saw along the way. Near Mt. Tsukuba we stopped to look at the scenery. We stayed in the car because it was freezing cold outside. Both my father and my aunt were impressed by the mountain, which was tall and stood out high over the fields. I told them it was one of Japan's most famous mountains. Makoto's parents' 120-year-old house impressed them even more, just as I had been impressed the first time I saw it and its enormous, well-kept gardens and the surrounding rice fields. For years to come, every time I brought friends to see the house the reaction was the same, it was like looking at a piece of history, like on a Kurosawa movie set.

Kurako was very moved by the meeting with my father and aunt. My father shook her hand warmly and thanked her for treating me so nicely. She smiled and asked that I translate her thanks to me for raising her grandsons. She served us tempura vegetables, sushi and *karaage* fried chicken. It was a typical traditional Japanese meal served on a low table, and we ate while sitting on our knees on pillows.

Later we took my father to the airport and my aunt stayed with me for ten more days. I thanked her for coming and told her she had enabled me to handle my new motherhood better. I still had a lot to learn, but what she had taught me in her short visit made all the difference. I had no neighbors or nearby relatives to talk to and her presence made me less afraid and gave me insight into how to behave with my son. I began to distinguish between his crying out of hunger, tiredness and pain.

Motherhood brought a drastic change to my life. When Kai was awake nothing else existed. I couldn't leave him for a minute, not even to go to the toilet. When he slept between feedings I slept next to him. Every day I waited impatiently for Makoto to come home from work so I could at last soak in the bathtub. Tomonori and Michitaka generally came home before him and helped me bathe Kai in his bassinette, which we placed in the middle of the living room. I loved watching him kicking the water.

As is customary in Japan, on the 45th day after his birth we held another party, this one at Meiji-jingu Shrine, for the traditional blessing. The baby is dressed in a white outfit, a present brought by the grandmothers. Kurako sent us one made of white satin decorated with lace. There was a little cape and a hat. It was a little too fancy for me but I accepted the tradition and dressed him in the entire ensemble.

That day a lot of children were being blessed and all of

them were wearing the same outfit, cape and matching hat. According to instructions, before the ceremony we fed him and changed his diaper so he would be calm. Then we sat in a row, all the parents in a straight line with the babies on the laps. A Japanese priest intoned a long blessing, none of which I could understand, and was later told no one could understand it either since it was in ancient Japanese.

When Kai was four months old I asked Makoto to let me take him to Israel for the Passover celebration. He knew I wasn't feeling well and thought it would be good for me. I made a lot of preparations because I didn't know how Kai would react to the long flights and I didn't want to leave anything to chance. I packed a suitcase with everything I thought we would need and hoped for the best.

My father, brother and sister were waiting for us at the airport in Israel. When I entered the arrivals hall and saw them I became so overcome with emotion that I began to cry. It had been more than a year since my last visit to Israel and I had been terribly homesick. I had come for Passover and would have the chance to meet everyone at the Seder[2].

Being married to Makoto and living with two adolescents and an infant changed me. I no longer felt the anger I had during my first year of marriage. After Kai was born my priorities changed, and now the four of them were the center of my life. When life in Tokyo became challenging I went on vacation to Israel. My family and friends were waiting for me, and welcomed me with open arms. For the first time I didn't feel I was bothering anyone.

---

2   Seder, (Hebrew: "order") religious meal served in Jewish homes on the 15th and 16th of the month of Nisan to commence the festival of Passover

My friends said it was thanks to me that they met each other again. My strongest relations were with the friends who had come to visit me in Tokyo before Kai was born, and over the years our friendship grew even stronger. We had so much in common to talk about. We had all begun new lives, become wives and mothers and learned to adapt, each of us in her own way. It was a comfort to know that we all had similar problems regardless of where we lived and of the fact that I was now responsible for two step-children. I could understand Tomonori and Michitaka, probably because I had also lived in a house with my father's second wife. I felt the need to protect them and save them from the unpleasantness I had faced as a child. I had a few rules I lived by, such as to always speak to them directly, never through their father; not to disclose to him things they had told me privately, especially when there was no need; not to be emotional around them; and not to bicker with Makoto or show him extra affection in front of them. I wanted to avoid all the mistakes my father and Charlette had made during my childhood. When my father and Charlette fought all I wanted to do was to run out of the house and escape from life. After their fights they would reconcile, hugging and kissing in front of me, and that bothered me just as much.

In Israel emotions are displayed openly. Everything is exposed, and people also communicate through facial expressions and body language. In Japan on the other hand, it is almost impossible to tell how someone feels by looking at his emotionless expression, whether he is happy, angry or sad. I learned from observing them how to hide my thoughts. I had to learn it the same way I had to learn Japanese, because expressing emotions always made people feel uncomfortable.

However, I preserved some Israeli customs, and one of them was inviting people to the house. I encouraged the children to invite their friends whenever they liked, as opposed to other Japanese mothers. Our refrigerator was always full of food the children liked, their favorite beverages and desserts. I ignored the mess they made when they played with their friends. Order at home was important but it was more important that Tomonori and Michitaka smiled at the end of the day.

In Israel people always told me I was lucky they were boys, because girls always envied their stepmothers and made their lives miserable. I think they were right, because I know Charlette always got along better with my brother than with me. He never complained about her and never cared about her relations with my father. My sister and I, on the other hand, were always angry when she yelled at my father and wanted to protect and defend him. We were also covertly in competition with her for my father's attention and demonstrations of love, and it was frustrating because she won every single time. That made us bear a grudge against him because of his weakness, but in retrospect I can understand it was hard for me to accept that he loved her and was willing to let her yell at him.

It was like living on a ship in mid seas never knowing when the next storm would hit. I didn't want Tomonori and Michitaka to grow up in the same atmosphere so I restrained myself around them and tried to give them the feeling that their father loved them very much.

After a wonderful time in Israel, Kai and I returned to Tokyo, right on time for the cherry blossom's season and as always, I was overcome by the splendid beauty. The white blossoms were everywhere and every neighborhood park became a place for people to enjoy them. Every year in spring we met at the local park with friends from the neighborhood. We celebrated *hanami*, which is a traditional custom of enjoying the beauty of the cherry blossom, called in Japanese *Sakura*. Makoto was in charge of getting there early to find us the best shady spot before the park became crowded. The national flower of Japan, Sakura, also has an enormous influence on the Japanese economy, because tourists from all over the world come to Japan in the spring to see the trees, and tourism flourishes.

Finding Myself

When spring came I felt it was time to put Kai into kindergarten; in Japan *kindergarten* was the name given to the educational framework for children from the time of birth until the age of six. I wanted to carry out my plan of finding a job and developing myself as a person, all of which was put on hold because of my pregnancy and birth. A working mother in Japan could put her children into kindergarten any time during the first year. Since getting married I hadn't worked at all and I didn't know how to begin looking for a job. I had worked very hard to learn Japanese but my command of the language was still fairly weak. There were nine kindergartens scattered around our neighborhood and Makoto and I were requested by the local district city hall to visit them and rank them according to our preferences from one to five. We visited them all and I couldn't find any real differences between them. The buildings all looked the same and nothing stood out that would make me choose one over another, and in the end I numbered them according to their proximity to our house. Makoto filed the forms while I was visiting Israel, and Kai was supposed to start kindergarten the first week of April. After

I got home we waited to be notified which kindergarten had accepted him.

We got a long list of instructions to follow and equipment to buy. We had to prepare bed linen according to the exact dimensions of the kindergarten's futon size where the children napped, a blanket cover and both summer and winter blankets. I was supposed to embroider his name on everything, including his first name, last name and the number he had been given. This would be used throughout his entire six-year at kindergarten. We also had to prepare cloth bags for dirty clothes, towels and diapers. We bought small towels with loops which were hung on a hook with his name and was changed after each use. He also needed a set of towels for wiping his hands and face at meals, and three bibs, one for each meal. There were seamstresses who specialized in sewing what the kindergartens demanded. We chose the material and a seamstress and gave her all of Kai's information, and she prepared the order.

Every child had his own cubbyhole with a card bearing a picture; Kai's was a picture of a helicopter. Every day parents had to put two sets of clothing into the cubbyhole, clean pajamas, disposable diapers and clean bottles. When we entered we had to take off our shoes, and for the first year parents could only enter the children's reception room, no further. Every morning we gave Kai to one of the kindergarten teachers after we had changed his diaper, and picked him up in the same room in the afternoon.

I had to take his temperature every morning, record it in his notebook and write a few sentences describing his general condition, what he ate the previous evening, when he went to sleep, how many hours he slept, how he slept, etc. The teacher also wrote a summary of his day, things like group activities, food he had and naps took. The notebook followed Kai for his six years of kindergarten.

It was difficult for me to get used to the strict instructions and took a lot of energy from me. Every weekend I had to change his bed linen, wash them and return them the following Monday. Monday morning was rush time where all the parents arrived before they went to work and scrambled to change sheets and blanket covers.

I brought Kai at nine every morning and picked him up at four-thirty in the afternoon. He adapted quickly and seemed to enjoy the other children's company. We parted with a smile every morning as I handed him over to the teacher without a problem. The place was clean and well maintained and all the children wore clean clothing. I felt he was in good hands and in a positive, safe environment. The teachers were very nice to me, and since they knew my Japanese wasn't fluent they wrote in *hiragana*, the phonetic alphabet used by children, so I could understand what they had written.

While looking for work I remembered my walks with Kai in the park not far from our house. Whenever we went I stopped at a clothing store I frequented and looked for something interesting. The store was owned by two friendly Korean women, Toki and Yuki, who liked me and were always happy to see me. Their parents came to Japan after the Second World War and settled in Tokyo, where they had both been born. However, they were both proud of their Korean heritage. They and their children had gone to Korean schools and kept their Korean identity; it was not an unusual practice. There were a great many Koreans living in Japan and they preserved their traditions and culture, which kept them separated from their surroundings.

Toki and Yuki wanted me to teach them English. I told them I was Israeli, not American, and they said every foreigner knew English better than they did. They wouldn't leave the subject alone, and a month after Kai had become acclimatized to kindergarten I went to the store, and told them I was free and willing to teach them English. They were overjoyed and we set our first lesson for ten o'clock in the morning at my house. The time was ideal for me and for them as well because the store opened at eleven.

To prepare lessons I contacted Cai, my Australian friend, who had been teaching English for a long time and asked her to send me a list of books. She sent me a list of elementary books for teaching English as a foreign language published by Oxford and Cambridge. I went to a bookstore in Tokyo and bought a set of books, workbooks, audio cassettes and the teachers' guide. I prepared lessons every day for a week and read all the books from cover to cover. It wasn't particularly difficult because the books were for beginners.

I thought the lessons would keep me busy and help me learn how to teach, and since I was learning myself I told them they didn't have to pay me. However, they refused and in the end we settled on a nominal sum. Each of them paid me $10 per lesson, and they paid me at the beginning of every month, $80 in an envelope.

I decided to post an ad on the bulletin board at the

community center in my neighborhood where I studied Japanese. That same month two other women also sked for English lessons: Shu-San, who had come to Tokyo from Taiwan two years before, married a Japanese man and stayed in Japan. The other was Kobayashi-San, who was 65 and a widow, and spent her life studying. She said she had studied English for a number of years and wanted to practice conversation. I took both of them as students and told them the charge would be $100 a month each. They both accepted the offer and we agreed I would not have other students join them. So now I had four students and was making $280 a month.

At that time I met Mitani-San, the wife of one of Makoto's good friends from the university. They played golf together and all four of us occasionally met. Mitani-San and I became good friends. She was a good sportswoman, regularly playing golf and tennis and going to the gym. Since I wanted to lose the weight I had gained during my pregnancy I joined her at the gym, and she suggested I learn how to play golf. She said that way I could join them and we could play as a foursome.

Makoto liked the idea and supported my learning golf. He said the game could be played at any age and the lessons would benefit my health when we got old. Not only would I learn a new skill, but I would be able to join the circles of people who traveled around the world to play the game, and there were golf courses in beautiful locations in the mountains and near the sea.

The monthly cost of golf lessons was exactly the price I took from each of my English students. I was happy that for once I could pay for something myself. I was one of 15 women learning the sport, and the lessons were taught in the same meticulous order that everything else was done in Japan. At the beginning of the lesson we stood in a long line and each of us received a bag of golf balls. The instructor demonstrated a technique and each of us practiced it standing in our own individual square, hitting the ball towards an open field. The instructor passed among us, corrected our hold on the club or our stance, and showed us how to improve our technique. In that way, one stage after the other, I improved my golf skills and managed to hit balls more than 109 yards away.

As time passed I got to know the other women in the group. They were all housewives and older than me, and were coming for lessons for the same reason I was, to be able to play well enough to join their husbands for their weekend games. I was a foreigner and that made them curious, and after I had told them something about my background I said I worked as a private English teacher. They were overjoyed and wanted me to be their teacher as well, which significantly increased my number of students.

By then I had 11 students and was making $1,100 a month. Before they started I tested their level and assigned them textbooks accordingly. Toki an Yuki were my most advanced students and were already working on their third textbook. Preparing for lessons involved reading and understanding the new material and I had to make a great effort. Thankfully, I didn't have to work that much every time, since I used Toki and Yuki's lesson plans for the new students.

I found myself surrounded by friends who were more like mentors to me. We played golf with our instructor, and they helped me a great deal with Tomonori and Michitaka. They had their own experience with adolescent children and knew how to deal with them, so they gave me some excellent advice which helped me understand the children better. An additional advantage was that by speaking with them I improved my Japanese, they taught me new words and I became more fluent.

That year I met with the therapist twice, and he was pleased with the changes in my life. He said that as soon as I had found work and something to do in my free time I was going in the right direction and there was no need for us to continue the meetings. He said if I ever needed his help again all I had to do was call him.

As usual, Makoto was busy with work most of the day all week long. He came home late, and perhaps because of the change in my life it didn't bother me as much. Tomonori and Michitaka helped me take care of Kai and were usually perfectly happy to babysit him. My students taught me Japanese cooking and the children loved the food I made and complimented me on it. Unfortunately, Makoto was having trouble communicating with them again. As soon as he came home they rushed to their rooms and closed the door behind them. When he was not at home they spent hours with me in the kitchen and living room. Clearly, they were under a lot of pressure, because their father wanted them to study, and not sit in front of the TV. Despite his expectations, I knew that behind their closed doors they weren't doing homework. As soon as they heard his footsteps they took out their books and notebooks and pretended to be engrossed in their studies.

Makoto's behavior towards them angered me. When I asked him why he was so strict with them he said a father that loved his children had to be strict to bring out the best in them. I, on the other hand, thought his strictness made them rebel and lie all the time. They obviously hated it. I tried to convince them that their father loved them and was doing what he thought was best for them so that they would succeed in life, but they didn't believe me. They thought he was angry because he didn't love them. Over the years they understood his motives and saw him behave the same way with Kai. But by that time they were older and had the confidence to confront and criticize him for the relationship he was building with their younger brother.

I became friends with other mothers from the kindergarten and invited them and their children to our home in the afternoons. What bothered me was that they came but never returned the invitation. Makoto told me that in Japan people didn't invite guests to their homes, and that meetings always took place in public places.

The changes I had in my life left me feeling I didn't have enough information to see the big picture. I was curious to know what other people's homes were like in order to understand their lives better. In Israel I had amassed an enormous amount of information as a child, as a teenager and as a soldier, but in Japan I always felt I was lacking knowledge. So when we went to the park and the children were playing I asked the other mothers questions about everything that intrigued and bothered me. Their answers made me realize just how different I was from them, how differently my way of thinking and my actions were, especially in regard to how children should be raised. I came to realize the enormous differences between married life in Japan and married life in Israel. I saw how lonely the Japanese were, how their rigidity kept them at arm's length from one another. They all told me that before they were married their relations with their future husbands were warm and loving, and lasted until a short time after the wedding. As soon as they became parents, their relationship with their husbands was pushed aside and the children took center stage. They went out as a couple very seldom, they had no babysitter to watch the children when they were little, and in an emergency they called the grandparents. They almost never hugged or kissed – especially not in public. To me that lack of warmth felt very sad. Life in our house was different, I hugged and kissed Makoto whenever I wanted to, because human contact was important to me.

The other mothers in Kai's kindergarten were young and like me, devoted most of their time to their children. They complained on Fridays because they knew the weekend was coming up and they would have to serve their husbands. They all said their lives were much easier when their husbands were at work and came home late because that way they only had to take care of the children. They were surprised when I told them Makoto helped me with Kai when he was at home, and sometimes cooked dinner. I said I was different from them and sad when Makoto didn't spend the evening with me. I waited eagerly for weekends because then all five of us were together as a family.

Sometimes I paid Tomonori and Michitaka to babysit Kai so Makoto and I could go out. I refused to sleep in Kai's room because sleeping together with Makoto was important to me; the Japanese custom was for the husband to sleep alone in order to be rested for work the next day. I didn't really understand the concept that the husband was the only one who needed strength for the following day because the wife worked at home and sometimes outside as well, and therefore also needed a good night's sleep.

Another thing that surprised me was their lack of interest in physical contact and were indifferent regarding hugs and kisses. They explained that the Japanese wife was responsible for all the chores at home, cleaning, cooking, paying bills and handling the checkbook. The husbands worked until late, received spending money from his wife and had no idea what the family's financial situation was. The wife signed the checks and only she could withdraw funds. The husband was secondary when it came to finances, but he gained by not having to worry about it.

That was how couples lived in Japan. The man was a father and husband on the weekends, when he would take the children to the park, take the family to a restaurant and on occasion help clean the house. The wife never knew if her husband was at work or in a bar and she never asked. At night they turned the lights off and went into their separate bedrooms.

For the first time I understood the effort my husband had to invest as soon as he married a foreigner. His entire way of life changed. Unlike other men, he slept in bed with me every night and I waited up for him to come home from bars at night. If he came in later than midnight I would be still up and most of the time it ended in arguments. I absolutely refused to accept the fact that he spent his time in bars until it was almost daylight. He preferred to avoid the arguments than going to bars, and most of the time tried hard to come home earlier.

Unlike in other Japanese households, it was important for me to hear about what he was doing during the day. I was also curious and interested to know about the previous chapter of his life. I wanted to know more about his first wife and his family. I told him about my family all the time, my life in Israel, my friends, I described everything in details. He, on the other hand, described almost nothing, which frustrated me. I finally found the key to getting him to talk about himself, it was going to bars and getting drunk, and then he would overcome his inhibitions and tell me about his life.

His mother's family was rich and owned a lot of land before the Second World War. After the war the new government passed land reform laws confiscating about two thirds of the territory of the landlord, leaving each family with very little of what it had formerly possessed. Kurako had been married to a physician and gave birth to Norio. During the war her husband served in the Japanese army and fell in love with a nurse who worked at the same base as he. He left Kurako and she had to raise Norio by herself; he was three when his father left.

The year after her divorce a marriage was arranged for her with Shizuka-San, Makoto's father. He adopted Norio and raised him as his own. Four years later Makoto was born and until they grew up they didn't know they were half-siblings. When Norio was an adolescent they told him about his biological father, telling him they didn't know where he was; in fact, they never did find out.

Makoto said his family name, Okubo, was his mother's, because in Japan children were given the last name of whichever parent's family was richer, and since his mother's family had more money than his father's, he was called Okubo-San.

Norio left home when he was 18, rented a room in Tokyo and started university. He was 22 when he graduated and went to New York where he worked at odd jobs. Japanese currency was weak at the time and the dollars he earned were worth a fortune when he came home and exchanged them to yen. He started a successful company for constructing pipes and channels for sewers. He was a canny businessman and the company is still flourishing to this day.

Norio married Fumie, who was his high school sweetheart. According to Makoto, the relationship between his mother and Fumie was difficult for many years. Fumie was a pretty woman, a dietician with an affluent lifestyle, who liked fashionable clothes. She traveled abroad and had many hobbies. Kurako was the complete opposite, she was a simple suburban woman. She had no financial problems but she didn't spend money on herself. She lived with her husband, didn't spend money on entertainment or travel, and had always lived like that, even before her husband's accident. She spent most of her time at home, helped her husband manage their land and had no idea what was on the other side of the ocean. The differences between them caused endless friction. Watching the way they interacted led me to believe Kurako probably wouldn't like me at all, but I was lucky, she was tolerant of me because I was a foreigner and didn't expect me to act according to the Japanese code of behavior. Moreover, I had married her divorced son and had taken it upon myself to raise her grandchildren. She maintained her tolerance throughout all the years I knew her. She never criticized my trips, not to Israel or anywhere else.

Like his brother, Makoto left Tsukuba when he was 18. He also rented a room and studied mathematics at university, and after graduation went to Europe with friends for three months. It was a trip, he said, he would never forget. He remembered the names of all the places he had been to, and over the years we visited many of them together again. It was surprising to see at what precision he remembered them, and even with the passage of time they hadn't changed much.

When he returned to Japan, he found work in the insurance company where he still worked 22 years later. He met his first wife, Yuriko, at one of the bars he used to frequent with his university friends. She was 21 at the time, exotically beautiful, and her appearance also represented the story of the people of Okinawa.

During the Second World War American and Filipino soldiers were stationed in Okinawa and fell in love with local women. That resulted in many children of mixed origin, who were beautiful. Yuriko came to Tokyo at the age of 20 with the intention of earning money, like many young people her age. Pictures of her reflected her beauty and I could understand how Makoto had fallen hopelessly in love with her. They were together for several months when she fell pregnant; the pregnancy was unplanned. Makoto absolutely refused to allow her to have an abortion and they got married. His parents objected to the marriage because they felt Makoto and Yuriko were too young and Yuriko had no education, and later they found other reasons which reinforced their objection. When Tomonori was born, due to their objections to the marriage, his parents refused to give them any help or support during the first years.

From the way Makoto spoke about Yuriko I knew they had both been very much in love and the first years were good. After they had been married for three years Michitaka was born, and life continued as it had before. Yuriko was a devoted mother and good household manager, while Makoto became a senior figure in the insurance company. His salary rose and their economic situation improved. In Japan at the time, salaries were automatically upgraded according to rank, and employees enjoyed high wages and excellent working conditions. In return they were loyal and committed to the company, working long hours, sometimes until late at night. Gradually the custom of going out for drinks with other employees became prioritized over going home and spending time with the family. That was when Makoto was absent from home more and more. He spent hours until late at night with other employees or with clients, and family time was reduced and limited to weekends.

Yuriko found her own pastime activity for her spare time and began going frequently to the neighborhood bar to drink with friends and bet at the local Pachinko parlor. Pachinko is kind of a cross between vertical pinball and a slot machine, which you put money. Pachinko parlors were very popular in Japan at the time. People spent hours looking at little metal balls and pulling knobs to get them into the holes and win. Like the slot machine in Las Vegas, they were addicting. The balls were exchanged for money. Yuriko was spending a lot of money at bars and losing more in pachinko parlors. For a while she hid her new hobby but eventually Makoto found out and they argued bitterly about it. He complained she wasn't taking proper care of the children and was wasting huge amounts of money on drinking and gambling.

Makoto's place of work transferred him to Osaka and he came home only on weekends. The children's school began calling him regularly because the boys always came in late. The relationship between Makoto and Yuriko got worse. They slept in separate rooms and stopped talking to each other all together. That came as no surprise to me, because I knew Makoto preferred not to deal with problems. He simply ignored them. I assumed that was what had happed with Yuriko. I thought that if he had discussed it openly with her he would have found out why her behavior had become problematic. He would no doubt have discovered what I knew without ever having met her, that she was lonely and isolated in Tokyo. Her husband was busy all day, she had two young children to take care of, and very young herself. It couldn't have been easy for her. On the other hand, I could see how the Japanese culture of restraint had led her to keep it bottled up. But it was apparently too much to bear and she found a way to relieve her frustration and anger through drinking and gambling.

Most foreign women married to Japanese men found their husband's behavior unacceptable, did not agree to their absences and demanded they do their share around the house. No Japanese woman would think of behaving that way. They had been raised differently, copied what they saw growing up and continued the traditions after they were married. Had I been Japanese Makoto would never have allowed me to go abroad alone and I certainly never would have been able to employ someone to clean the house once a week. None of my Japanese friends ever had help around the house, it was simply out of the question.

As Tomonori and Michitaka grew older they were busy with school and after-school activities, and Yuriko felt they no longer needed her. She was alone at home all day and one day she decided the time had come to leave Makoto and return to Okinawa, where she had been born. Makoto agreed to give her a divorce on the condition that he would have full custody of the children. It was a harsh and unusual condition, but to his surprise she agreed. He knew she had stopped loving him years before, but he never believed she would give up the children. She left home when Tomonori was 13 and Michitaka was 11 and returned to Okinawa. The children were allowed to decide with whom they wanted to live and they chose to remain in Tokyo with their father, mainly because that was where their friends were.

Yuriko left almost immediately and without warning. One day she simply disappeared. It was only after they signed the divorce agreement that Makoto found out she had lost a great deal of money gambling and had a lot of debts, which automatically became his responsibility.

She never returned to Tokyo and Makoto hadn't seen her since. That was considered normal in Japan; divorced women cut their ties to the past and moved on, but usually with the children. In most cases they didn't encourage the children to spend time with their fathers. It was all strange and unnatural to my foreign eyes. I had never heard of a situation in which after a divorce the children didn't spend time with both parents, one way or another, but in Japan it was the norm.

Tomonori and Michitaka spoke to their mother on the phone occasionally and in the beginning went to visit her twice a year during school vacations, but gradually they began going only once a year, and then once every two years. Once I moved in they phoned her very infrequently and the relationship petered out. It pained me that she didn't even call them on their birthdays, and it was evident that their feelings were hurt. As far as I could see, a child whose mother ended her relationship with him would spend the rest of his life with abandonment issues, it didn't matter what country they lived in. Mothers are mothers.

I wanted them to feel comfortable enough with me to share their pain. I spoke to them about their childhood all the time, and they described it in happy terms. They only spoke well of their mother. They told me about the food she used to make them and about family outings. I was happy for them, at least they had happy memories.

During the early years of our marriage Makoto tried to turn our relationship into the same kind he had known all his life and have me behave like an obedient Japanese wife. At first I found I enjoyed trying to do what he expected. When he was around I was quiet and submissive the way I was expected to on many issues, but that couldn't continue forever. Clearly, if I didn't tell him how I felt I would go crazy. The first time I was angry and complained about something he was surprised and he didn't know how to deal with it. He preferred not to say anything and wait until I had run out of steam. He learned there was always a quiet after the storm, and it was better to let me get my anger and distress out of my system without participating. I wanted him to be like Israeli men, who knew, in their own way, how to express themselves. I expected him to let me into his world. However, he wanted to keep his own life to himself and for me to take responsibility for my own life and actions.

I never really managed to change him. He was a Japanese man and I had to accept a lot of things. I learned he would never show me love the way I had hoped for, that his love would be without words, and I learned to feel it inside. I slowly stopped sharing my days with him and stopped asking him how his day had been. At first it was a challenge, but as time passed I got accustomed to the situation and even found it had some positive aspects. I learned to take control of my own life and stopped asking permission to do what I wanted.

Our first fight startled both of us, but we gradually learned how to appreciate each other's approach to life. He no longer became upset when I screamed and I stopped being upset by his silences. He came to the realization that his spontaneous reaction to my anger, which was to tell me I was hysterical, only fanned the flames, and he learned it was better not to say anything. Today I know he listens to every word I say when I share my frustration.

When Kai started walking at the age of 11 months we had more fun together as a family. By the time he was a year old he knew a lot of words and became the family clown. He loved being the center of attention and made funny faces, imitated animals, and repeated words again and again.

Michitaka felt more confident playing with him and helped me take care of him. Kai loved having everyone around him, and on an unconscious level I knew he was the glue keeping us all together. He filled the house with light. I loved watching Makoto take care of him. That was when I could see the softness, sensitivity and patience that had been hidden deep down inside.

Parting from Shizuka

Shizuka's condition deteriorated from day to day. He had been bedridden for many years but his heart continued pumping because, according to the doctors, he had been engaged in sports for many years. He couldn't function independently and was completely dependent on Kurako and her devoted care. To make things easier, Norio had constructed a hoist above the bed to help him move to his wheelchair. Every day for the past 15 years had followed the same routine: Kurako wheeled him into the kitchen, fed him and talked to him. Then they would watch TV together and in the afternoon she brought him back to bed for a nap. While he slept she cleaned the house, and when he woke up she returned to taking care of him with a dedication that was truly astonishing to me. I admired her patience. She never complained; it was her life and she had accepted it, despite the many sacrifices she had to make and the difficulties she bore. She made sure he was clean, and when he became incontinent and needed adult diapers, she was the one who changed them. Her internal strength was amazing, and I couldn't envisage myself doing the same thing.

When Shizuka's condition continued to deteriorate

the doctors decided to hospitalize him. Kurako spent every day sitting at his bedside and took care of him just as she had at home. They followed the same routine, she fed him and then they watched TV together. He gradually stopped communicating and finally no longer recognized her. She remained at his bedside and I was certain she was brokenhearted. For moral support we went to visit her at the hospital on the weekends. To raise her spirits, we took her out to lunch at restaurants and bought her food that would help her vary the hospital cuisine.

Shizuka no longer had an appetite, and within a short time he lost a lot of weight. From that point he went downhill quickly. I had never known him when he was healthy. From Makoto and the children's stories I tried to picture him as he had been, but it was difficult.

A number of months after he entered the hospital the doctors asked Kurako to gather the family because the end was near. She called Makoto and asked him to come that same day so we could say goodbye to his father. Makoto told me to get ready for the ride in the evening. I went to pick up Kai and waited for the children to come home from school, and told them about their grandfather's condition. Early that evening we drove to Tsukuba. We were halfway there when Norio called from the hospital to tell us Shizuka had passed away. We changed plans and drove straight to his parents' house.

It was a blow to all of us that we hadn't been able to say goodbye to him. When we arrived at Makoto's parents' house it was full of neighbors and family members who had come to help. Going immediately to the house of someone who passed away was a village custom. Everyone knew what they were supposed to do and together made all the necessary preparations for the funeral. Shortly after we arrived Kurako and Norio came home and she organized a memorial corner for Shizuka. His body was supposed to arrive shortly and the house had to be ready to receive him. The neighbors and relatives dismantled the doors and moved the furniture to the side, laying a clean futon in the middle of the room. Incense was lit and we waited in silence for the arrival of the body. A short time later, an ambulance parked in front of the house and Shizuka's body was carried inside and laid on the futon in the middle of the house. He had been dressed in an ironed kimono and his eyes were closed. When his lower jaw dropped Makoto rushed to close it. When it refused to remain in place Makoto took a handkerchief and tied it around his father's head to secure it. I was shocked by it all. I had never been so close to a dead body. I found a distant corner and observed the people around me. It was hard to believe it was really happening.

Somewhat later representatives from the burial company came and sat in a separate room with Makoto, Norio and Kurako to make arrangements for the funeral. Kurako wanted an elaborate, expensive funeral ceremony for her husband. It completely contradicted her frugal lifestyle, but she was willing to spend whatever it took. She wanted her husband buried with honor. She ordered flowers and decorations and gave detailed instruction for the ceremony. It was very late at night when we said goodbye to her and drove back to Tokyo. No one spoke during the ride, but I could sense Makoto was deeply sad and troubled. I wanted to comfort him but I didn't know how.

The next morning, we all got up early and waited for the neighborhood department store to open so we could buy clothing for the funeral. It was another strange custom I had never met before. Why did we need new clothes for a funeral? In Israel no one bought clothes for a sad occasion. Makoto chose black suits for Tomonori and Michitaka. The salesman helped him with the white shirts and black ties. We also bought them black shoes and socks. Kai got pants, a shirt, shoes and socks, all black. As I moved the hangers back and forth on the racks in the women's funeral clothing department I was sorry I hadn't bought a black suit while I was in Israel. Everything they had on sale was too small for me. I finally found something that would fit me, but the sleeves and pant legs were too short. For a considerable sum it would be altered, express. Luckily I had bought black shoes in Israel so I didn't have to try finding a pair in my size.

When we returned to Kurako's house, we found the entire area in front of the door covered with enormous paper flowers and the garden was decorated. A large stage had been erected inside the house, with a picture of Shizuka, and it was surrounded by flowers and colored lights. A bunch of women were in the kitchen, preparing food for people who came to offer their condolences. Shizuka's body was placed on a bed of dry ice and one after another people lit incense sticks, perfuming the house. Kurako spent the night sitting next to her husband, which was her way of saying goodbye to him. It sent shivers up my spine and I couldn't imagine doing it myself.

An enormous number of people came to offer their condolences. They sat on their knees facing the body, closed their eyes and whispered a prayer. Then they struck a Tibetan bowl and bowed. The children and I had to perform the ceremony as well and it took all my willpower, but I did what was expected of me as quickly as I dared. As the years passed I learned to become accustomed to the ceremonious nature of Japanese funerals when Makoto's relatives died. It got easier each time, and in the end I became fairly immune to the whole issue.

The funeral was held the following morning at nine o'clock. Guests continued coming to take their leave from him before the final long process of cremating the body took place. Friends from Makoto and Norio's childhood came, as well as neighbors and relatives. I was amazed by the number, but Makoto told me his parents were well-known throughout the village because of the land they owned and rented out to people far and wide. Kurako had managed the lands for the past several years so everyone knew and respected her. I understood how the size of the funeral reflected their status in the village.

When the day finally ended I was exhausted and depressed. On the way home Makoto prepared me for the following day, which only made me feel worse. It was the most important day and Makoto wanted me there with Tomonori and Michitaka, standing next to them and imitating everything they did throughout the ceremony. I promised I would, and that I would be able to deal with Kai as well.

When we got home Makoto asked the children to dye

their hair back to its normal black. The following morning we got up very early and wore our new black clothes. It was weird, because dressing up made me feel we were going to a party, not a funeral. Everyone made sure to look their best. The children shaved, Makoto asked me to use makeup, style my hair and wear the pearl necklace he had bought me years ago.

It turned out Kurako and Fumie woke up at four o'clock, two hours before us, to get ready. They had to put on kimonos, arrange their hair in a specific way and put on only a bit of makeup. Finally, they put on pearl necklaces and earrings. At that moment I was so happy to be a foreigner because it meant I was saved from having to wear a kimono and all it entailed.

At eight o'clock people started arriving at the house again, everyone wearing black and looking elegant, holding white envelopes decorated with bows made of black wire. A neighbor was sitting a long table near the door and as people came in they gave him the envelopes, which contained money for the mourners. Then they signed the guest book, removed their shoes and entered the house. I looked at the long line snaking along the path and again wondered at the patience they had for the long, slow walk into the house.

Shizuka's body had been moved to a coffin with a window in the upper part, through which his pale face could be seen. People walked silently around the coffin and then sat on their knees facing it. They closed their eyes, said a prayer, then lit an incense stick, stuck it into a bowl of sand and struck the bowl with a stick. After the sound of the gong they clapped their hands together and went to sit on pillows in the large room. The ceremony lasted about an hour and symbolized their parting from Shizuka.

A priest came in wearing an orange kimono and said a long prayer. When he finished the guests began humming a song; it sounded as though they were mumbling. When I asked Tomonori later he said he also couldn't understand the words. Later my curiosity prompted me to read about the ceremony and I found out that the priest had asked Buddha to take Shizuka's soul. According to Buddhism, the soul of the departed remains in the home for 49 days, so the prayer is very important because it releases the soul for its journey to the next world.

After the ceremony several men carried the coffin to the hearse waiting outside, and Makoto and Norio sat up front for the last ride with their father. There was a small golden temple on the roof of the vehicle. Tomonori explained to me that the car will be taking his grandfather to the crematorium. Other people, including the children and myself, went there by bus. The drive took only about ten minutes, but with everyone staring at me it felt much longer. They kept asking me questions, and said that while they knew Makoto had married a foreigner it was the first time they were meeting me. Mostly they wanted to know how I communicated with the children.

One by one we entered a large hall in the middle of which was the coffin. Everyone stood in silence, the priest murmured a prayer again, this time much shorter. Then he opened the door to another room and Shizuka's coffin was placed inside a chamber on a metal slab. The door closed, the priest pressed a button and asked everyone to move into a large room.

We sat at tables for an enormous meal of sushi, tempura, fried chicken, soba noodles and large quantities of sake. Makoto and Norio eulogized their father and thanked the guests for taking time out from their busy day to come and say goodbye to their father. They spoke a little about the accident that crippled him so many years before and reflected on his last months. Watching from the side, I couldn't help but compare the event to a wedding.

Then everyone was called back into the main hall. The priest waited until everyone was inside and opened the door to the chamber and removed the metal slab, on which were a pile of ashes and what looked like small pieces of bone. It made me nauseous and I was afraid I would pass out. Makoto sensed my reaction and sent me an angry look that said I had better get ahold of myself immediately. I went outside for some fresh air. While we were sitting and eating, Shizuka's body was being cremated in the next room. The smell was awful and nausea was my immediate physical reaction to it. After a few minutes one of the guests came out and said Makoto wanted me back inside. The immediate family stood in two rows across the table facing each other and formed couples. Each couple at their own turn raised long wooden sticks and pulled over pieces of bone which they then put into a large urn. When I went back inside Makoto signaled me to stand next to him with the children. When our turn came we performed the ceremony, which showed last respects to the departed and was considered a duty in Japanese culture. I did what was expected of me without protest. Kai was outside with the bus driver, and happily he provided me with the excuse needed to go check on him. When the bone-gathering ceremony ended we went back to Kurako's house. People who were not close enough to the family to participate in the actual ceremony were waiting for us outside.

Makoto and Norio asked me to join them with the children and we walked from the house to the cemetery, which was about 300 meters away. The priest led the way, followed by Kurako, Norio and his family, and us. The guests, of whom there was an enormous number, followed behind.

Shizuka's grave had already been prepared. There was a headstone with the family name engraved and urns, including the urn with Shizuka's ashes. Later, whenever I got the chance, I'd tell Makoto as well at the children, that under no circumstance would I accept being buried this way. I told them that when I died I wanted my body shipped back to Israel for a Jewish funeral and burial. They enjoyed teasing me about it, perhaps because they realized how serious I was, and they kept telling me that as soon as I joined the Okubo family I was one of them dead or alive. I didn't find it funny at all.

According to Japanese tradition the eldest son went to live with the parent who was widowed and took care of that parent until he or she died. Norio told Makoto he would do what was expected of him and moved in with his mother the following week. According to the same tradition, he was also his mother's sole heir. Nevertheless, I thought the sacrifice Norio would have to make as the eldest was excessive, especially since according to statistics, the

Japanese had a very long life expectancy, and taking care of an aged parent was not easy at all. It turned out that for that reason a lot of Japanese women refused to marry the eldest son, because one day they would have to take care of one of his parents. Kurako was 69 years old, and she was a strong, stiff woman. But Norio loved the house and was willing to endure whatever it took, if only to inherit the property he had kept up and taken care of for so many years before his father died.

We all wondered how the women would get along, Kurako and Fumie, who had been at odds with one another for so many years. Actually, we worried more than wondered. Makoto even said so to his brother that morning, but Norio answered unequivocally, "If Fumie doesn't treat my mother with respect I will divorce her." I had my doubts, although I knew how much he wanted to inherit his parents' property.

There was, however, a change in plans, and Fumie didn't carry out the family expectations. Norio and Fumie lived in a modern house about 15 minutes away by car. After Norio moved in with his mother, Fumie moved in, but only partially. She left all her belongings in their modern house and went to her mother-in-law's house at night to sleep with Norio. In the morning she ate breakfast with them, helped clean the house, and then returned to her own home to get organized before she left for work. She continued meeting with her friends in the afternoon, then went home to take a shower and rest, and only returned to Kurako's house before dinner.

The arrangement made Kurako very uncomfortable,

and she called Makoto almost every day to complain. She demanded Fumie behave in the fashion expected of the wife of the eldest son and live with them, as she should. For Kurako everything was black and white, she couldn't understand that a problem might have more than one solution, or a partial solution, and as far as she was concerned, a partial solution was no solution at all.

Every weekend we went to visit Kurako to help raise her morale, and she saved a week's worth of complaints for us. We tried to bring some joy to her life and encourage her as much as possible.

Norio was helpless in the face of his mother's displeasure, and he insisted his wife come to live with them. She conditioned it on having the house renovated and modernized to provide her with the kind of life style she was accustomed to. Norio went from one contractor to another and invested time and money in the renovation. The kitchen and bathroom were remodeled, a two-story wooden structure was built in the garden for Fumie to live in and decorated in a modern rustic style. He bought her a large TV set and expensive modern furniture, and had air conditioners installed in every room. A corridor joined the new house to Kurako's, so to a certain extent the 2 houses became one building.

Kurako lost control of herself. She was furious, she screamed, she cried and complained. She didn't like change and clung to the way of life she knew. She liked the old kitchen and bathroom she had been using her entire life, and she was furious that her daughter-in-law was living on her property but not in her house. Her anger was reflected in the weight she lost, seemingly every day, and we worried about her a great deal. She started transferring money from her bank account to Makoto's and putting some of her lands in her grandchildren's names, all to keep her daughter-in-law from getting her hands on it. She became introverted and angry all the time, and was no longer the loving grandmother the children knew.

Norio knew the land had changed hands but seemed apathetic. The most important thing for him was the house. That was what he was after. He and Makoto were very different from one another. Norio was active and always doing something, and if he wasn't doing something he found something new. I was impressed by him, he seemed indefatigable and completely successful. He was prosperous, his company was thriving, and he had a cadre of loyal, devoted employees who ran the company for him so he could allow himself to go to the office only a few times a week to see how things were going. Most of his time was devoted to his hobbies.

We thought that once Shizuka had passed away Kurako would be able to visit us in Tokyo, but she always had an excuse for why she couldn't come. Finally Norio convinced her, and he drove her down to stay with us for a couple of days. She hadn't been in Tokyo for 15 years. She was uncomfortable in the city and liked the countryside better, but she was impressed by how Tokyo had changed. Every day we drove her to a different place and walked around. She asked to visit the most famous temple, where she wanted to buy a good luck charm that would preserve her health. And while she was enjoying herself, she was still obviously tense.

Her first visit to us, however, was not very successful. No matter how hard we tried to make her happy, she was always nervous. We decided that the next time we would suggest she join us on a trip to the mountains. We wanted to make her life more pleasant and agreeable after so many years of taking care of Shizuka.

Kurako taught me how to make the simple Japanese food Makoto liked. Every time we visited her, before we drove home she filled the car with rice, vegetables and fruit. Going to visit her became part of our routine and we enjoyed it very much. She was Kai's only grandmother and she worried about all of us. Even after her death we continued thanking her for the money she had given us, because it made our lives far easier. Makoto paid off the loan on the house and paid all the children's tuition and other educational expenses.

Happily, Kurako and I had a great relationship. I knew that if she didn't like me I would sense it immediately. She never hesitated to criticize anything she didn't like, and I was happy that distance separated us. It made the relationship easier, and I knew how unyielding she was regarding her daughters-in-law, both Fumie and Yuriko, and what they had had to put up with. It couldn't have been easy living with her, and she was never satisfied with them. She appreciated me because I was raising her grandsons, I got positive feedback for that and not only from her. Jaws dropped when people heard I had married a divorced father with two children. I was happy they reacted that way, and besides, I enjoyed

Tomonori and Michitaka's company. They helped me raise Kai and taught me a great deal about life in Japan.

Mentality: A Test Case

For years I wandered in a fog through a culture and way of life I couldn't fully comprehend and a language I could barely understand and speak, but I wanted to make them my own. I can't put my finger on the exact moment it happened because it was a slow and gradual process, but after four years of marriage and children aged two, 17 and 20, I began to finally think I was getting a grasp of Japan. Or, that's what I thought, anyway. I have been told that when you leave the country of your birth for another country, you will always feel you are neither here nor there. But while I am Israeli and will always be Israeli, something about me is Japanese as well.

Some things became 100% mine: Makoto, the children, the house, my friends. But there were also things I never dreamed I would miss so much, simple things I took for granted like spending the holidays with my family. The holidays in Israel were just ordinary working days in Japan, not marked in any way. I tried to make the holidays and Saturdays special, at least for me, but with no success. Even my birthdays were nothing special and that depressed me. Makoto tried everything he could think of to make me feel better. He sent me flowers, bought me presents and a birthday cake and took me out to dinner. At such times I felt I was as distant as could ever be from Israel. During the 1990s communications weren't as developed the way they are today, international calls were very expensive and the Internet wasn't widely used, so calling Israel meant conversations that were short and purposeful with little time to express feelings.

Every time I felt homesick I didn't understand why. After all it was my own choice to live on the other side of the world, my choice to marry a man from a different culture who had two adolescent sons. But, knowing that this was my life and would be my life forever was stressful. I kept encouraging myself to keep positive but there were times I thought I was losing my mind in the process of trying to find the path to my happiness.

I decided to listen to my internal voice telling me not to let go of my authentic sabra self, and I did it in various ways: I celebrated holidays with other Israelis living in Japan, visited Israel once a year, even twice a year when homesickness overcame me. I also refused to surrender to Japan's strict rules of conduct, I couldn't stand them. I respected and endured the local culture when I was outside of the house, but kept true to myself at home. I would be an Israeli, cook the food I knew and loved as well as Japanese food for Makoto and the children. I would do everything to maintain my happiness.

My greatest difficulty was the Japanese approach to education. I had immense problems with it, especially when it was related to Kai. I couldn't stand the way children were brought up in Japan, and as time passed my objections increased. One difficulty was mother love, which is powerful and cannot be stopped or prevented from influencing the way a child is raised. I wanted Kai to have a good life and be happy, and I couldn't bear the thought that he would be raised the way Tomonori and Michitaka had been. That was what guided me in everything I did, and from a very early age Kai understood his mother was different from other mothers.

The absurdity was that Kai kept trying to make me be like the other mothers. It bothered him that I didn't act like everyone else. He took it upon himself to be my mentor and when he was young, for example, he demanded I obey the rules they taught him in kindergarten. As far as I was concerned it was ridiculous. The rules were illogical in my opinion. But they were important to him and when I criticized him for obeying them or objected to them, he was surprised and confused. He was being given two conflicting sets of messages because I allowed him to do things forbidden by his kindergarten teacher and father. I refused to give in and tried to teach him not to be afraid of the strict environment he lived in. I wanted him to understand he could be free and that openness was a wonderful thing. But it wasn't simple or easy because every hour of every day he saw Japanese who didn't dare go beyond the accepted limits. Everyone, except his mother, adhered to certain norms and there were no exceptions. Young and old, everyone reacted the same way and obeyed the rules blindly. Asking for a reason to the rule I didn't understand or didn't want to follow was unacceptable.

Kai came with me on my visits to Israel, and kept telling me, "Mommy, I'm Japanese, not Israeli." He insisted I speak Japanese with him and refused to let me speak Hebrew. Whenever I spoke Japanese, he corrected my mistakes and often told me, "There is no such word."

He was only five years old but he tried to fit me into the Japanese mold. When we went up an escalator he insisted on standing on the left-hand side, as was customary, and became angry with me if I stood on the right. When we waited for an elevator he demanded I stand at the side of the door behind the yellow line. I felt my spontaneity embarrassed him, and it was for his sake that I learned how to behave like a Japanese woman. I became more restrained and polite. I became more aware of my surroundings and respectful of the social codes. I tried to attract as little attention as possible, and in that way to my surprise discovered that when there is order, and everyone respects the rules, life becomes very organized and efficient.

Externally I behaved as was expected, but internally there were moments when I was giggling. I had no one to share my humor with when I waited for the light to turn green at the crosswalk. It could be very late at night without a car in sight, it made no difference, the Japanese stood and waited for the light to change. None of them dared break the rule and simply walk across the street. That reflected their approach to life in general. They always seemed weird to me, predictable, so uncreative. But sometimes along with the fun I made of it, I could admit, at least to myself, that there was something reassuring about being able to predict people's behavior. I knew I would never be surprised and yet, sometimes I missed the Israeli sharpness, the creative thinking and flexibility, and the ability to improvise.

Ultimately, Kai's attempts to educate me had their influence and as time passed I became more serene and less stubborn. I learned, with a certain amount of self-surrender, to accept and understand behavior that was different from what I was used to. I opened my heart to Japanese culture and stopped being so judgmental. I looked for the light at the end of the tunnel and found insights into the power of the well-oiled Japanese machine.

From within the way of life I had adapted myself to, there were always Israeli idiosyncrasies that flared up now and again. Small things that didn't escape the eyes of my Japanese friends. One of them was the way I arranged shoes just inside the front door, or rather, the way I didn't arrange them the way I was supposed to. The Japanese take their shoes off when they enter a house, and I did also. But then they arranged their shoes pointing outward so they could easily slip into them on the way out of the house. I never did, I kicked my shoes off and left them where they fell.

The custom of removing shoes was preserved in public buildings as well, local restaurants, hospitals, schools and kindergartens. It frustrated me every time. I couldn't bear the idea that I had to keep acting like a robot and put my shoes one next to another pointing to the door. To this day, I take them off and just leave them. Over the years I got rid of all my lace-up shoes so it would be easier to take them off and put them back on. I also bought lots of new socks so I wouldn't be embarrassed by wearing socks with holes in them.

Japanese consumers have a penchant for name brands. Almost every woman had a purse that had come from either Gucci, Prada or Chanel. They wore expensive watches, clothes, and shoes from the most famous international designers. However, they were completely lacking in creativity. They looked the same, as though they had all come off the same assembly line. I tried to understand why they never tried to break out of the mold, especially since they had the financial ability to do so, and dress more originally. Makoto said it was because they didn't understand fashion, they merely copied what famous people were wearing that year. That was the way they did things, he said, they preferred to copy their favorite actresses and singers.

He explained other things I had no answer for. He told me for the first time why my friends never invited me to their homes. It was because, he claimed, their houses were full of the things they bought and didn't have time to put away. That was absurd, because clearly it was important for them to look good, but didn't they want their homes to look nice as well? One day I happened to enter the home of Ryoga, who was a friend of Kai's, and I saw with my own eyes that Makoto was right. The entrance to the house was full of boxes with fancy brand labels holding purses and shoes bought by Ryoga's mother. A quick look told me the house had three rooms, one for Ryoga and his mother, one for his father and a living room, as well as a kitchen, bathroom and toilet. In the center of the living room was the kotatsu table, a low table surrounded with pillows, similar to the one I saw for the first time in the home of Makoto's parents. In the winter a heater is placed under the table and it is covered with a large cloth, almost a blanket, and everyone sits around it, covered and heated while eating dinner. In the summer the heating unit is removed, the blanket is removed, and both are stored for the following winter.

There was almost no furniture in the house. I imagined it was because the house was so small they preferred not to have too much clutter. There was an enormous closet in every room full of clothing with designer labels and piles of things in every corner. There was another reason the Japanese saved all the boxes. When they got tired of what they had bought they put them in their original boxes and sold them to secondhand stores for half price. With the money they received they bought something else to wear at the same store, something that had barely been worn and thus saved a lot of money. That way, even women who couldn't really afford expensive things could still have a Rolex watch, a Prada bag or Gucci shoes. On several occasions I also bought secondhand goods and got real bargains.

Another thing I learned from my Japanese friends was that most of them spent their free time outside the house, usually meeting friends in the city for shopping or sitting in a restaurant. I, on the other hand, liked hosting in my own home. When I was at home there were no time constraints and we could sit comfortably. They kept apologizing that they couldn't invite me to their homes. But once Makoto had explained why, I stopped caring it and I told them I was happy to have them in my home and let the topic drop. They never came empty-handed and always brought fruit or a cake or something they had cooked. That was fine with me, it made my life easier, and in addition, not only was it a cure for my loneliness, it helped improve my Japanese. They helped me find the kind of speech that was appropriate for my status. Differences in status are expressed in forms of speech, children have a lower status and speak more informally, while adults have a higher status and speak formally. People with certain professions, such as doctors, lawyers or teachers, are called Sansei and are highly regarded, and their speech is the most formal. Since I was a foreigner they indulged and forgave me, and I was the only parent who addressed the kindergarten teachers inappropriately. I also allowed myself to joke and talk to them as though they were my friends, which the other mothers did not.

It might all seem trivial, but the rules were very clear and strictly followed. For example, when I returned from a visit to Israel I brought Kai's kindergarten teachers a box of chocolates. They absolutely refused to accept it because they were forbidden to receive gifts from parents. I tried to convince them it was only chocolate, but I had no success in breaching the wall. That was the last time I tried to give them a present.

What happened at home stayed at home, mainly to preserve Makoto's honor. For example, his mother never knew he helped me cook or that a maid cleaned the house. Makoto asked me to keep it a secret because his mother would come to only one conclusion, that I was spoiled. When we visited Kurako's house I kept my traditional-wife face on. I let Makoto watch TV while I helped his mother in the kitchen, and I served him tea and rice cookies.

The children gradually adapted and got used to me, and eventually Tomonori and Michitaka accepted me for what I was, and also found the advantages in having a foreign stepmother. They began to boast that their father was married to an Israeli and their half-brother was half-foreign. They thanked me in their own way for the trips we took abroad and for opening a door to other cultures, and for arguing with their father on their behalf to allow them more freedom of choice.

Nevertheless, the sensation of being a stranger in Japan never left me, and if there was something that preserved my sense of balance it was calling my friends and family in Israel. I needed to talk to them, it kept me in touch with my roots. I think Makoto was able to accept and understand that, but he couldn't accept how expensive international calls were, and when the phone bills came he couldn't contain his anger. He demanded I call less frequently, but those calls were my lifeline and I couldn't do without them. More than once he told me that if I behaved with my Japanese friends the way I behaved with my Israeli friends they would have nothing more to do with me. Japanese women, he insisted, didn't want to talk about personal things, and certainly didn't want to hear my complaints about the Japanese culture. Happily, my friends also included Sandy, Cai and Sophie, and I could talk to them about things I would never dare mention to my Japanese friends. They listened to me and I listened to them, and tried to help them with their problems. One day I came up with a theory to explain the difference between the Japanese behavior compared with the Israeli. The Japanese use their heads, they are logical and rational and blindly obey rules like machines. Israelis are also logical and rational, but they use their hearts as well as their heads, and they always question everything.

When Kai was three, the other mothers pressured me into joining the kindergarten committee. Membership in the committee was based on voluntary rotation and changed every year. Those who wanted the best for me told me that in any case at some point I would have to volunteer, and the sooner I did the easier it would be. "The older the children get the more work the committee parent has to do," they explained, and that convinced me to volunteer that year.

Since I was a foreigner I went to committee meetings but didn't dare say anything. After the first meeting they invited me to go to a local bar with them. Just like the men, a couple of cups of sake released their inhibitions and they were frank with me about their problems. Since I had no inhibitions, with or without the sake, I felt perfectly comfortable. Alcohol, I said to myself, was a good friend, especially when I looked at how it influenced the Japanese. It enabled me to really get to know those women better. Their drunken state helped me ask them personal questions about the relations with their husbands and to learn more about what really happened in Japanese homes.

I learned a lot of things outside our home that were never put into practice because of my agreement with Makoto, such as managing the family budget. That was left entirely in the hands of the wife, and she had the important task of deciding how much would be spent and on what. Some of the money went for daily expenses, some was deposited in a savings account for the children and some for a house. Wives even decided whether to buy a house or continue renting.

From the very beginning Makoto and I decided we would do things differently. Obviously, he would continue being responsible for the budget, exactly as he had done since his divorce. He was responsible for Tomonori and Michitaka's future, and of course there was the language barrier, which meant I couldn't understand the fine print. I was happy to let him be the family banker and in control of our finances.

The other mothers had guessed that the way Makoto and I led our lives was unlike the typical Japanese way in many respects. That didn't surprise me. Being different wasn't painful, quite the opposite really. In reality, in many respects I felt sorry for them, and would never have changed places with them. While they did have the status of CFO at home, they knew no warmth from their husbands. I also pitied their husbands, whose reception every evening was so apathetic and lukewarm at home and where the atmosphere was particularly depressing. Every day I was thankful I had managed to navigate my relationship with Makoto along a different course, and I hoped it would continue that way.

When I was single everything in Japan seemed wonderful, but now, as a mother, when I had a more comprehensive overview, I understood the price the Japanese paid and it depressed me. Suddenly, the strict order made me anxious and the courtesy seemed hypocritical and inhuman. I wanted to return to the warmth I had known and I was homesick for Israeli openness and spontaneity. It was most likely motherhood that was making me feel that way and I was worried about Kai. It was difficult for me to accept the Japanese aspects of his upbringing. I despised the educational methods used in his kindergarten, the strict obedience demanded of such small children that turned them into little soldiers. For me, the kindergarten teachers' expectations of two-year-old toddlers, that they internalize and adopt the behavior of older children, was weird. They were repeatedly told not to cry, because only infants cried. If something hurt or was difficult, they were expected to act with restraint. They were always being told, over and over again, not to show emotions. *Self-control* was the mantra they heard repeatedly, in kindergarten and at home. It was an extremely important part of the Japanese education. When Kai cried Makoto would tell him, "You're a boy. Learn to control yourself. Boys don't cry." Later, when he entered first grade, Makoto and the children told him, "You're a big boy, you aren't supposed to cry."

The demand for restraint and self-control was also expected of me. If I lost my patience or showed dissatisfaction, the first thing Makoto would always say was, "You're already a mother. You have to think about your child, not about yourself. Restrain and control yourself."

Another Japanese trait is the almost-complete avoidance of physical contact. Sometimes entire months went by and the only people I touched were Kai and Makoto. Luckily, at least I could recharge my batteries during my visits to Israel. In Japan it is unacceptable to even shake hands, people merely bow to one another. Tomonori and Michitaka were always embarrassed when people came to visit us from Israel and our natural reaction was to hug and kiss each other. They kept begging me to tell my guests that in Japan it was unacceptable behavior. When I picked Kai up from kindergarten I always hugged and kissed him. Very quickly the other children began standing in line for me to hug and kiss them as well. It was very apparent they liked it, and probably needed it as well. Japanese mothers stopped kissing their children when they were quite young, and at a certain point Kai's friends began to laugh with embarrassment, but that didn't deter him in the least, it had the opposite effect. When he was in kindergarten he seemed to like making other people uncomfortable and became demonstrative when they were around. When he grew up things had changed. I just wanted to give him the same love and warmth I had received as a child.

Reactions to my insistence on Israeli education were mixed. My Japanese friends couldn't get used to it and warned me Kai was in danger of becoming spoiled, and in the end I would be the one to suffer the consequences. His kindergarten teachers were amused by the way he showed his fondness for the girls in his group. They told me he was the only child who hugged and kissed, but I already knew that.

Every time I showed Makoto affection he was terribly embarrassed, especially in the beginning before he got used to it. When I kissed him in public he would check to see if anyone was looking, as if estimating the damage I was causing. He would protest but I discounted it and told him there was nothing to be ashamed of. He was my husband, I loved him, and it was only natural that I express my love.

Over the years we became friends with many mixed couples. My persistence and the fact that our immediate environment changed eventually had an influence on Makoto. He surrendered to the warmth I showed him and began demonstrating love and tenderness as well. He influenced his Japanese friends, who showed they were capable of smiling more and speaking much more freely.

When Kai was five and in preschool, he asked me to have a big birthday party at home. That had never happened before and I was happy to comply and finally had the opportunity to do something I was familiar with and capable of doing. I immediately got into gear and began planning. After searching for a while and consulting with my American friends I found a clown, decorated the house with balloons, ordered Kai a birthday cake decorated with his favorite superheroes, prepared little party favors for the children and invited his friends from preschool and my foreign friends and their children. The Japanese guests were amazed; they had never attended a birthday party like the one I held for Kai. On the other hand, I was amazed by the presents he received, which were fairly weird. He got bags of cookies, candy or stickers. It was ridiculous. They had no idea about birthday parties in people's houses. The only birthdays they knew were the ones celebrated in the kindergarten. The child sat in front of his friends with a crown on his head and the children came up to him in turn and gave him a drawing they made for him, and wished him a happy birthday.

After having been to Kai's party, several mothers told me that thanks to Kai they had greatly enjoyed, the opportunity to experience other cultures and customs.

I turned his birthday parties at our home into a tradition which I followed for many years, and eventually I moved it to a park or a nearby restaurant. The children surprised their parents by learning to play the games I remembered from my youth. Kai's friends came with their parents, who took loads of pictures, and even their siblings joined in the fun.

Every year during the party preparations Makoto followed my every move and didn't hide his disapproval. He kept telling me I was simply insane. I smiled to myself and thought that for someone who was insane I was doing just fine. Besides, I also heard the enthusiastic reactions of Kai's friends, who mentioned his special birthday parties for years to come, and I was happy for the joy Kai felt. As he grew older I saw how he learned to follow the Japanese custom and ceremony. I wanted him to be familiar with and become part of the Israeli tradition as well. I wanted him to know the festive aspects of the Jewish holidays such as Purim, Passover and Rosh Hashana, not the religious duties. I wanted him to know about Jewish customs and traditions.

Makoto had no particular religious identity. When I asked him what his affiliation was he said he was not a Buddhist, not a practitioner of Shinto and not a Christian. He was Japanese, and religion had no interest to him. Only the traditions were important to him. To this day I know that Makoto's traditional approach saved Kai a lot of confusion. That way we could celebrate both Christmas and Hanukkah, and the children got presents for Christmas, finding them under their pillows, and we lit the menorah and ate jelly donuts for Hanukkah. Kai liked the combination.

New Year's Eve is one of the most important holidays

in Japan. The last day of work for most employees is December 29th, and on January 1st the stores close, the only day during the year when they do. The Japanese tend to spend vacations with relatives who live far away, and sometimes they travel abroad. At that time the demand for international and domestic plane tickets and trains is high.

Our family custom was to visit Kurako's home, and she followed all the traditional customs, one of which was eating long buckwheat noodles called *soba* at midnight on New Year's Eve. Soba are made by hand and symbolize long life. The demand for them before the holiday is enormous. The following morning Kurako served the traditional New Year's breakfast, each dish with its own symbolic meaning. Sweet red beans were for strength and health, fish in a sweet sauce for a good rice harvest and fish eggs for fertility. There were eggs rolled in sweet seasoning, ozoni soup with mochi rice cakes, and other sweet dishes symbolizing the hope for a sweet new year. To a certain extent, they reminded me of what we ate at a Jewish New Year's meal.

Japanese tradition varied widely from one region to another and every district had its own special dishes with their particular significance. However, all the TV stations broadcast entertainment suitable for the whole family. Every year we sat close to each other on the floor around the *kotatsu* table, warming ourselves on the heater beneath it while eating and watching TV.

It seemed to me it was more of a holiday for men and less for women. The men enjoyed three enormous meals every day while the women worked to prepare and serve them. The first time we went to Tsukuba to celebrate New

Year's Eve and the holiday I returned home unhappy and exhausted. For three days I had washed piles of dishes, helped prepare meals, served the food and cleared the table without a minute's rest, working around the clock. When the nightmare ended and we went home I took all my frustration out on Makoto. It infuriated me that he had sat with the men and not lifted a finger to help me. I swore it was the last time I would ever celebrate the New Year that way. He said that if his mother had seen him helping me she would have been profoundly shocked. Men didn't help in the kitchen.

The holiday made it clear to me how inferior women's status was in Japan. I was angry I had been forced into the situation and hated the thought I would have to repeat it the same way every year. At home we were all equal. I made it a custom for the boys to help me and after we finished eating everyone took their own plate to the kitchen and put it in the dishwasher. Makoto did the cooking on the weekends and everyone helped clean up. Makoto accepted the majority of the changes I had enforced, but still found it difficult to watch the children clean. He pitied them to no end and said children helping their mothers was out of Japanese common sense. The difference in our approaches as to how a mother should raise her children was one of our main points of contention and that never changed. Makoto claimed Israeli mothers were selfish, egotistical, spoiled and didn't know how to raise their children, and I though Japanese mothers were ultimately cold, bitter housemaids. It was something we never managed to agree upon.

During the week of the New Year, Japanese went to

the temples to pray to the gods for prosperity and health for the upcoming year. The temples sold good luck charms and it was customary to give them as gifts to relatives. The charm was kept in a wallet or a bag, and the Japanese genuinely believed in their power. There were charms for warding off sickness, accidents and other catastrophes, and there were charms for luck, income and love.

Every year good luck charms were exchanged for new ones to deal with the needs of the coming year, and the old one was returned to the temple and burnt. Every year Makoto bought each of us a good luck charm, plus one for the car to protect us from accidents, and one for health and one for income. I was surprised by the great faith the Japanese had in the charms because they weren't otherwise religious people.

The custom of housecleaning before the holiday reminded me of the preparations for Passover. Japanese women began cleaning a month before and used steam cleaners, vacuum cleaners, special brushes, soaps and other products. The supermarket shelves were emptied of cleaning products. People sorted through their things that had piled up during the year and threw out what they didn't need and cleaned every corner of the house. They did it every single year. Children waited impatiently for the New Year, to receive from their relatives envelopes filled with money; sums that varied according to their age. They obviously hoped for a lot of money. Kai, Tomonori and Michitaka spent their money on all sorts of little luxuries throughout the year. Makoto also filled envelopes for his nieces and nephews, which were distributed during rounds of visits to relatives. People wished one another a happy new year and gave the children their presents.

Makoto respected my tradition, and joined me during the Jewish holidays, which we celebrated at the Chabad center. It was a nice gesture on his part, especially in light of the fact that Jewish tradition was utterly foreign to him. He didn't understand Hebrew or the blunt Jewish mentality, and in his opinion the meeting was nothing more than a free-for-all. The Israelis who came to the center were young, most of them just out of the army, they had long hair and piercings and they were everything that completely violated the conservative appearance Makoto valued.

For me it was almost like being at home, although it made me homesick for my family in Israel. Meeting Israelis like me at the Chabad center didn't fill the void I felt. I realized that Makoto was making a great sacrifice just to make me happy on the Jewish holidays. At some stage I told him he didn't have to come with me anymore and this actually made me feel liberated. I got closer to the community of Jews married to Japanese, and after a number of years I stopped going to the Chabad center and began celebrating with these people in their homes. As time passed the fluctuation between the two traditions, Jewish and Japanese, became balanced, and once I stopped comparing them, I could enjoy them both.

Days of Crisis

The year Tomonori graduated from high school he said he wanted to study interior design at a professional school. He didn't want to go to university, and I thought it was probably because he was afraid the entrance exams would be too hard. Michitaka was in high school and was an excellent student and Makoto was satisfied. He often repeated that at least Michitaka would go to university, and it turned into the main topic of conversation at home. Countrywide exams were held every three months and the results were considered a way of predicting whether a student would be accepted by a prestigious university or one that is less prestigious.

I could see Michitaka slowly internalize his father's message. He knew how important it was for Makoto to boast about a son accepted by a good school and knew the responsibility was his because Tomonori wouldn't be able to fulfil his father's expectations regarding higher education. It was very important for Makoto that his sons trained for desirable professions at high-ranking universities and lead good, respected lives according to the Japanese standard.

I was shocked by Makoto's obsession with education.

I was often angered by his lack of sensitivity to his sons' souls. He had one objective and he never understood he was breaking their spirits. I meddled as little as possible. They weren't my biological children, and I didn't feel I had the right to channel their education according to what I believed. I didn't want to cause any damage and most of the time I kept quiet when the issue was raised. Nevertheless, on the rare occasions when they did consult me about their studies or anything else regarding their future, I allowed myself, after carefully considering my words, to say what I thought. I always conveyed the same message to them, and it was to follow their dreams. I said they had to listen more to their hearts and less to the people around them. I gently tried to have them be less influenced by their father's pressure, because in the end they would be the ones who would have to live with the consequences of their decisions. They were responsible for their future and there was nothing wrong with learning a profession that was considered less prestigious, or not prestigious at all. The really important thing for them was to study something that interested them.

Makoto was aware I was meddling even though he was never present at any of the conversations I had with them. He could see their new approach and understood it could have only come from me. We argued a lot about their schooling. I was in favor of complete freedom of choice, and he argued that it was a parent's duty to direct his children's choices in life, but his children were terrified of failure. I thought Makoto's pressure made them doubt their ability to succeed, leading them to believe they could never be accepted by a university. In the end, both chose to learn something useful rather than something academic.

University and professional school tuition was $15,000 a year, generally speaking for four years. There were other expenses as well, such as train tickets, food and textbooks, and the expenses kept piling up. Japanese parents saved for years to be able to send their children to good schools because they wanted them to have good lives and comfortable economic prospects. Interestingly enough, the level of studies in Japanese universities was lower than in other countries. It troubled me that from a young age children devoted what should have been the happiest years of their lives solely to studies. When Kai was four years old, my English students explained to me that if I wanted him to succeed in life, I had to send him to private tuition that would prepare him for the first grade. Makoto was happy that my students has worn down my objections and explained how the Japanese educational system worked. He was afraid I wouldn't let Kai have extra lessons, especially in view of my evident distaste regarding the many hours Tomonori and Michitaka devoted to their homework. I asked several people I knew about Japanese education, and they all told me the same thing. The dream of every parent was for his child to study in a national school and from there continue to one of Japan's leading universities. As soon as the child was accepted by such a school his future was assured.

Makoto wanted Kai to take the exam for one of the national schools in Tokyo, and in retrospect his chances of acceptance were low. Each one accepted only 80 pupils for the first grade and there were thousands of candidates.

Everyone told me he should take the exam because it was the best road to success.

My friend and student Yoshida-San, with whom I played golf, ran a well-known neighborhood school which prepared children for the first grade. I asked if Kai could study with her, and I was relieved when she said yes. For the first two years he had two-hour lessons twice a week in the afternoon. She said that in the third and final year, before the exam, the children had three-hour lessons three times a week. Ninety percent of Japan's population didn't speak English, and it was very important for me that Kai have a command of the language and fluent.

I searched until I found an American kindergarten close to our house and enrolled Kai for two days a week, eight hours per day. The public kindergarten was willing to allow him not to attend on those days. He started when he was four years old, and three times a week he had classes in the afternoon to prepare him for the first grade. We also enrolled him in swimming lessons, so at a young age he was already very busy. Throughout that period, I consulted with my friends and students about how to deal with the stress of his daily schedule and how to create a balance to keep him from being miserable. I kept watching Tomonori and Michitaka try, unsuccessfully, to satisfy their father all the time, and give up in the end. I wanted Kai to be a happy child who would remember having enjoyed his childhood.

The changes in Japan's economy came gradually, approaching like dark gray storm clouds. Shu-San, one of my English students, told me financial difficulties were plaguing the company her husband worked for. One day he received notice that his salary was being cut by 10% and the bonuses he received twice a year, in the summer and in the winter, wouldn't be forthcoming. She kept apologizing, because she would have to stop taking lessons. I told Makoto what I heard from Shu-San, and he told me, for the first time, that the company he worked for was also experiencing difficulties and that we might be in the same situation.

At that point we had a very high standard of living and a lot of expenses. Tomonori was studying at a school for Interior design and the tuition fees were high, Michitaka was taking lessons in the evening with a private tutor who was preparing him for university admission exams and Kai had classes to prepare him for the first grade, we paid the mortgage on the house every month, Makoto ran an expensive car and would pay installments on it for the next two years, we went abroad on vacation twice a year, once the entire family went and once I took Kai with me to Israel. My income as an English teacher paid for the trips to Israel and for family entertainment.

Life at home became tense. Makoto became bitter and nervous, and that repelled me. He distanced himself and refused to share his problems with me. Inevitably, our standard of living declined. He stopped buying me presents every weekend and didn't give me money for what I needed. He complained about the water and gas bills and how much the housekeeper cost. I understood I had to start spending less, but I absolutely refused to do without the housekeeper. I couldn't clean up after Tomonori and Michitaka, who were both very messy, and besides, it was thanks to her that my relations with them had improved.

Makoto refused to save money on the children's education and suggested we spend less on entertainment and the luxuries we had become accustomed to. It meant cutting down on everything, and my Japanese friends told me they were in a similar situation. The first thing employees had to give up was their annual bonuses, each of which was equal to two months' salary, which meant 25% less income, a significant blow to many households.

It was only years later that Makoto told me that before the economic crisis, most of our money originated with his investments in the stock market. It never occurred to him that one day it would all be over, and in one month he would lose almost everything and would have to rely on his salary, which didn't cover all the installments he had to pay. In retrospect, I thought it was a pity I hadn't known from the beginning. If I had known I would have used money more wisely, but he always made me feel we had a lot of money coming in and there was nothing to worry about.

Every day the TV and radio news programs reported heavy stock market losses and large companies firing thousands of employees, but I didn't think it had anything to do with me. I didn't know Makoto had invested in the stock market, I had no idea how much he earned, and he never told me how much money we had in the bank. He had a very senior position in the company he worked for and believed he would remain there until it was time for him to retire, and it never occurred to him that he might be fired. A number of our friends were in fact fired and found it very difficult to find other jobs. The work market was a shambles, salaries were low and there were no bonuses.

We started to feel the consequences of the economic situation. Makoto was bitter and frustrated and took his anger out on all of us. He yelled about everything, even stupid little things, and we understood something was going on but we didn't know what. We argued more frequently, almost every day, and eventually I couldn't tell the difference between simple anger and unbridled, furious aggression. He spoke to me as though I were a servant and dictated orders, and I in return yelled that he had no right to talk to me like that. The children and I joined ranks and he became a policeman, pursuing us mercilessly. He kept looking for faults, especially mine, and seemed to enjoy sneering at me and finding proof I was deficient in some respect. He insulted all of us and was angry all the time so we confronted him as little as possible. Sometimes he came home drunk, and we were both angry from dawn to dusk. There were times I threatened to divorce him, and I wanted to return to Israel and take Kai with me. Every time I threatened to divorce him, he would treat me better, but it never lasted more than a week. I remembered what my father told me before I married Makoto, that the day would come when I understood why his wife divorced him.

Makoto kept sending his poisoned darts in my direction and it hurt terribly. He made me feel I was being a lazy, spoilt child who couldn't do anything on her own. It was so different from the respect and admiration I had received in the past for raising his children and being a second mother to them. Apparently, his crisis was so serious it colored his every thought and action.

I thought about personal development and studies,

and Makoto blocked my path. He said, "You're too old to go back to school. Concentrate on raising Kai," clipping my wings. He thought private tutoring was easy, well-paying work and preferred I remain with what I knew and was good at. He didn't know I was incapable of doing the same thing all the time. Routine bored me. The need for change every few years was a concept unknown in Japan. They trod the same path forever. Once they finished university, they joined a large company and stayed there until they retired. Anyone who moved from one company to another was considered unstable and found it difficult to get a good job.

The younger generation was tired of the tradition and strongly objected to the ideology of their parents' generation. Tomonori and Michitaka thought differently from their father, but I thought the way they did. They didn't want to see themselves stuck in the same company for twenty years, like their father. The issue of our future, theirs and mine, was one of the main reasons Makoto and I argued all the time. He simply disliked change and couldn't stand people who kept changing and reinventing themselves. He thought such people would never advance in life. I tried to explain that the Western world had a different approach, and people who felt they had done all they could in one place of work moved on and looked for new challenges and found new jobs, but he couldn't accept it.

One evening when only Makoto and I were in the living room he told me management had called a meeting of the employees and suggested they resign voluntarily, in return for which they would be well compensated. He wanted to consult with me before he made his decision. I was very moved because it was the first time he had shared his concerns with me and wanted my opinion.

We examined everything we knew all over again. He had worked for the insurance company for 22 years and was a dedicated employee. The company was organized like the military. The employees were ranked and were treated according to rank. The younger employees worked very hard, and the more mature, and more experienced employees worked far less and had a lot of power. Makoto had reached the stage where he didn't work too hard and managed 120 employees who feared him and obeyed his orders without asking questions.

The job was perfect for him. He didn't like change and he liked being obeyed. On the other hand, he was 45 years old, and it was his last chance to change careers. After the age of 50 the chances of finding a new job with a high salary were very slim.

Makoto told me his gut feeling was that the situation at the company wouldn't change. It was hard for him to decide whether to remain, with a lower salary and no bonuses, or resign with excellent conditions. He tended towards resigning, and I supported him wholeheartedly.

From the time he handed in his resignation he had one month to tie up loose ends and get organized. We knew that economically we would get by in the short term because he was entitled to eight months of unemployment insurance, which would be 70% of his current salary, so we had time to think of what our next steps would be.

The recession that came after the stock market crisis was felt in the streets of Tokyo. Every employee was afraid of finding himself without a job. Ready cash dried up and people started saving money instead of spending it. Very few people visited the department stores, restaurants closed, and bars went bankrupt. In a very short time, everything in Japan had changed.

The news on TV was full of reports of people who committed suicide. Employees who received pink slips jumped from roofs or lay down on railroad tracks rather than facing their wives and telling them they had been fired, which was a terrible humiliation.

I had faith in Makoto and believed he would find something very quickly. However, I had no idea how long the road ahead of us would last. It was the first time I was actually involved in Makoto's life decisions, and I was happy he had shared them with me honestly and openly.

Surviving the Economic Crisis

The economic crisis was felt in every corner in Japan. Salaries plummeted, fewer and fewer people had money for luxuries, the real estate market crashed, and Japan entered a recession. Everyone tried to survive, and like Makoto, his friends either resigned voluntarily or were fired and looked for a new niche. I realized that anyone who did manage to survive the recession would be stronger once it ended. However, some people were unlucky; they lost everything, and their relatives had to help them. Women who had been stay-at-home moms now had to go to work, and even 17-year-olds found jobs and helped support the family. The recession made me realize I couldn't rely on the present because it could change overnight, and that the unexpected, whether personal or national, for better or for worse, was part of life.

One change was quickly followed by another. Makoto could no longer use company credit cards – he had to return them when he quit – and with them went all the unlimited evening entertainment he had been used to. He could no longer spend hundreds of dollars of company money at bars and clubs. Instead of working long hours and then taking his employees and clients out drinking, for the first time since we were married, he spent his evenings at home with us.

Staying at home made him restless so he looked for something to do. He discovered things at home that were broken or didn't work and set about repairing them. It was wonderful, but it also revealed a side I hadn't known existed in him, as I had never known he was so good with at repairing things. He replaced the tatami mats in the guest room with parquet flooring, painted the walls, replaced the screens and faucets in the kitchen and bathroom and replaced all the ordinary incandescent light bulbs with LED bulbs.

We had to make other changes. We stopped going to expensive bars with friends and instead invited them home. That reduced our expenses considerably and made it possible for us to maintain friendships.

It was customary to send presents and greeting cards to friends twice a year, once in summer and once in winter, purchases that enriched the department stores. It was all orderly and typically Japanese: friends received presents that cost between $30 and $50, and the department store wrapped them as gifts, added a card and sent them to the recipient. In summer the present usually consisted of food like fruit conserves, beer or fruit juices, and in winter, soup, expensive coffee, hand-made noodles, etc. While Makoto was still working for the insurance company, he had a list of 80 people with whom he always exchanged presents and there were years when the house was overflowing with presents, and for months we ate and drank what was in the boxes. All this ended the moment Makoto left the company and the list shrank to 20 people, after I added my students to it. Makoto continued the custom by sending cards reading, "May you have a warm, healthy winter," or, "May you have an easy, enjoyable summer." Many, many households were forced to spend less but no one abandoned the tradition entirely. It had been part of their childhood and had to continue, regardless of how life changed, and I felt that was a good thing.

Eventually we learned that everything we had done extravagantly could be done modestly. Instead of flying to ski or play golf, with all the attendant indulgences, we organized the same with a group of families and went to vacation sites just outside of Tokyo. Instead of five-star hotels we stayed at traditional Japanese inns called *ryokans*. They were cheap, very large, and suitable for ten guests. We reserved three rooms for two nights, one room for the women, one for the men and the third for the children. In addition, the women had a room to ourselves where we could talk, the children loved having their own room to play in, and in the evening we could all meet for drinks. We spent time in the *onsen* thermal pool inside the hotel, but there were also outdoor pools and we – women only – used to bathe naked and talk and gossip. It was a lot of fun unless the water was too hot. Everyone else went straight into the hot water, but my heartbeat increased dramatically, and I felt woozy. Outside the pools was a row of faucets and stools where one could fill bowls with hot water to pour over one's body to get used to hot water before going into the pool, and I tried it myself.

I rubbed my body with soap and a rough washcloth and then tried inching my way into the pool, sometimes only halfway. Eventually I got used to the heat and learned to enjoy myself. The combination of the hot water and the spectacular view was relaxing and calming. Eventually, we got out of the pool and wrapped ourselves in hotel robes which were similar to kimonos called *yukata*, which we wore throughout out stay in the ryokan, as was the custom.

The festivities continued in the dining room where we were served seafood, sashimi, rice, and miso soup. After dinner we met in one of the rooms and drank wine and sake, we had brought with us, and talked until the early hours of the morning.

The ryokans cost $40 per person and included an overnight stay and two meals. Entertainment and how we spent our time was up to us. One of the attractions the children especially liked were the fireworks, which we had brought with us, and we allowed the children to light them themselves. It was a very popular summer pastime in Japan, and a special area was set aside for it outside the hotel. We filled pails of water to extinguish the fireworks and there was always an adult present. Activities usually depended on the season. In summer we went fishing and held barbecues, and in winter, we went to the nearby ski slopes.

Our circle of friends changed according to Kai's friends. At first, we became friendly with couples whose children were in kindergarten with him or who were in his afternoon preparatory class. When he began playing basketball our circle of friends changed. There were 12 children on his team, and we got to know the parents. Makoto was usually the oldest person in the group and the only one who had two older children. Everyone treated him with respect and regarded him as a mentor in issues regarding parenting, work, raising children and education.

He enjoyed his position and meetings with the other parents encouraged him a great deal, especially during that uncertain phase of his life. The basketball coach, Shirai-San, was the only person older than Makoto, and that gave them a lot of common ground. Makoto had a great respect for him and helped him with the team for many years. Shirai-San's wife came on trips with us and took it upon herself to be the team's accountant. That made all the other women afraid of her. I was the only one who spoke to her directly. She wasn't threatening in the least and I found her to be very friendly and sharing the usual curiosity about me and where I came from. She was interested in other cultures and wanted to know how Makoto and I, who came from different countries, could exist under the same roof. We often invited Shirai-San and his wife to visit us and introduced them to other mixed couples.

In the summer of 2000, I took Kai with me to Israel again for two happy events. My friend Sandy got married and my nephew celebrated his bar mitzvah. Both made me remember things that over the years were pushed to the back of my mind. I was happy to feel the joy I had always associated with weddings and bar mitzvah celebrations, talking to people in my mother tongue, and the excitement of people dancing to familiar music. It immediately made me compare Israeli customs to Japanese and made me realize how much I missed them.

The last two weeks of my vacation I devoted to my father. I loved spending time with him. We visited his sisters and brothers, went on trips and sat in restaurants, and now that he was retired, he had all the time in the world for me. The day after the bar mitzvah we agreed to meet in Tel Aviv with all the family and go to the Carmel Market and the Flea Market, both places my father and I were very fond of. We were on our way to the Central Bus Station to pick up my father when he called and said he had tripped and fallen down the escalator and apparently broken his leg and had been taken by ambulance to the Hospital.

At the hospital they told us he had torn a ligament in his leg, and they would have to operate. At that moment we abandoned our happy plans for the rest of the day and changed direction to the orthopedic ward. The doctors examined him and told us they couldn't operate immediately, only after his heart had been catheterized because they were afraid it wasn't strong enough for surgery. That month there were strikes and sanctions in all the hospitals and the waiting time for a catheterization was particularly long. The entire situation depressed my father no end. He asked the doctors to release him and let him go home until he could have an appointment for the procedure, but they were afraid the strain would be too much for his heart.

Man proposes God disposes. The last two weeks of my vacation in Israel, which I had planned to spend enjoying life with my father, were spent waiting anxiously in a hospital. My father's appointment for the procedure was set for the day I was supposed to fly back to Japan. I said a very sad goodbye and wished him the best of luck.

Twenty-four hours later, when I was already back in Japan, my sister called to tell me the procedure hadn't been successful, and the doctors ordered immediate open-heart surgery. He wanted to talk to me before the operation, but I was already on the plane, and he was now in the operating room. I sobbed and prayed and hoped everything would be OK. After several nerve-wracking hours they told me the operation had been a success and my father would remain in the hospital and then move to a convalescent home.

My brother and sister sat next to his bed most of the time and it took an entire month before he recuperated enough to being doing the simplest things, like walking. He couldn't accept the fact that he could no longer move around freely. He had always been active, and overnight he had lost his independence; it upset him a great deal. But he wasn't about to give up easily and despite the restrictions the doctors had imposed on him he went back to driving and walking around the city, although with the aid of a cane. We spoke on the phone all the time and he told me his relations with Charlette were getting worse by the day and she was sleeping in the spare room. "Ever since I was released from the hospital," he said, "she's rejected me, she said she doesn't want to be with me anymore and isn't interested in me." He felt alone and insulted. Sometimes he said he no longer had a reason to live. It was awful to hear that from my father, whom I had loved and admired my whole life. I knew the reason behind it all was that they had had a big argument about money. He transferred all the money he had to my sister, so she could manage it, invest it for him and deposit the monthly interest in his account. We knew about it and agreed to it, but Charlette wasn't involved. That made her very angry, and she rejected him.

She suggested that she buy his half of the house and asked him to leave. But that would have been out of character for him. My brother and sister tried to convince him to accept the offer and said they would help him buy an assisted-living apartment. He was terribly offended and said, "What do you want me to do, go to a nursing home?"

As the relationship with Charlette worsened so did his health. Not only did he have medical problems, but his heart was broken. My sister asked me to fly to Israel again so we could find him a place to live. We couldn't bear the fact he was living in a house where he felt rejected and miserable. We all wanted to see him happy and return to his old optimistic self.

The next time I saw my father was about half a year after the accident on the escalator, and the change was drastic. He was thin, his face was wrinkled, and he was unusually quiet. Before I arrived, my sister told me she had found an assisted-living complex near her home and asked me to convince him just to take a look at it. She said she had spoken to several people who lived there, and they were all satisfied with the conditions. It was important for her to live near him so she could visit him every day and make sure he had everything he needed.

We went to visit the complex and to me it looked like a five-star hotel. Happily, our father was surprised by the atmosphere, especially when he discovered that people he had known when he was young were living there and heard how pleased they were. After a thorough examination he decided to move in for a three-month trial period, and that same week we moved him into his new apartment.

Half a year later I flew to Israel again to see how he was doing. I had mixed feelings. I was very angry with Charlette for ending their relationship. She was 18 years younger than he and clearly she didn't want to be with an old man she would probably have to take care of. I was happy to see my father happy again despite his painful separation. The staff loved him, everyone was captivated by his charm, his childhood friends introduced him to new people, he swam in the pool every morning and became stronger, learned how to use a computer, went to lectures, joined various groups of people with common interests and profited from everything the place had to offer. His apartment had two bedrooms and we slept in one of them and were allowed to use all the facilities. Within a very short time my father was his old self again.

During his first days there his younger sister Esther came to visit him with her friend Elizabeth, who was a widow looking for a new relationship. My father liked her immediately, and after three months, when he had to decide if he was going to stay in assisted living or not, he decided to stay and asked Elizabeth to move in with him.

He was 67 and she was 60. Old age isn't a stage anyone is particularly eager to reach, but nevertheless Elizabeth taught my father how to deal with his age and accept it for what it was. He learned how to enjoy doing things more slowly, which made it possible for him to do the things he liked. They enjoyed their time together and learned things he had never time for.

I looked at them and wondered at the way life changes sometimes. For a long time, it had seemed they were both going down dead-end paths, but then it became clear that change for the better was always possible. Both of them had been lost, each for their own reasons, and now they had found each other and had a reason to smile. My father was happy, he smiled all the time and his eyes sparkled.

He introduced Elizabeth to his family and friends, took trips with her and showed her places that were important to him, like the old house in Herzliya, the beach and his favorite fish restaurant. They went on trips all the time, and every time I called, he told me where they were and what they were doing. It seemed to me they were on the road all the time, and it was wonderful.

Before he entered the first grade at school Kai was already engaged in a lot of educational activities, and one of the things I especially liked was that he was learning to speak English. It was a skill he was learning at the American kindergarten. I also spoke Hebrew with him whenever I could. Most of the time he didn't answer in Hebrew, but when we visited Israel, I could see he had been absorbing the language, because he spoke to my family and friends in Hebrew. He wasn't fluent by any means and made a lot of mistakes, but he managed to communicate with them, and that was what was important. Hebrew verbs have both masculine and feminine forms, and he would refer to himself using the feminine form, which amused everyone. They corrected him and explained the differences to him; Japanese doesn't distinguish between genders. I knew it was difficult for him to get used to the difference because

I was the only person speaking Hebrew to him, and he imitated me.

The last year Kai was in kindergarten was a difficult year for us all. Makoto wanted him to go to a national school, which would prepare him to be accepted into the best universities. That was every Japanese parent's dream, and Makoto was determined. Due to the great demand for those schools, every parent had to visit schools near their home, and pay each of them a fee to join the lottery. That was the only way to give their kid the chance to participate the school's entrance exam. The week after Makoto paid the fee, we received postcards from each school with a number and the date, a different day for each school. Thousands of tense parents came to the lotteries, which were held in the school playgrounds, hoping to hear their number called.

The school principal began the ceremony by wishing luck to all the parents, took three numbers between one and ten out of box and read them out over a loudspeaker. If one of the numbers was on your postcard, your child was accepted. For example, if the number 2 was called, 12, 25, 1002, etc., were winners and the parents remained in the yard, the other parents were asked to leave. Kai's number came up only once, which meant only one school opened its doors to him to begin the long process of acceptance.

The next stage was yet another postcard with a new number and the date for an interview, to which applicants and their parents were invited. Specific preparations had to be made before the interview. Kai was only five but he had to sit up straight throughout, look confidently at the interviewer and answer all the questions in a loud voice.

What is your name? How old are you? What is your full address? What do your parents do for a living? How many brothers and sisters do you have? What is the name of your kindergarten? What do you want to be when you grow up? etc., etc., etc.

We kept rehearsing with Kai and the atmosphere was tense. A lot of the time I was sorry I let Makoto dictate how Kai would be educated. The prep school for the first grade had gone into high gear with a lot of information, some of which seemed utterly unnecessary for such young children. Childhood is a wonderful time and I wanted Kai to enjoy his, but once we had started the process I had no choice. All of us had the same objective.

On the fateful day we got up early and dressed him in a blue suit with a white shirt. A crowd of children and parents had assembled in front of the school, all of the children dressed the same way. We stood in line according to the number we had received and waited to be called. Only one parent could be present and in our case, it was naturally Makoto. After that Kai went into a different room alone.

An hour later, when it was all over, we took him to his favorite restaurant. Makoto told me some of the questions, one of which was why Makoto had chosen to send Kai to that particular school, and he answered that he wanted him to get the best possible education and have a secure future. Most of the other questions were trivial, such as which university Makoto had attended, where he worked, what his salary was, how many children he had, etc. Kai didn't volunteer much information, he only said it was OK and that the interviewers had played games with him.

We waited anxiously to hear from the school. And in fact, he had successfully passed the first interview and would now receive a date for the entrance exam. He had been preparing for it for two years and it covered a lot of information in many fields. He had been taught the seasons, Japanese holidays, geometric shapes, animals and more. The children had been given rhythmic lessons, which used movement to teach them how to follow instructions.

And another fateful day arrived, and we again dressed him in his blue suit and drove to the school. This time far fewer children and parents were waiting. Kai was taken into a classroom as part of a group, and we waited outside with the other nervous parents. They came out an hour later, and when we asked Kai how it was, he said "Easy." I was happy it was over, and now all we had to do was wait for the results of the exam. Makoto said that passing the exam didn't mean immediate acceptance because there would be another lottery, this time of the names of the children who had done well, and only 80 would be chosen. Every year they opened four first grade classes with 20 children in each.

A few days later we received a postcard saying Kai had passed the exam, and now we were waiting for the date of the final lottery and the tension at home increased. When the date arrived, Makoto went by himself and I wished him luck. Actually, I wished Kai luck, and said I would be sorry if his name didn't come up, but it was a matter of fate, and you can't argue with it.

This time the parents were waiting in front of the school without their children and there were fewer than the time before. The principal gave a short speech, which everyone success, and started the lottery. He once again pulled three numbers out of the box and called them out over a loudspeaker. None of them was on the postcard Makoto was holding. He was very, very disappointed and called me immediately with the news, which for him was terrible.

I tried to comfort him and said there were advantages to Kai's not being accepted, the first of which was the distance between our house and the school. If he had been accepted, he would have had to get up at six in the morning to get to school on time, and take the subway an hour in each direction. The public schools, which were not prestigious, were a fifteen minute-walk from our house.

Makoto was terribly upset that a random number was all that separated him from realizing his educational dream for his children. He said he wasn't going to give up, he would do everything necessary to prepare Kai for the junior high school entrance exams. That meant extra tutoring, which would begin when he was in fourth grade. Such lessons are a thriving industry in Japan, the tutoring schools are called *juku* and almost every child in Japan, male and female, attends them. Tomonori and Michitaka attended them throughout their educational career, and privately I thought it was an awful thing to do to a child. When Kai was born, I didn't want it for him, but now apparently there was no choice.

I had barely recovered from the tension of the final lottery when Kai scared me half to death by waking up in the middle of the night with a 104°F temperature. We immediately drove him to the hospital. The doctor who examined him prescribed antibiotics and something to reduce the fever and sent us home. The next day he was worse. He woke up with sores in his mouth and all over his legs and his temperature shot up to 105°F, almost 106 degrees. I could sense something terrible was happening to him. He lost consciousness and we took him back to the hospital where this time we demanded a thorough examination. A young doctor hooked him up to an IV drip and took blood samples. We waited for two nerve-wracking hours and were then called into a specialist's office. He said Kai had Kawasaki disease, a form of vasculitis named after Professor Kawasaki, the doctor who had found a way to treat it. The specialist said it was a disease which affected the blood cells, and if left untreated, could migrate to the heart, in which case it could prove fatal. He had us sign a form agreeing to a blood transfusion.

Kai spent two weeks in the hospital and was in the ICU for the first couple of days. He was very week and slept most of the time. Intense pain was one of the symptoms and he cried a lot. I was with him 24 hours a day and was frantic and cried with him. The first days were the worst. He kept asking me, "Mommy, am I going to die?" and I kept telling him that no, he was not going to die, but deep inside I was terrified.

He was given an enormous number of injections and countless blood samples were taken from him. Every time a nurse came near him holding a syringe or a test tube he began crying and screamed he didn't want another injection. It was heart-breaking and I wanted to scream along with him, but I knew I had to remain calm and help the nurses perform their duties.

After 48 hours his condition began to improve, and

continued improving as the days passed, and finally he was no longer in danger. The first indication was that he smiled at me. He also began chatting with the medical staff. At that point the doctors decided to move him to the children's ward. On the one hand I was happy, but on the other, there were visiting hours and parents couldn't spend entire days and nights with their children. We could come between three in the afternoon until nine at night. I couldn't accept that and demanded I be allowed to stay with him from six in the morning until nine at night. From the fact that I started talking and didn't stop, they must have thought it would do no good to become embroiled in a shouting match with the crazy foreign woman, and agreed I could stay with him.

Before Kai was released from the hospital the doctor told us the disease might return because his immune system was weak. He said Kai had to stay home for two months and not play with his friends. During the morning, while I was teaching, he would watch movies in his room. My conscience bothered me for leaving him alone and during my free time I would do jigsaw puzzles with him and help him build things with Lego. In the afternoon his brothers came home, and they spent as much time with him as they could.

Because Kai and I spent so much time at home we both gained weight. In addition, the entire atmosphere at home was very tense, and Makoto and I were full of recriminations and accusations towards one another. Makoto blamed me for not paying enough attention to Kai's hygiene, claiming that was why Kai fell ill. I blamed him for exerting so much emotional and psychological pressure on Kai regarding the school exams, saying that was why his immune system had become weak. In reality, both of us wanted to know why he had become ill, and no answer was forthcoming from the doctors. They said medical science still didn't have enough information about the disease, which surprised us, because at the time ten thousand children were catching it every year, all of them between the ages of two and six years old.

I was as angry with Makoto as I had ever been, and at times I wanted to simply get up and leave everything. He often lost his temper and behaved cruelly, accusing me of ridiculous things. Since I had spent so much time cooped up at home, I had neither the strength nor the will to deal with him. Not that I didn't answer, I would say things like, "I'm sorry I married you...you're such a disappointment." He wasn't about to let me have the last word and would hurt me in my most sensitive spot, telling me, "You're a terrible mother!"

Kai had weekly medical examinations and we were finally given permission to let him resume his normal activities. We were extremely relieved. The first thing I did was register both of us at a sports center so we could get rid of the two months' worth of pounds we had amassed. While Kai was taking swimming lessons I went to the gym, and within a few months I could recognize myself again in the mirror.

Relations between Makoto and me didn't improve, and during one argument I said I was leaving him. I had already planned what I was going to do. I would tell my family that in light of my current situation I would remain in Tokyo because I didn't want Kai to be torn between two parents.

I bought two plane tickets to Israel and told Makoto

that when I returned, we were separating. For me there was no way back. The trip was scheduled for the month before Kai entered the first grade at school and I was in a terrible emotional state. I had to get away from Japan and Makoto to put things into perspective. Makoto was persistent. He called from Japan every day, asked after Kai and begged me to forgive him. I could sense that this time he understood he had gone too far and that I was serious about separating from him. In an extraordinary gesture he said he loved me and Kai and missed us. Instead of melting at his rare gesture of emotion, I replied with all my resentment and grudges.

In Israel, everyone embraced me with love and concern. But to my surprise they also defended Makoto and reminded me of how hard it had been for him, hoping I would forgive him. The only thing on his side at the moment was his sincere apology, which he repeated every time he called. I, on the other hand, found it very hard to turn my loathing into something positive.

The Purim holiday fell while we were still in Israel, and it was the first time Kai celebrated a Jewish holiday away from Japan, that reminded Kai of Halloween. My father's assisted living complex invited all the grandchildren to a Purim party, and everyone came wearing costumes. Kai was happy and blossomed over the next few days. On Purim morning we went swimming in the pool, had breakfast, and then joined my friends and their children in the celebrations in the streets. It was one of our most enjoyable vacations in Israel.

In addition, I had space to think about my life and my future. When I was no longer furious, I could look at the situation objectively. I realized I couldn't take Kai away from the country of his birth and bring him to live in Israel. I knew for a fact that Makoto would never let me do it. I knew how important his children were to him, he had fought for them in the past and he would do it again.

The tension between Makoto and me was hard on Kai. When he arrived in Israel he told my sister, "Mommy and daddy are mad at each other." My sister was sorry to hear about the crisis in our relationship and supported me wordlessly. There wasn't much more she could say.

The time came to return to Tokyo. I didn't expect Makoto to be waiting for us at the airport. It was a two-hour round trip and Makoto always complained about how much time he wasted on the drive. I was therefore very surprised to see him waiting in the arrival's hall. Kai ran and hugged him; I remained cold and distant, but I was moved to see Kai run and hug his father.

When we got home Makoto hugged me and said, "You can't imagine how much I love you and how much I missed you. You're my angel. Please forgive me, I promise everything will be fine." I burst out crying and couldn't speak. I asked him to leave me alone for a while and give me time to think. We returned to make preparations for Kai's first day at school, and we had a lot to do. It kept my mind off what was troubling me and allowed me to concentrate on positive things like the preparations we made before he entered kindergarten. Here again instructions were clear and precise. Following them pushed aside my thoughts about the future with Makoto, but I couldn't ignore the small gestures he made. Every afternoon he called from the office to ask about Kai. He wanted to know what we had done all day and told me about what had happened at work, which was something he had never done before. Before Kai had gotten sick, he resigned from the insurance company and opened an import and export company of his own, and the only connection I had with his office was correspondence regarding shipments from Israel. But beyond that I didn't know if his sales were successful, how much profit he cleared every month and which stores sold the most merchandise and all the other things he dealt with every day. To tell the truth, he had never shown a willingness to discuss such things with me, and if I tried to get him to share them with me his replies were short and cold. But now his attitude had changed completely, he began speaking to me as a friend, not a dominant, irritable husband. He was the old Makoto I knew, nice to be with. Not only that, he came home in the afternoon, but he also helped me cook.

The change in his behavior took the edge off my anger, but I couldn't forget the terrible things he had said, which hit me like waves every time. The only thing that really functioned was sex, which was terrific. But that was nothing new, even when our emotional relationship hit bottom rock, the sex just got better. Eventually his persistence won me and I decided I would make the effort and give him another chance to prove the change was real and lasting.

The tension at home influenced Kai and on occasions he imitated us when we fought. We explained that our arguments were like his arguments with his friends, and that our anger at each other didn't mean we were angry with him or didn't love him. I don't know how much he understood, but when our relationship improved, one day he asked us, laughing, "Have you made up?" and he was very happy.

Days turned into weeks and at the end of the school year the kindergarten held a graduation party for the children leaving to go to school. We got dressed up again and I bought a fancy outfit for myself. Graduating from kindergarten and entering the first grade was considered a very important event and many parents invited the grandparents to the ceremony.

Kai's class had only 20 pupils, and there were only two classes in his grade; that was the Japanese custom. Every school had 240 pupils, and I was surprised by the small number because I was used to Israeli schools, where classes were much larger. Japan had a fairly low birthrate, and most of the inhabitants were middle-aged or older. Japan's life expectancy is one of the highest in the world and that became and has remained one of Japan's foremost and most-discussed problems. A large number of older people and very few children mean there is no one to take care of the aged, meaning the heavy burden of their care falls on the government.

We lived in an area with a relatively large number of young couples with children. Most of the parents worked until late in the evening and if necessary, left their children in after-school centers run by the local municipality where the children played or did their homework until their parents came to pick them up.

I had different priorities. I wanted Kai to learn English in the afternoon and shortened my workday. I also signed him up for tennis and piano lessons, which he continued during the first grade. He came home every day after school and did his homework, and then went to one of his after-school activities. He liked school. There were children he knew from kindergarten, and he made new friends. My Japanese studies now proved themselves more important than ever because I could help him with his homework. The children had to learn a lot: In the first grade they learned 46 hiragana letters, 46 katakana letters and 80 kanji symbols. In the second grade they learned 160 more kanji symbols, and by the time they finished elementary school they were required to know one thousand symbols, and then learned another thousand during junior high school. Every symbol had one meaning in Japanese and another in Chinese, and the children had to remember the difference. After studying kanji for ten years, I knew 1,500 symbols.

When Kai was in the first grade, I volunteered for class parents' committee; I was one of four volunteer mothers. It would be an important experience for me because I would see what was going on behind the scenes in the school and for the first time understand how things were done. It increased my understanding of the great difference between me and the others and showed me how they strictly observed all rules. Rules were also observed at the committee meetings. No voice was raised, business was conducted calmly, and everyone came on time and participated fully without making excuses. The committee had a lot of work and devoted an enormous amount of time to preparing the events of the school festival. It was amazing to see how everyone joined in and contributed, quietly and calmly. No one complained if someone else got the job they wanted, everyone did exactly what was necessary without arguing. It is impossible to describe how that lowered the level of tension. I enjoyed the meetings and apparently, I wasn't the only one, because at the end of the year some of the mothers said they were planning to volunteer the following year as well. For me one year was enough and I stepped down.

The children were interested in me because I looked so different and foreign. The second I entered the school I heard the children whisper, "That's Kai's mother." Kai was also a subject of their interest. They knew he was half Japanese and were very curious, especially the girls in the upper grades. They didn't know which country to place him in and automatically asked him if his mother was American. As far as they were concerned, every foreigner who came to Japan was American. Most of them had never heard of Israel.

I couldn't explain it to them, but I kept telling Kai that I was a born and bred Israeli and would always remain Israeli forever. Israel was and would always be my country, my home and the place closest to my heart. I promised him I would always do my utmost to respect Japan and follow the rules and social conventions. As time passed, I learned how to enjoy both worlds, Japan and Israel, and finesse my way between them. I hoped Kai would be able to do the same and find a way to live harmoniously with two countries and profit from what both had to offer.

Sometimes Kai was glad I was a foreigner, and when I asked him why he said, "Because of you I get to travel a lot. My friends have never been to as many countries as I have."

I laughed and told him I was happy he liked to travel, so did I, and I promised him we would see the world. I wanted him to know there was a universe beyond Japan where the sun rose, and people smiled. Ironic as this may sound, Japan is known as the Land of the Rising Sun, but everyone always looked expressionless.

Japan had an ancient tradition of celebrating certain ages. For boys, it was when they turned five, for girls two birthdays were important, three and seven. The *shichi-go-san* festival was held every November 15, a rite of passage that celebrates the growth and well-being of young children and comes from the tradition of celebrating children's survival, because in the past many children died of various diseases before they reached the ages of three, five and seven. The children dressed in festive kimonos and had their pictures taken in a studio.

So, when Kai was five, we rented a kimono and made an appointment to have his picture taken. Makoto and I didn't feel the ceremony were particularly important because its original significance had been lost, but nevertheless we followed the custom, mainly for Makoto's mother. She was so fond of ceremonies and tradition, and attending every event was important to her. Since she didn't like coming to Tokyo, we went to Tsukuba to celebrate with her there. We also invited some of Makoto's cousins to a traditional Japanese restaurant after the ceremony.

Everyone congratulated Kai and he loved being the center of attention. He also received envelopes full of money from the uncles, enough to cover the cost of renting the kimono, the studio photos and the bill at the restaurant.

Later on we bought him a bicycle, a present from the whole family. In accordance with Japanese custom, immediately after the event Makoto sent the guests gifts that cost 10% of what they had given us. That was customary after every large event like a wedding or funeral or hospitalization or some celebration for children. It was conventional for guests or visitors to bring money with them and receive a gift in return. I left such things to Makoto to deal with.

The Death of My Father

Every year in December we planned a ski vacation at the holiday cottage of our friends, the Watanabe family, which was in the Nagano Mountains. I had just finished making all the last arrangements for the trip when my sister-in-law called. I was surprised to hear her voice because we were not in the habit of calling each other. I asked her what was wrong, and she said she had bad news. "What?" I wanted to know, and she said, "Your father."

"What about my father? What happened to him?"

After a moment that seemed like forever, she said, "He passed away an hour ago."

I could barely take in what she said, and all I could say was, "Wait for me! Don't do anything without me! I have to get a plane ticket." Before I hung up I asked if my sister knew and she said my sister was in class teaching and the principal would tell her.

My worst fear was how my sister would react. She was so attached to my father and spoke to him every day, especially during the past year. She worried about him all the time and went to see his doctors, always making sure he received the best possible care.

I walked down the stairs to the living room where Kai and Makoto were watching a comedy. "My father is dead," I cried. Makoto's jaw dropped, it was the last thing he expected to hear; actually, it's the last thing anyone expects to hear. He got up, hugged me and whispered, "Don't worry, I'm here with you." I sobbed and sobbed and trembled out of control. I put my head on his shoulder and felt the first stabs of the terrible pain.

It was New Year's Eve, December 31, 2002, and it was too late to find an open travel agent's office. The next day began the five-day New Year's holiday. That meant it would be almost impossible to book a flight out of Japan. I called Daniella, a friend who always got me out of the most complicated situations, and I knew she was the only person who could help me on such short notice. She was in the middle of preparations for her parents' 30th wedding anniversary party, which would be held that evening.

Sobbing throughout, I told her about my father and my trouble getting a flight out of Japan. She said, "Give me a couple of minutes and I'll get back to you. In the meantime, start packing." I called Watanabe-San and cancelled the ski trip; she offered her condolences. She had met my father when he came to Japan, and we spent a couple of days with her in the Nagano Mountains. I remembered my father had a good time and liked the view of the mountains from her windows. I had wonderful memories of the visit and when we spoke on the phone he often asked after her.

I went upstairs to pack, and Daniella called back a short time later, as promised, and said the fastest way to get to Israel was to fly to Turkey and catch a connecting flight.

The flight left the following morning and landed in Israel at midnight. I gave her all our information and she took care of everything.

The night before we flew out was very difficult. I was impatient to arrive in Israel and help my family make preparations for the funeral. I was so upset I broke out in hives. I couldn't sleep, I couldn't sit down, and all I could do was wander around the house. Kai and Makoto went to sleep, and the living room was empty. It all came back to me, reminding me of my mother's funeral.

My sister called at midnight, and I was surprised at how calm she sounded. She said she was on her way to our father's apartment where she would meet his brothers and sister and my brother for a final goodbye. She said she was afraid to go alone and told me not to hang up.

My father's brothers and sisters were waiting for her. They had covered my father with a blanket and sat on chairs placed around the room. My sister began sobbing and I joined her. She brought her phone close to my father's ear and asked me to say goodbye to him. I told him I loved him, and missed him, and hoped he would meet our mother, who had been waiting for him for a long time. "Daddy, you always said mommy came to you in your dreams, now you can meet her."

I remembered when two years after his oldest brother died of complications of diabetes, the third brother died of long-term heart disease. My father, who was the second born, was very angry when he died. He kept saying, "I should have been next, it's not right." Even then I had the

214 • Tokyo Tales - My Journey

feeling my father didn't have a long time left to live, because like his brothers, he had severe diabetes and heart trouble.

It was kind of a chain of bad luck. His parents also died young. My grandfather died at the age of 58, and my grandmother died blind from diabetes when she was 69. Over the years all six brothers lost their wives to cancer. My aunt died of bone cancer and a month later, the day they unveiled her headstone, my uncle died. The short time between their deaths rocked us.

My family suffered so many losses sometimes I had the terrible feeling death was stalking us. And as cruel as it sounds, gathering in cemeteries, offering condolences and meeting at memorial services were the events where everyone turned up. Every member of the family tried to do whatever they could to avoid becoming a family statistic. They didn't eat junk food, took vitamins, and never missed a routine doctor's checkup. My father was the odd one out. He began taking care of his health far too late, and only when his test results were incontrovertibly disastrous did he start worrying about himself. Until then he ate and drank as pleased. He mostly ignored doctors' warnings, devoured fried food and red meat and super sweet desserts. He used to say, "Better to live a good short life than a boring long one."

Between the time he got sick and the time he died he suffered very little, and people used to tell us that only the righteous died that way, with no suffering or long months of pain; it brought us very little comfort. Anyone who knew my father knew how typical of him it was to just get up and disappear without any forewarning. The night prior to his death, he said to my sister, "For your birthday I'll get pizzas, cheese pastries and drinks, and Elizabeth and I will come over to your house." My sister loved his visits, and he always came bringing gifts. She said, "We'll be waiting for you, daddy." Not for a minute did she imagine it would be the last time she spoke to him or the first time he didn't keep a promise.

He died in his apartment in the assisted-living complex; he was 69 years old. He had lived there for two wonderful years, going swimming every morning, participating in activities, his calendar full of interesting events. Knowing he was busy and happy kept us from worrying.

The morning of the last day of his life began as usual. He went shopping at a nearby store, went swimming and then went back to his apartment to read the paper, and all of a sudden, he felt he couldn't breathe. He pushed his panic button and within a few minutes a doctor arrived. The doctor later told us that he found my father unconscious on the floor. He tried to resuscitate him, but it was too late, a heart attack had killed him within a few minutes.

My sister was waiting for Makoto, Kai and I at the airport when we landed. She was strong and composed, and just seeing her and knowing she was making arrangement for the funeral made me feel more confident. She told me to write a list of all of his friends I thought should be invited. We knew he had a lot of friends and was always in contact with them, more than either one of us could remember. That evening my sister went home with his address book and called every number in it, and my brother took care of the preparations for the burial. My father had a plot next to my mother with one headstone covering both. It had to be removed so he could be buried and so his name and the dates of his birth and death could be chiseled into it. It had been made specially to look like their house, the house my father built for my mother. He always used to say, "When I die you will have to get a winch to move it," and he was right. The man who made it had his office on cemetery property and he knew my father because he visited my mother's grave often. We didn't realize what a project it would be to move the headstone, and neither did the man who had made it. In the end he decided to destroy part of it and rebuild it later.

One evening, sometime before my father's death, we finished dinner. Makoto and Kai went to have a shower and I cleared the table and tidied the living room. Suddenly I saw a ball of gray hair on the floor near the armchair and realized it was a mouse. I screamed and ran, terrified, into the bathroom and locked the door behind me. Makoto didn't understand what had happened, and when I could breathe again, I told him, and he said it was impossible. "We have never had mice," he insisted, but I wasn't convinced, I knew what I saw, and I refused to leave the bathroom as long as there was a mouse on my living room's floor. Just at that moment the mobile phone in my pocket rang. It was my sister, and she couldn't understand why I was so upset. I was crying and screaming, and she told me to drink some water and calm down. "There's an enormous dead mouse in the living room. What am I supposed to do? I can't touch it!" She laughed but then stopped because she realized I was having a panic attack. She told me to calm down, which had no effect at all. Then it turned out Makoto also couldn't stand mice, and the three of us stayed locked in the bathroom until we were rescued. By a fluke Tomonori came home from work early, and he was an animal lover. When he was young, he had a terrarium in his room with an iguana and a snake, and he fed them dead mice he bought in pet stores.

"I'll take care of it," he said from the other side of the bathroom door. He wrapped the mouse in a sheet of newspaper and threw it into the garbage bin outside the house. He reported that the threat had been removed and only then did we come out of the bathroom.

I was stunned and tried to figure out how a mouse ended up in our living room. The only thing I could think of was that Makoto and I had gone to the airport that morning to release goods from customs, and the airport warehouses were notorious for having mice. When Makoto had loaded the merchandise into his van, the mouse must have joined us for the ride. When Makoto came inside, he laid his coat on an armchair, and in fact I found the dead mouse on the floor next to it. That was the only explanation I could think of.

When my sister told me our father had died it reminded me of our adventure with the mouse. My sister, Makoto and I thought it was an omen, a warning that my father was going to die. I was surprised that a mouse had caused such a panic attack, and the way I screamed then was the same way I screamed when my father died. Maybe the dead mouse came as a warning of what was going to happen.

My mother's sisters came to my sisters' house to help prepare for the funeral. It had been twenty years since my mother's death, but they kept in contact, with my father as well. I was 15 years old when my mother died and two women stepped in to help: my sister, who was 9 years older than I, and who became my second mother, and my aunt, by mother's older sister, who supported me and helped me with whatever I needed. I needed their support because my father was in crisis. After mom's death he wasn't himself. He went to singles' bars looking for a woman who would fill the void left by my mother's death, and the month after my mother died, he met a woman working at the checkout counter in the supermarket. She was 18 years his junior, but he liked her and asked her out for months before she finally agreed. He talked about her all the time and prepared us for bringing her home for dinner so we could get to know her. The first time we met her we thought she was nice; she certainly looked nice. He told us she had a daughter my age. She married when she was very young and divorced shortly thereafter, and she and her daughter went to live with her parents. My father stopped going to singles' bars because Charlette was the only one for him. He wanted to formalize their relationship as fast as possible, but since he came from a family of cohanim, who had been high priests in the Temple since Biblical times, and according the Jewish religion are prohibited from marrying a divorcee, they had a lawyer draw up a legal agreement. He bought her a ring to symbolize their union and she came to live in our house.

Silvie had been our housekeeper since my mother died and I adored her. She kept the house running, and cleaned and cooked for us, but in general I just liked being around her. A month after Charlette moved in, my father fired Silvie and put Charlette in charge. Around that time my sister got married and moved out and my brother went to the United States to see what life there had to offer. I was still in high school and had nowhere to escape to. I was forced to live at home with my father and his new partner, and most of the time I was angry at him. I didn't understand him at all. Everything he did seemed stupid to me, especially the way he was weak and fulfilled all of Charlette's demands; the only thing that interested him was getting into bed with her. They never behaved unkindly to me, but I couldn't stand the idea that someone had replaced my mother and was in bed with my father.

I also hated the way they wasted money, especially since I knew how much he owed to the banks. His debts grew from year to year, as did their arguments. I couldn't keep myself from telling my aunt, time and time again, how awful I felt at home, and how unhappy I was. She told me to pack my bags and come to live with her, at least until I finished my military service, and that was exactly what I did. She had a large house with a spare bedroom, and she made sure I lacked nothing. She washed and ironed my army uniforms, cooked what she knew I liked, and sometimes told me about my mother when she was a child, when they were both growing up in Israel during the 1950s.

I stopped going to visit my father and he understood, and so he came to my aunt's house to see me, and always made sure to give me my allowance. Despite the difficulty of losing my mother and all the awful things I did as an adolescent, he continued showing me how much he loved me, my sister and brother.

The last two years of his life, when he was living with Elizabeth, were a way of coming full circle. He began talking about meeting childhood friends and he went to visit them, even when they moved far away. Moreover, he told me stories about my mother again, something he stopped doing almost entirely when he was living with Charlette.

Kai didn't understand what all the excitement was about and went to hide in his cousin's room. Makoto sat silently in the living room, unable to participate in the conversation, which was in Hebrew and dominated by three women related by blood. My aunt, my sister and I sat at the kitchen table until the early hours of the morning, planning the funeral, which would be held at one o'clock in the afternoon. We made a shopping list for at least the first two days of the Shiva and decided who would do what, and by the time we had finished it was almost time to get up.

In the morning we went into the city to go shopping, trying to buy the same things my father had bought for my mother's memorial service because those were the things he liked to eat, and bought enough for the whole week. On the way home we stopped for a short visit to the assisted-living complex to show Makoto where my father had lived. Makoto hadn't been to Israel during the two years my father lived there, and since we were there anyway, we spoke to the director and the doctor who had tried to revive my father. They both said they were surprised by his death because there had been no preliminary signs to suggest it. My father had returned from the pool in a perfectly good mood and went, as usual, to chat up the receptionist.

"He didn't seem weak or tired, he looked just fine," said the director.

I thought about putting a notice on the notice board, but the director asked me not to because death was a very sensitive topic for the residents, and death notices upset and depressed them. We therefore cancelled out plan to hire a bus to take the residents to the cemetery. We promised the director that as soon as the Shiva ended we would come and collect my father's things from his room.

When we arrived at the cemetery we were surprised by the large number of people. There were people we hadn't contacted, but one way or another they found out and came. Distant relatives, old neighbors, friends from work, a lot of my friends, and my siblings' friends. That was the point when it started to sink in that my father was really dead. Charlette and her daughter with her son-in-law also came to pay their last respects to my father; my brother had informed her of his death.

Makoto also wanted to say goodbye to my father before they buried him, and the responsible caretaker for the funeral allowed him to enter the room where my father had been laid. When the cloth covering his body was removed Makoto was shocked and horrified to see his hadn't been shaved and his mouth was open. In Japan the dead are prepared for burial, they are shaved, their mouths are closed, and make-up is applied. I explained that in Israel the dead are not exhibited and nothing cosmetic is done. My father's face had the same expression as it did at the moment of his death: surprise, and that stunned me. The funeral was held but I was miles away, mourning my father's death and the hole it left in my life.

The funeral ended and we all went back to my sister's house. Her friends went into the kitchen to help with the refreshments and people kept coming, offering condolences, snacking, and leaving. Makoto sat helplessly in a corner, uncomprehending, with the same expression on his face as I had at his father's funeral. He was a foreigner just as I had been, and as helpless as I had been. Happily, friends of mine had promised to keep him busy during the week.

For the entire week of the Shiva the house was full of people all day long. People came who had known my father at various stages of his life, some of whom I hadn't seen for years. The week passed quickly, Kai was entertained by his cousins, and I almost never saw him. Every morning Makoto sat on my sister's porch, enjoying the winter sun and reading books he had brought with him from Tokyo. In the afternoon my friends came to pick him up and show him the sights of Tel Aviv. In the evening he sat with us and spoke to people who had come to pay their respects, some of whom he knew because they had visited us in Tokyo.

On the last day, only close family came to sit with us, so we took the opportunity to go to the cemetery to thank the man who made the headstone for making it possible to bury my father. He promised my parents' new headstone would be taken care of and there would be plants all around the gravesite, just the way my father liked. From there we went straight to the airport to say goodbye to Makoto and Kai, who were returning to Japan via Turkey, where they would have a ten-hour layover in Istanbul. I had hired a Japanese-speaking guide for them who picked them up at the airport and took them on a tour of the city. I would be flying back in three days and wanted to spend the time with my brother and sister.

The next day, as promised, we went to the assisted-living complex, where we spent two days sorting and packing my father's things. We made two piles, things we wanted to keep and things we were going to give away. His brothers wanted mementos, something to remember him by, and we let them choose what they wanted. Elizabeth received the furniture; we bought it only two years previously, when they started living together. I took family pictures, kitchen utensils and things my father bought on the shopping channel; both of us loved gadgets.

We worked quickly considering what we had to do. The heavy things went to my brother and sister, so that after two days we could return the keys. I had only one day left, and I spent it with my sister and some close friends, and the next day I said goodbye to everyone and returned home, to Japan.

Arriving in Tokyo I was tired and confused. My head was still in Israel, and I kept having flashbacks. For years I had suppressed memories and concentrated on my life in Japan, but all of a sudden, they came flooding back. Subconsciously I had always feared the day someone would call me to tell me my father had passed away, and it came a lot sooner than I imagined.

A lot of my memories were about our old home. My father, who had a small construction business, built his dream house near the sea with his own two hands. He liked silence and he liked the sea. Financing the house wasn't easy because real estate by the beach was very expensive, but he didn't care because he was making his dream come true. I was seven years old when we moved there, and I had a lot of friends at school

Many memories of my mother's illness surfaced, and I tried my best to suppress them. When the first symptoms appeared we didn't recognize them for what they were. She went to many different doctors to find out what was wrong with her, and eventually after several years she was diagnosed with ovarian cancer, which in the meantime had metastasized throughout her body. First, she had a hysterectomy, then chemotherapy, which was awful for her and only helped a little. For a short time, we thought she was getting better, she felt and looked much better, and my parents took the opportunity to travel abroad and returned to enjoying themselves like a young couple. They met when my mother was 17 and got married the following year. My father called her the love of his life. Years later my aunt told me that my mother, like her sisters, had married young to escape from their parents and the strict upbringing they also had.

I was optimistic and in denial and refused to listen to my father when he told me the truth, that her condition would deteriorate. He said the cancer was in remission and it was only a matter of time before it returned. She was in constant pain and was taking prescription painkillers. She spent the last year of her life in bed at home, praying for death. She said she wanted us to go on with our lives and to take care of our father, who was 48 at the time. I couldn't imagine how empty my life would become. The house was always full of people who came to sit with her, her sisters, her parents. She suffered a lot, and slowly faded away. It embarrassed her to have people come and see the state she was in. She asked my sister to polish her nails and comb her wig, but she never lost weight and her face was always beautiful. She was 42 when she died. We had been prepared for her death but not for what would happen afterwards. My father surprised us all with his strength. He didn't cry, at least not when we were around. After the Shiva he announced he had no intention of remaining alone. He said my mother kept making him promise to move on with his life and not be alone.

The change in him was surprising, to say the least. He consulted us about what to wear when he went on a date, and he went out on a lot of dates. I don't even remember the names of all the women he went out with, it didn't matter, as he didn't like any of them. He was looking for someone like my mother and he never found her. The only one even slightly looked like my mother was Charlette. She was 35 when she moved in with my father and he was 51 and head over heels in love. I was very young at the time and couldn't believe someone my father's age could fall in love. Today I realize how young he really was.

Eventually my father went into debt, he spent more than he earned, and he owed the Israeli income tax and social security a lot of money. That led to repossessions, the bank took a lien on the house, and it couldn't even be sold. He made an enormous effort and worked very hard, but everything he made went to cover his overdraft. I wanted to go to university but there was no money to pay for it, and I knew that once I finished my military service I would have to work and pay the tuition fees myself.

One thing led to another and laid the foundation for the change I made in my life. Once out of the army I went to work at the diamond exchange. My first job was as a clerk in the export office. At that time I was living with my aunt, and I was doing fine. I was near friends; I bought a small car which I drove to work and used to go out in the evening. I hated my job. Most of the day I counted and weighed diamonds, and I was forbidden to talk to anyone because it would ruin my concentration. My boss invaded my personal space far too often, breathing down my neck and looking at me like a pervert. Once I understood nothing good would come out of the diamond exchange I quit and looked for another job, something more interesting and better paid. I soon found work in a small construction company near my father's house. It was a very different kind of job, very demanding, but the work atmosphere was excellent, and I was surrounded by nice, professional people, most of them architects and engineers. I learned how to use a computer, which back then were reasonably new in Israel and ours had only recently been installed in the office. There was no Internet, and we were all working with a primitive operating system. Nancy, the office manager, took me under her wing and taught me how to manage the office myself. The company was in a villa overlooking the beach, and I enjoyed every minute of what I was doing. But as the year passed, I began to think it might be a dead-end job. Filing started to bore me, and I had already gotten used to the view from the window. After a year my body begged for change. This time I wanted to get as far away from everything as I possibly could. I was dissatisfied and felt hemmed in, and I didn't see any way out. My salary wasn't high enough for me to rent an apartment and I knew my father couldn't help me. That was when I decided I had to go abroad and see what was waiting for me over there.

Today I think that if my mother were still alive, I wouldn't have run away. Who knows? Even my father was certain I couldn't stay away from home for such a long time and gave me his blessing when I left. He didn't think for a second, I would go away and stay overseas forever.

Staying Strong

Returning to my daily life in Japan was extremely difficult. I didn't see how I could possibly start preparing my English lessons. I called my students and asked them to take some time off from our lessons, and each one asked to meet with me, as is customary in Japan. I invited them over one evening and they brought an enormous bouquet of flowers and a silver-paper envelope, also a Japanese custom when there is a death in the family. Makoto served green tea and rice cookies and I sat with them, utterly incapable of speaking normally with them. They offered their condolences and I promised to let them know when I felt I could continue our lessons.

For the next month I stayed home most of the time. I had no desire whatsoever to do anything at all. I had no appetite and I lost weight. The only thing I did was cook for Makoto and the children and drive Kai to his after-school activities. I spoke to my sister on the phone a lot and she told me she felt the same way, exhausted and wanting to be left alone.

However, time passes and dulls even the worst sorrows, and I slowly began to understand that from now on I had no parents. I knew I had to be strong and keep moving forward. The first thing I would do was to put my life in order, starting with the house. I opened all the closets and arranged them. I threw out clothes I didn't need and arranged all the photos from our vacations in albums. I felt I was getting back on my feet. After two months of inactivity, I called my students and told them I would begin teaching them again. Of my 13 former students, only three said they would continue our lessons. It seemed that while I was putting my life in order, they were doing the same thing, and wanted to do something new and different. That made me rethink everything, and I was grateful to them, because I understood I was going backwards instead of forwards, and the time had come to change directions.

I decided to focus on teaching school-aged children. Every time I met Kai's friend's mother in the street she asked me, "When will you teach my children English?" so I called her. She was happy to hear from me and asked if I would be willing to teach English to a small group of children, and I agreed and said that I would. She made several phone calls and arranged a study group of seven children. Each student didn't pay a lot of money, but with all seven together the sum was quite respectable. We decided to meet every Wednesday at six p.m. in the evening, which was when Kai had his karate class.

I felt wonderful, the idea of a change breathed new life into me. That week I went to the largest bookstore in Tokyo and bought some books, file cards, tapes, and worksheets. I searched the Internet for English-teaching materials and found a lot of information and free downloads. I prepared for the first lesson all week long. I was nervous because I thought I might not be able to teach children, but when they entered the house, I realized I knew all of them from Kai's class and relaxed immediately. They sat attentively and were happy pupils.

I had prepared games and children's songs for a pleasant learning atmosphere, and I did the same in the following lessons. I added a new activity to each lesson to keep them from becoming bored. Until then I had been working with adult women, and I was surprised how smart the children were and how quickly they grasped the language. My adult students forgot what I taught them from one lesson to the next, but the children remembered and made excellent progress.

The news that I was teaching children spread and other mothers asked me to teach their children. I formed another group and continued teaching my three adult students. A few months later Makoto received a notice from the local municipality regarding the need for English teachers in elementary schools as children would now begin learning English in the lower grades. There were only two conditions, a knowledge of spoken English and good connections with children. Makoto convinced me to go for an interview. He prepared for me a resumé, called to find out what else I had to bring with me, and when everything was ready, I submitted my application. I had to pass Five interviewers and all the questions were in English. They asked me why I wanted to teach in a Japanese school, and I said that as the mother of a school-aged child I knew how important a knowledge of English would be for him later in life. I told them about the children I taught at home and how impressed I was by their ability to absorb a new language so quickly. A week later I got a letter saying I had been accepted.

I began teaching three times a week and was surprised to find that the teaching staff strongly objected to the introduction of a foreign language into the curriculum. They wouldn't let me use notebooks or pencils to teach the written language, and I was only allowed to teach spoken English. I constructed lessons based on songs and games and told them about other cultures, what foods people ate in other countries, and what their customs were like.

The school principal was concerned lest the children develop resistance to the language and demanded that I teach only nouns, no verbs, and no grammar. Since in any case I had experience from teaching children at home and I had a lot of material already prepared, I managed to construct lessons based on his demands. I taught a different subject every time, sometimes the names of animals, sometimes food, sometimes colors, and sometimes numbers. I slowly overcame any barriers there might have been and felt confident of what I was doing and liked the hours. We slowly merged into verbs and basic grammar, but only after the principal saw that they had assimilated what they had learned so far and were having no problems.

I got an enormous amount of satisfaction from my new job, and my paycheck gave me a sense of security. I no longer needed permission from Makoto to visit Israel or to justify what I bought. Teaching made me feel closer to Japan. Until then I felt there was an invisible wall separating me from the country I lived in, and I was anxious because I had no real roots – my roots were still firmly planted in Israel. Now for the first time something changed. My relationship with Makoto was stable, open, and deeper. He expressed his esteem for everything I did. Japan became my home in a more significant sense. The only thing that bothered me was that Kai was turning into exactly the opposite of what I wanted. He had juku lessons three times a week until ten at night to prepare him for the junior high school entrance exams. He was more Japanese than the Japanese. Every suggestion was met with his assurance he was fine and was doing what was right for him. He wanted to succeed, and as far as he was concerned the juku lessons were the correct path for every Japanese child. He told me again and again that his studies were more important than playing with his friends. Makoto was extremely proud of him and compared him to Tomonori and Michitaka. He was so happy Kai was ambitious, studied hard and wanted to be a success.

"My Mother has Cancer"

At the end of May 2007, I had my annual checkup; Makoto and I were very responsible about medical examinations and health. Given my family history, Makoto made sure I underwent every possible exam. I was never worried about the test results, I was young and healthy, and two months before my 39th birthday, I went alone, riding my motorcycle to the doctor's office. I was depressed about our finances and constantly tried to find a way of improving them.

At the clinic I was given a white a hospital gown and a number, and I went from one room to another, having my eyes and hearing tested, giving blood and urine samples, having a mammogram, chest X-ray, stomach X-ray – preceded by a particularly revolting barium cocktail – and finally an internal gynecological exam. The last was given by a woman doctor who asked me the questions they asked me every year. In the middle of the exam she said in surprise, "You're bleeding a lot, I don't understand why, I'm going to give you something to absorb the blood and send you to the hospital for further tests."

I was as surprised as she was. Nothing hurt, physically I felt fine. I didn't panic and I thought she was overreacting. I was fairly certain she had nicked something during the exam without noticing, and there was nothing wrong.

She told me to get dressed and wait, and after a couple of minutes she came back and said, "I want the test results as soon as possible. If you're willing to pay, I'll have them by tomorrow afternoon. If your insurance pays for it I won't have them for ten days, and I think it's in your best interest to have a quick analysis." I agreed, and when I left the clinic, I called Makoto. I told him how alarmed the doctor had been and he told me he would call me back as soon as he had more information.

Then I called my sister. I told her about what the doctor said and about our terrible financial situation and she tried to get me to calm down and be optimistic. "Call me tomorrow after you get the test results," she said, "and let me know if they found anything." I promised I would. In the meantime, Makoto called me back and said he has spoken to the doctor. She told him I had a large lesion on my cervix, and it didn't look good.

We waited for the test results. Makoto was shaken, but our only option was to wait patiently for the doctor to call. The lab results were sent to her on Saturday evening and she called Makoto. I had had a Pap test at the hospital and the results weren't promising; on Monday I had to go back to the hospital. I couldn't understand what he was telling me. I sat there smiling, as though he were talking about someone else, and it took me until the next day to fully understand what I was being told. I tried to be optimistic.

The exam at the hospital on Monday took only a few minutes. The doctor read the paperwork I brought with me, asked me to lie on my back for another exam and said, "I'm admitting you to the hospital immediately for treatment." He asked me if I had come alone, and I said no and asked Makoto to join me. The situation was changing fast, too fast and I kept thinking Kai left for school in the morning and I hadn't even told him I was going to the hospital, and now his father would have to tell him I was being hospitalized. Makoto suggested he tell him, in a way that wouldn't make him worry, that I had to undergo a minor procedure.

I asked permission to go home and pack some things for a hospital stay and then return, and permission was granted. The doctor told me to come back to room 302 on the third floor. On the way home the fog that had been clouding my brain cleared and for the first time I realized what was happening: "I have cancer." Tears rolled down my cheeks, and I couldn't stop them. The very word terrified my whole family, we had lost so many people to the disease, and now I panicked. What was going to happen to me? What would happen to me in a Japanese hospital? What about my students? What was I supposed to tell Kai?

I went home and packed towels, pajamas, soap, toothpaste and a toothbrush, a book and a laptop, crying the whole time. Then I remembered our financial difficulties, which Makoto had only recently told me about, and it was like I was sinking in quicksand. Makoto was terrified, lost in a sea of trouble.

At three o'clock in the afternoon a nurse welcomed us on the third floor of the hospital. She showed me my room, the bathroom, shower, telephone card, TV, and laundry room. She explained the hospital rules to me, one of which was that patients were forbidden to use cell phones in their rooms. I listened to her in shock, trying to absorb it all in.

Makoto stayed with me for the first couple of hours and then he went home to wait for Kai to come home from school and get ready for his juku lesson. He returned in the evening and when he entered my room, he looked stunned. I couldn't blame him, because I was in a ward with patients who had either undergone radiation treatments or chemo, and they were all bald. They were all perfectly friendly and pleasant, and one after another told us how they found out they had cancer, what happened after that, what treatments they had received and what their condition was.

It was a completely new world for me. From the moment the door opened into this unwanted world I had understood nothing, and I hoped the test results would be ready as soon as possible to let me know I could get out of bed and leave.

Makoto called his brother and told him about the tests, and Norio said he would talk to a friend who worked for the Ministry of Health to find out which hospital would be best for me; I was touched by his concern.

I was afraid my condition would keep Kai from his studies, but he was too busy to be distracted. I called him in the evening, and he sounded fine. He promised to visit me the following day. I however, had nothing to occupy me except thinking about what could happen. I thought about what to tell Kai, how to explain to him and how to be strong enough not to lose my mind. Time passed very slowly.

On Friday morning they said I could go home for the weekend. They were not willing to tell me anything specific, but I could tell the overall picture was unfavorable. In the meantime, Norio found an oncology hospital and said he would help get me a transfer; the hospital was an hour away by train from our house. It didn't even take me a second to make up my mind. I wanted to stay near Makoto and Kai, and I was willing to forgo a better hospital if it meant being close to home.

The weekend was nerve wracking, and I could find no peace. Most of the time I was on the phone with my sister and my best friends. They were all very worried and were afraid of what the doctor would tell me.

On Monday morning Makoto and I met with the head of the oncology department in his office; my test results were on his desk. We sat down facing him and he said, "You have a cancerous growth on your cervix, about the size of ping-pong ball." He showed me the MRI result, which revealed the growth on my cervix near my bladder. He recommended a series of three chemo treatments to shrink the growth and then an operation to remove my uterus and ovaries, and then three more chemo sessions. The entire procedure would take about six months, and without even giving me a chance to swallow he asked me when I wanted to start. "As soon as possible," I answered.

On the way home my brain was foggy again. I couldn't stop crying and all I wanted was to be hugged by my sister and friends, but all I could do was talk to them on the phone. They all told me the same thing: get on a plane and have everything done in Israel. I smiled to myself but knew it was impossible. I couldn't leave Makoto and Kai for half a year and besides, I had no medical insurance in Israel.

It made me feel better to know that everyone was on my side. My friend even asked an oncologist if the treatment in Japan would be the same as in Israel, and he said the doctors in Japan act according to international protocol and there was nothing to be worried about.

At that point I knew I had to tell Kai the truth. I told him, simply, "Your mother has cancer." His eyes opened wide, and he said, "Are you going to die?" "No way," I said, "I will have to go to the hospital sometimes, and after a year I'll be perfectly healthy again." He looked at me skeptically and didn't say anything.

I called the parents of all my private students and told them what the situation was. As is customary in Japan, I asked for an unlimited leave of absence. They were shocked and promised to pray for me. "Take your time and don't worry about the children, only about your health."

I only found out about what our private health insurance covered after Makoto sent them my medical documents. Once the doctor signed the forms, I was supposed to receive $10,000, an additional $20,000 for the operation, and $300 for every day I stayed in the hospital. I breathed a little easier and was glad Makoto had insured me as soon as we got married. He had worked for an insurance company for 25 years and had seen policies save clients' lives and understood the importance of medical insurance.

I did what I could to make my first hospital stay as pleasant as possible. I bought new summer pajamas, got books, downloaded movies and TV shows to my laptop and bought a wireless Internet connection. I had no idea of what chemo really was or how it would affect me. All I knew was what I remembered about my mother, that after every session she was terribly nauseous, her hair fell out and she lost weight.

For my first treatment I was assigned to a room near the nurses' station. They hooked me up to machines and stuck tubes in me and began feeding the drugs into a vein. It wasn't so bad, although inserting the catheter was awful. I had to lie in bed, but I could read or watch movies on my laptop. After three hours they gave me a different drug in a different bag; from start to finish it took six hours. The doctor told me that the second drug might make me sleepy. He was right, I fell asleep. The preparations, the chemo itself and being monitored afterwards took a full week. I made friends with the other women in the room, learned about the hospital and what kind of treatments they offered, and consulted with the doctor treating me, who explained what I could expect later. In the afternoon there were visiting hours and people came to see me, which raised my spirits immeasurably.

Once the week was up, I went home and got into bed immediately. My whole body ached, I had a high temperature, and I was exhausted. In the evening Daniella called to tell me she was getting on the next plane to Japan. I was happy and moved by the effort she was making for my sake.

The visit forced me to stand on my aching legs and occasionally go with her for short walks. My hair fell out and whenever I went out, I looked for hats; I must have spent at least an hour a day trying on hats. In the meantime, Makoto ordered a wig for me; it came a few days later. He had to measure my head exactly and send the measurements to his friend who imported wigs from China and gave it to me as a present.

Her visit lasted for a week and raised my morale a good deal. Every day Makoto took us to the city for a couple of hours and we walked around the markets and went to coffee houses. It was exactly what I needed to prepare myself for the next chemo session. It was also an excellent opportunity for me to avail myself of their professional knowledge because Daniella was an economist. One day I told her about the financial fix we were in and asked for her advice, but she immediately said, "Now you have to think about your health, not money." She said, "When I get back to Israel, I'll transfer $150,000 into your account, I'll take out a bank loan, don't worry." I sobbed tears of relief.

Before she flew back Daniella told me to have Makoto make a list for her of all our debts and the business' routine expenses, and she would analyze the problem. I also decided to do something positive myself. I called my students' parents and told them that from now until I finished with the hospital, I would teach two weeks a month. They were fully supportive and said I should teach as many lessons as I felt I could; teaching made me happy.

The second chemo session was like the first, but this time there were other women in the room with me. I was in a better mood than the first time. The other women were friendly, and we got along well, and I was popular with the nurses and doctors because I spoke English fluently. They wanted me to practice their English with me and I was happy to accommodate them. During the day I surfed the Internet, found funny things to look at and in the afternoon went with my visitors for coffee in the hospital cafeteria. Everyone who worked there knew me and even remembered some of the people who came to visit me every day. They tried to speak to us in English.

The hospital routine was calm but the situation at home was catastrophic. Kai couldn't bear seeing me without hair, and he wouldn't come near me unless I was wearing a hat or my wig. He stopped talking to me, was angry all the time, and provoked me whenever he could. He said, "You have no right to talk. You sleep all the time, you're lazy." Sometimes it was a lot worse, and he would say, "You annoy me, you're ruining my life." And once he said, "Don't go near my school, my friends or my basketball team. I'm ashamed of you. You're ugly." I was shocked and very hurt and called Daniella to complain and tell her how miserable I was. I knew it was difficult for him and his reaction reflected his fears. She recommended a child psychologist in Israel, who agreed to counsel me over the phone.

The psychologist was a woman named Lora. She explained that Kai was worried about me, especially since he knew my mother died of cancer when I was 15. She said he made the connection, cancer was cancer, and he was positive I was going to die. My telling him that my mother's cancer was different from mine and that mine could be cured didn't convince him. He simply didn't believe me. She said, "Your bald head is a daily reminder for him that his mother is going to die."

Until I got sick Kai was my best friend. He used to hug me and laugh with me, and we always had a wonderful time together. Everything changed overnight, he was angry, he kept away from me and shut himself in his room. He rarely spoke to me, and if he did it was only to tell me I annoyed him, and he was ashamed of me. Almost every day he told me he hated me.

Lora told me to work on myself, not to be hurt and not to become anxious. "You have to show him you're strong," she said, "and most important, don't feel guilty for being sick. It wasn't your wish and it's not your fault." She encouraged me to be assertive with Kai to make him feel more secure with me. It was absurd, but when I was gentle and tried to reconcile with him, it only frightened him more.

Despite Kai's objections to appear with me in public she said I should go to his basketball games as usual. She said as soon as he saw that people treated me the way they always had he would understand that my disease didn't interest anyone and that would make him more secure. I did what she suggested, I put my wig on, a hat on the wig and went to the game. Adults and children alike, everyone was happy to see me and acted normally. That evening at home, he didn't mention the game but acted almost as he had before I became ill. Every time he had something to say about the wig I said, "It is what it is, and you will have to get used to it until I finish being treated and my hair grows back."

Being in the hospital was the hardest part of having cancer. I hated the way the hospital smelled, the iron bed, the strange, strict rules. We couldn't shower every day, only every other day. We weren't allowed to make phone calls inside the building. The lights were turned off at nine at night and we were awakened at six in the morning.

Sometimes Makoto came to take me from the hospital and return me for procedures in the evening. I could never fall asleep at nine, I would go into the lobby with my laptop and telephone to talk to friends and family members.

In September, after the first three courses of chemo, I went for an MRI. The results showed the treatments had successfully reduced the size of the tumor and the next stage would be the removal of my uterus and ovaries.

It was hard for my sister to accept my illness. She went to various rabbis and spent a lot of money buying charms and amulets. She began praying and keeping the Sabbath, and eventually became ultra-Orthodox religious. She believed in an omnipotent god who would decide if I lived or died, and that her prayers would help me overcome the cancer. I respected her new faith, but I asked her not to force it on me, and that she accepts the fact I was married to a man who wasn't Jewish, and I hadn't been observant for many years. I told her I would lead my life as usual, meeting friends, watching comedies, and trying to keep my morale up.

The operation was difficult, and recovery wasn't easy. After having my uterus and ovaries removed, I began having hot flashes, and despite being only 39 years old, I was already post-menopausal.

After the Operation

As promised, my sister landed in Tokyo the day I was released from the hospital. She brought a suitcase with her full of Israeli products and cooked me healthy, tasty Middle Eastern meals every day. The house was full of the familiar aromas of soup, beans, and chicken, all the things she remembered I liked. Kai loved her cooking, proof to me he had Israeli blood in his veins.

The visits from Israel made my life much easier, especially since with visitors around Kai had to restrain his rudeness towards me and he did calm down somewhat, but it did flash up from time to time. Makoto was grateful to my sister for coming and drove her to the market every day. It was her third visit to Japan, and she liked Tokyo very much. She claimed it was cheaper than Israel, with a lot of good-quality bargains. She bought her children designer clothes and presents for the ridiculous price of one dollar. The dollar stores were very popular in Japan, and tourists waited in line to enter them.

During the second week of her visit, I began to feel a little better and I could go back to doing things if I didn't tire myself out, and I felt better from day to day. At that point eight weeks had passed since my last chemo treatment and my hair began to grow back. However, I still had three more rounds and I knew my hair would just fall out again.

My fourth chemo treatment was scheduled for the day my sister flew back to Israel. I was tired of being hospitalized and fed up with their strict rules. I also felt guilty about everything Kai and Makoto had to deal with, I wanted it to be over and done with. The three last chemo sessions were the worst. Each one made me weaker than the previous one and I gained a lot of weight from the steroids they gave me, even my eyebrows and eyelashes fell out, and I looked exactly like a classic cancer patient undergoing chemotherapy.

Kai kept away from me as much as he could and barely spoke to me. Makoto, on the other hand, was wonderful. He changed completely from the moment the cancer was diagnosed. He surrounded me with love, hugged and kissed me, and a month after the operation he wanted to have intercourse again. I was too terrified to even try, but I took it as a compliment that fat and bald as I was, he was still attracted to me.

A childhood friend said she would come to visit the week after my final chemo treatment, and we would have a party to celebrate. I suggested we go to Club Med in Okinawa, a south-Japanese island located near Taiwan. She thought it was a great idea, so I reserved two plane tickets, paying with Makoto's frequent flyer miles.

In the meantime, I still had my final chemo session, and it was a nightmare. The hospital and its smells made me sick to my stomach. I couldn't tolerate seeing doctors and nurses anymore, even though they had done me no harm. Even the hospital cafeteria, which I liked in the beginning, had become unbearable. I was in a particularly bad mood and kept having hot flashes, one after the other. I asked to cut my hospitalization short and promised to rest at home, but the doctors refused.

Makoto came to visit every evening and took me to a nearby restaurant for dinner. He knew I couldn't eat hospital food anymore, and without the restaurant I would have eaten nothing. I kept dreaming of going to the hotel with my friend; I really needed a vacation.

I was finally released from the hospital, and my vacation was just around the corner. I deliberately didn't tell my doctor. He probably wouldn't have recommended it but something inside me said it would cure my soul. Makoto was worried about my going away so soon after treatment, but I decided not to make it a topic of discussion, I just promised to take good care of myself.

My friend landed in Tokyo the week after I was released, and we flew to Okinawa. The flight was worth it. The island was breathtakingly beautiful and the hotel, which was built along the Kabira Beach in the East China Sea, was an oasis of tranquility. We arrived at the perfect time, off-season in December, and we were virtually alone. All I wanted to do was rest on the beach, read, eat non-hospital food, and talk to my friend.

The day she returned to Israel, I returned to teaching. I was happy to be with the children again. They always made me feel good. The reception they gave me was wonderful and renewed my energy. None of them knew about my illness and all of them wanted to know if I had dyed my hair and had it styled differently.

After three months my hair started to grow back, and I began to forget how awful things had been. The unbearable hospital smell, the needles they stuck into me, the frequent gynecological exams, the long nights, the appearance of the women whose cancer remissions had ended, all taught me it had been hard but now I was strong. I found people who showed they were true friends, and I will never forget them.

The more my hair grew, the more Kai returned to his normal behavior, and we became close again. In retrospect I realized that distancing himself from me made him invest more in his studies and in basketball, and he became both an excellent student and an outstanding basketball player. Everything came together at the end of the school year when we were considering enrolling him in a good school in preparation for acceptance into a good university.

Makoto and Kai went to several open school days at the prestigious schools so Kai could enroll in one. Kai was upset that not even one of them had a good basketball team. One day he said, "I'm not going to a school for geniuses. I want to be a basketball player." Makoto absolutely refused. He said basketball was temporary, studies and a career were permanent. Kai remained unconvinced. He cried and told me, "My dream is to play basketball, and nothing can change my mind." He convinced me he knew what he wanted, and I decided to fight Makoto and this time not to let him overrule me. Unlike the days when we were raising Tomonori and Michitaka, this time the child was mine as well, and I decided to save him from having to go through what they had.

Kai found two good schools in Tokyo and Makoto opposed to both. He said to Kai, "You're going to destroy your future. You're an excellent student, and you want to waste everything you've achieved over the past few years." I told Kai to do what he wanted, and I will handle Makoto. Kai kept crying and Makoto refused to back down. We consulted Shirai-San, Kai's basketball coach, and he recommended we send him to a school close to home. He knew the coach there and knew they had a good team. He said they began training at seven in the morning, which meant Kai would have to get up very early. Kai kept insisting on going to one of the schools in Tokyo, which were further away and whose academic level was lower. After repeated attempts to convince him Makoto enrolled him in the school he wanted.

But then things changed. Several weeks later Shirai-San called to tell us that the school closer to home didn't have enough basketball players on his grade and the coach was searching high and low for good players. The coach had appealed to Shirai-San to encourage Kai to switch schools and join the team, and he promised to put him on the court during his first year, which was a very rare promise. In addition, since Kai was an outstanding player, he had a better chance of getting into a good high school without an entrance exam. Makoto was enthusiastic and after talking to Kai a couple of times, the ongoing saga of school enrollment ended.

If for a minute I thought we could relieve Kai of daily juku lessons because the road to a good high school was already open to him, it ended when Makoto told him there was no way he would stop juku. "I don't believe you will be accepted without an exam," he kept telling him. "You will not just play basketball and ignore your studies."

Kai looked at me pleadingly but, in this case, I stepped back and told him I couldn't help and he would have to make room for both basketball and juku. I wanted to help him, especially because I knew juku was the nightmare of every Japanese child who parents wanted him to have a brilliant future. My hands were tied, and I knew that in this case Makoto would decide and nothing would make him change his mind.

Discipline, Japanese Style

During the first week of April 2007 the junior high school year began in Japan. Exactly 15 years previously I had arrived in Japan and Michitaka had begun junior high school, exposing me to the burden the students shouldered. And now here I was, with my own child going down the same road. Before the school year started, I bought Kai two suits, one for summer and one for winter, which would be his school uniform, plus a lot of button-down white shirts, a tie, and a pair of black shoes. Every morning I watched my adolescent son go to school, looking like a groom going to his wedding.

The second week of school there was a parents' meeting, and we met the school basketball coach for the first time. His reputation was terrifying. He explained the team's agenda and rules, and the role of the parents. I couldn't believe what I was hearing. Kai had to be at school at seven every morning for an hour of practice, and on Saturdays and Sundays they either trained or played at various locations around Tokyo. The players would not be given any days off and the only cause that justified absence was a high temperature.

He said the rules were not negotiable and there were no exceptions. He added, "I don't take any vacations because I have committed myself to training your children. I gave up my personal life for the team, which will be in Tokyo's opening ten. To reach the goal both parents and children have to work towards achieving it." He was silent for a minute, and then he said, "Anyone who thinks it is unsuitable can leave the team now. I'm not forcing anyone to stay, it's your decision."

I came home in shock and told Kai everything. He understood how upset I was and said, "I hope you behaved well and didn't make any inappropriate comments." I said, "I sat quietly and listened to that crazy person speak. And I think you're crazy for agreeing to go to that school. I hope you'll be able to cope with the pressure." He said, "Don't worry, I'll be fine."

In May our new routine began. Every morning Makoto and I got up at six, I woke Kai, we helped him get organized and made him breakfast. He needed three changes of clothes every day, two for basketball and one for school, and I had to iron everything to perfection. He also had more books and notebooks. His backpack was so heavy I forbade him to walk around with it all day.

On Saturdays and Sundays, the players took public transportation to games and practice, and even though we also drove to the same locations the coach forbade players to go with their parents and didn't even allow us to take his heavy backpack in our car. It was hard for me to watch Kai walk to the train station regardless of the weather – rain, snow, heatwave – and go with his friends to wherever practice or the game was being held. The coach was very strict with them and told them that anyone caught breaking the rules would be punished. Kai was terrified of him and apparently all the other players were, too. However, as promised, within a few months he was playing on the court, and thanks to the coach's strictness the team became one of the best in Tokyo.

Almost every evening Kai came home exhausted after a long day of school and later practice, and he barely had ten minutes before he was out the door again for juku, which began at seven in the evening on Mondays, Wednesdays, and Fridays. On the other days he came home smiling and in a good mood. When he was free in the evening, he lay on the couch in the living room and watched TV.

The change in him was amazing. Within a few months he lost weight and became taller, broader, and interested in girls. And girls became interested in him. He was no longer embarrassed by having a foreign mother and loved his uniqueness, which for the first time seemed like an advantage.

Junior High School studies were difficult. The teachers were very strict, and anyone who pushed the boundaries too far was punished, and that included corporal punishment for rebellious children. The slightest infraction of the rules, including not having your shirt firmly tucked into your pants, was considered a serious offense. Corporal punishment was also used on the court. The coach struck or cursed every student who angered him. Violence was never hidden, and parents saw it as well. It was humiliating. Kai didn't care if the coach yelled or hit him, which made me feel marginally better, and I'm sorry to admit I learned to accept the situation.

At the end of May I planned to fly to Israel for two weeks and I wanted Kai to come with me. He said, "Go to Israel and have a good time. I'm too busy, all I care about now is basketball." I thought it over and decided to go anyway and leave Kai with his father. I needed to get away and breathe different air, especially after the terrible year I had just gone through. Israel was celebrating the 60th anniversary of the founding of the State, and it was one of the best visits I had since leaving the country. I was welcomed with great warmth, and everyone was so happy now that I was well. I went to Eilat with my sister and some friends, and we had a wonderful time, not just because we were on vacation, but because I felt I was finally well again. My hair had grown back, I had gained weight – more than I had lost, but it didn't bother me – I was physically stronger because I had been working out and eating well, and I had changed my approach to life, allowing myself to enjoy simple pleasures.

I returned to Tokyo full of energy and a positive feeling I could now move on. I would still have routine medical exams, and there was stress before each one, but as soon as the results came back negative, I could get on with my life. That year we also made progress in regulating our finances. While I was still sick Makoto followed Daniella's recommendations, he closed his business, paid his debts with the loan we received from her, we used my insurance money to live on and somehow managed to survive. Obviously, I would have to be patient until Makoto found a new source of income. I knew him well enough to know that he would find his way and not pressure him. Pressuring him always backfired. And this time I had sympathy for him. I knew how difficult it was to feel helpless in the face of an unknown future.

I felt strong enough to return to work. I went back to teaching English at home in the afternoon and at school in the morning. But I wasn't making a lot of money and I had to look for something more profitable to help Makoto pay Daniella back. I updated my resumé and uploaded it on employment websites. It took me hours, with Makoto in the background giving a running commentary of his opinions. He said Japanese companies would not contact me even though I had a good command of the language. They would prefer, he said, people whose native language was Japanese and could read and write it. I didn't pay too much attention because I knew how pessimistic he was. He was a glass half-empty kind of person, and I had been married to him long enough to know I wasn't going to change him.

Initially no one contacted me, and I was hurt. I knew it wouldn't be easy for me to find a job with an Israeli company that had offices in Japan, and I felt I had wasted valuable time investing so much effort in learning the language, which hadn't done me any good, at least not yet. Still, I didn't despair. I surfed the Net looking for simultaneous translation jobs, and that was where I started getting responses and I was occasionally sent to accompany Japanese businessmen at meetings with Israeli businessmen. Those meetings were fortuitous because they opened the door for me to the Israeli business community. I stayed in touch with them even when they went back to Israel and every time, they arrived in Tokyo they asked me to accompany them to their meetings.

The pay was excellent. Even Makoto was surprised by how much I earned, and he started looking for simultaneous translation's jobs for me. One day I got a call from one of the manpower companies Makoto had contacted in my name. They wanted me to translate at interrogations in the customs department at Narita airport. The invitation came the same week I finally got rid of my wig. My hair was short, but it was thick and healthy, and it was my own hair. Happy, finally, with my appearance I took the train to Narita, a two-hour trip. A customs officer was waiting for me and asked me to accompany him to an interrogation room, where I would translate. I asked him who had been arrested, and why, and he said they had arrested three Israelis on suspicion of smuggling drugs. Each one had a lawyer and translator, and I would be the translator for an 18-year-old boy from a mostly religious city in the center of Israel. They also asked me to spend the next week in the airport hotel, for which they would pay. I called Makoto and he said, "Stay there," he said, "I'll send you clothes, they'll arrive tomorrow." Delivery services in Japan were reliable, readily available, and cheap.

I told the customs officer I could stay and started working. Every day I came at nine in the morning and stayed till noon. Work stopped at noon and resumed at two o'clock, ending at six in the evening. Sometimes I met with the investigators in the evening.

My first task was to examine the young man's suitcase,

read and translate every document. Since I couldn't write Japanese well enough, I was accompanied by a man who would write for me. It took me the entire morning, and in the afternoon, I met with the investigator, and he explained the procedure in the interrogation room.

In the afternoon I met the suspect. He impressed me as a nice enough young and innocent man who said they found eight kilograms of drugs in his possession, and knew nothing about them. He explained that the person who gave him the box told him it was full of Jewish religious objects and he should not open it, just to take it with him to Japan. He seemed innocent to me, but I knew there were legal procedures to go through, and he wouldn't be able to simply walk out the door on my say-so.

I worked for a week, at the end of which I was told I could go home for the weekend. Three weeks passed quickly. Once the investigation had been completed the customs officials asked the manpower company to send me again, this time to the police station in the city center. They would need me between two and three times a week until the judge had decided whether the accused would be handed over for trial or set free.

The whole procedure lasted for more than a year and the pay, which was excellent, helped us financially. Once I had finished working for the police, the lawyer of one of the defendants asked me if I would come to the jail with him as his translator, so I continued for another year and our financial situation improved considerably.

Kai's 13th birthday was approaching fast. He knew what it meant in the Jewish tradition, that he was Bar Mitzvah, no longer a child and responsible for his own actions, and because he had attended his cousins' bar mitzvah parties in Israel, he was eager to celebrate his own in Israel, too; he said he needed a vacation. For the past two years, between studies and basketball he hadn't gone abroad at all. I wondered how he would work it out with his teachers and basketball coach, and he said not to worry. They liked him. He would ask for time off.

I told Makoto, and his immediate reaction was, "Absolutely not! He's not going to miss classes or juku because of a Bar Mitzvah!" I called my sister. "You don't have to come exactly on his birthday, you can come the following month, it'll be during the Japanese Christmas vacation. It's only the year that's important, not the date." I asked Kai to check with his coach when he could be released from training, which he did without hesitation. He told the coach about what being bar mitzvah meant and how he felt it was his duty to undergo the same rite of passage as other Jews. Once the coach understood the significance of the ceremony, he released Kai for the Christmas vacation.

Makoto was not pleased what Kai and I had done behind his back, and he said, "You're not normal! How are you planning to pay for all this?" I said, "Don't worry, there's money for it, and besides, he'll be getting presents which will cover a lot of the expenses." I insisted Makoto would join us, even though he wasn't interested at all.

My sister was excited when I told her we would celebrate Kai's Bar Mitzvah in Israel. She promised to take care of all the arrangements and said she would go with her family to see reception venues and find the best one for us.

She asked the rabbi of the synagogue near her house how a child who couldn't read Hebrew would be able to say his portion of the Torah at his bar mitzvah, and the rabbi promised to help him learn a few sentences. She prepared everything and it only took her a few days. She convinced me to keep all the preparations secret and to surprise Kai before we flew out of Tokyo. Together we made a list of 150 guests, and she later said all of them would come. Japanese boys didn't come to Israel for their Bar Mitzvah celebrations very often.

So, one Saturday morning all of Kai's aunts and uncles, with their children, and my childhood friends with their children, my friends' parents who also wanted to come, my sister's friends, and my brother all gathered in the synagogue. Kai's reading of his Torah portion went smoothly. Outside, my aunt prepared refreshments for the guests and I was very moved by it all and pleased as well as emotional that so many people came to celebrate with us. I was so very proud of my only son. I was only sorry that neither of my parents had lived to see the day their Half-Japanese grandson would become a Jewish man.

Five days later Makoto returned to Tokyo full of stories about his experience. I had also made sure the ceremony had been videoed and photos had been taken as well, and he was thrilled. He kept telling everyone in Japan about the ceremony and the Jewish rite of passage from childhood to adulthood. It was moving to see how pleased and proud he was, especially after initially having been so opposed to the idea.

While we were in Israel Kai played basketball with his

cousins and they were impressed by his ability. They were amazed he was so young and so skilled. They didn't know he had been practicing for at least four hours a day for two years. Since we had two more weeks of vacation, I looked for a place in Israel where he could continue playing. I found out that the Wingate Institute had a boarding school for exceptional basketball players. I called them and was transferred to the director, who was very interested in Kai's background. He asked me to send him a video of Kai's games in Japan. As my sons' most ardent fan, I immediately sent him several videos I had taken with my phone.

The next day he called me back and said, "Your son is an athlete and has all the potential to turn into an outstanding player." He suggested we meet, and I told Kai, who was overjoyed.

The director turned out to be charming, in love with his work, and with years of experience in coaching young athletes. He took us to a court and while I watched them he tested Kai to see how he played. When he finished, he offered Kai a week at the boarding school so he could see what it was like and participate in some of the activities. Kai was overwhelmed and immediately agreed to the proposition, and we agreed to return the following day with Kai's things. On the way back Kai was in seventh heaven.

The next day the director and one of the resident athletes were waiting for us and got Kai settled, and we said our goodbye. When I came to pick him up a week later one glance at him told me how happy he was. He said, "Mommy, it was fantastic, I want to stay and play basketball in Israel." The director said he could enroll the following year. I thanked him and told him quite honestly what his father's reaction would be, that he wouldn't agree, and we couldn't accept his offer without Makoto's permission. I had a lot of questions, and while I could see how excited Kai was in the boarding school, I wondered how he would deal with the Israeli lifestyle over time. Moreover, since he was half Japanese, he might not grow tall enough for professional basketball.

When we returned to Japan Kai told Makoto about the boarding school, and as expected, his father didn't like the idea. In fact, he was angry I had let Kai spend even a week there and that I thought he could abandon his assured future in Japan, including juku, and move to Israel. For him Israel had been and remained an uncivilized country which would destroy his son's future. I found that amusing, and I said, "He is also my son and I also have the right to say something about his future." I had seen how Tomonori and Michitaka had been raised and where it had led them, and I didn't want the same thing for Kai. In the meantime, Kai told everyone he was leaving Japan and going to live in Israel. Everyone asked Makoto and me if that was true; I said, "Yes" and Makoto said, "No."

Kai wanted desperately to go to Israel and began confronting his father. He tried to convince him to release him from juku and allow him to just train. He said, "I'm not going to go to the genius school where everyone wears glasses, four-eyes, all of them. I'm going to play basketball and I want to live abroad, not in Japan."

It took a while, but Makoto finally realized Kai was serious and changed his approach. He spoke to him kindly, avoiding confrontations, and tried in every possible way to explain his own position. He said, "Of all my children, you're the smartest. You have good grades and you'll be able to get into any school you want. You can't make a living as a basketball player and becoming a professional and making a good living is especially hard." He begged Kai to listen to him and stay in Japan and promised he would find him a high school with a good basketball team. Kai was not appeased. He said he didn't want to play basketball as an amateur, and he didn't care if the school was good or not.

Makoto continued pressuring him, saying he didn't think Kai would ever succeed as a basketball player because he didn't have what it took. Kai said, "Why do you think you can decide for me if I will be a good player or not? Let me find out for myself. If it turns out I was wrong, it'll by my problem, not yours. I want to go my own way; I don't want you to decide for me!"

Makoto stormed out of Kai's room and said angrily, "See what you've done! What a waste! He is a good student, and you destroyed his future!" I replied, "Maybe in your opinion I'm destroying his future, but in my opinion, I'm saving his future. Israel is not a third-world country, and remember, he is half Israeli." I really believed Kai would flourish in Israel and someday come back to Japan as an adult, and then he could choose where he wanted to live. He would be bilingual and have self-confidence, and for me that was far more important than a university degree. I knew that what awaited him in Japan, the pressure to be accepted by a good university, would be intolerable.

I Find a New Profession

Kai kept begging me to save him and help convince his father. "I want to go to Israel. Don't let me have to continue juku. I can't stand the pressure, and I want to be a basketball player, and not live in Japan." I promised I would do what I could to get Makoto to agree to a six-month trial period and see where it led. For months we tried to convince Makoto, and Kai threatened he would stop studying altogether. Eventually Makoto caved and when Kai was 14 and in junior high school, we sent him to Israel for a three-month trial period. Makoto was certain he would be disappointed and return to Japan, and that he would understand Israel was not the right place for him.

As summer approached my sister said she was planning to visit Tokyo with her children; the trip was a bar mitzvah present for her son. I was excited they were coming. She hadn't come to visit since my operation, and then she only came to take care of me, not as a tourist. This time we would devote all our time to having a good time.

During the vacation Kai's time was taken up with basketball practice and juku. He didn't have school in the morning, but he had double the number of basketball hours and then juku as usual, so he had almost no free time during the day. My sister and her sons pitied him, and when we were alone, she said it was inhuman to force that kind of day on a child. They couldn't believe the coach hit the players and pulled their hair. They told Kai that if it happened in Israel the coach would have been fired immediately.

At around that time my friend Daniella introduced me to her friend, who lived in Tel Aviv. She told me about a successful Internet site called Tokyo Top Guide that worked in collaboration with tourist sites like TripAdvisor, providing information for tourists from all over the world who travel to Japan. She got a commission from TripAdvisor when hotel rooms in Japan were booked through her as well as when tours were booked for other sites. She heard I was coming to Israel and asked Daniella to introduce us. I couldn't have been happier.

She told me that for the most part the people she worked with spoke English and the next time she travelled to Japan she wanted me to show her special places in Tokyo, and recommend restaurants, hotels, and other attractions. We became friends at our first meeting.

Every so often I got a call from the jail asking for me to come and translate for them. It happened about twice a year and the jobs lasted about three weeks. I was also teaching English, and the parents knew that sometimes I needed to take time off. I met Daniella's friend at a time when I felt I needed a change. She suggested I start an Internet site for Israelis and offer translation services for businessmen in Japan. She recommended I learn how to construct a site by myself, and it took me two months but eventually my site was up on the Web. I hoped it would reach the right people and provide me with work and continuous income.

In the meantime, my nephew came to Japan for a visit. He came all the time, sometimes alone and sometimes with friends. He told me his best friend's parents were planning a trip to Japan and wanted someone to be their guide while they were there. There would be eight people in the group. He told me I would be the best person for the job. That made me smile, and I told him he knew more about tourists' sites than I did because he visited them all the time, and he promised he would help put a program together. Excited, I went to tell Makoto, but he, skeptical as usual, said, "You have never guided a group, you aren't at all familiar with Japan, how do you propose to do it?"

I like challenges and this one seemed to be perfect for me. First, I spoke with the couple planning the trip to see what they wanted. They told me they were less interested in Japanese history and more in touring and having a good time. They wanted good hotels, good restaurants, and didn't want the kind of program they got on ordinary guided tours. They just wanted me to accompany them, they needed someone who spoke both Hebrew and Japanese.

Makoto was of course pessimistic from the beginning and generally objected to the whole idea, but as usual in the end he always helped me. We planned the trip together, and he arranged for transportation and drivers, arranging things with them in advance to prevent problems later. They reserved hotel rooms by themselves from Israel, and the agency reserved a room for me as well for locations outside Tokyo.

The trip was a success. They knew it was my first time as a guide and confessed they enjoyed every minute. "You were exactly what we needed," they said, and promised to recommend me to friends who were planning to visit Japan that year. Without previous planning or investing in marketing, that year I guided three groups of Israeli tourists, and suddenly, I had a new profession.

I also knew I had to have more of a foundation, I had to have information for tourists who wanted to know about Japanese history, so I began studying. I also went on trips with Makoto to explore new places and continued working on improving my spoken Japanese to make it easier to communicate during the tours. I also expanded my Internet site to include simultaneous translation for tourists, and people showed a lot of interest.

Every time I had a new idea, I could see it made Makoto anxious and nervous, he would retreat and try to keep me from trying it out. Eventually I realized that sharing things with him was detrimental. I decided to do everything by myself and tell him when it was done, thereby saving myself a lot of useless arguments with him. When he saw that the first steps had already been taken there was no reason not to proceed. He became calmer, cooperated with me, and helped me a lot.

The website started bearing fruit. Israeli companies sending staff members to meetings or exhibitions hired me to accompany them as their translator. Since I also offered sight-seeing tours, they often asked me to be their guide and show them a little bit of Tokyo. I was so happy to be earning money from something I really enjoyed doing.

Makoto's fortunes were not progressing so rapidly, and things didn't seem to work out for him. I began to feel he was looking for something that didn't exist, and it depressed him. He sat on the couch watching TV for hours at a time and refused to discuss the subject. He wouldn't speak about his financial difficulties or how he felt. From the little he did tell me, however, I understood that the manpower companies had offered him work paying one third of his former salary. I tried to convince him to accept one of the offers, but he refused and said he would keep looking. I became angry with him for wasting time when he could be earning something, at least, which would help us pay back Daniella's loan. I was furious that he allowed himself to sit doing nothing, but the more I pressured him the more he withdrew into himself or attacked me in return. That again led us to argue about various disagreements, and again our relationship began to break down to the point where we almost weren't speaking to one another. It was my good fortune to be busy most of the time, and I invested more and more energy in marketing my website to generate enough work so I could at least pay the household expenses.

I knew Makoto sometimes met with old friends from the insurance agency. They kept him updated on what everyone was doing and talked about what the market had to offer. On one occasion someone told him the company he was working for was hiring and gave Makoto the details. The salary was low, but Makoto was open to suggestions because his friend worked there. I was glad to know there was someone he was willing to listen to and I begged him to give the company a chance. Tomonori and Michitaka were independent, and we no longer had to support them, so Makoto didn't have to earn as much as in the past. Nevertheless, he still wasn't convinced. We again bickered and argued, and since I didn't stop begging and crying, he agreed to sacrifice his self-respect and took the job.

He discovered the company had employed at lot of people his age who were in similar straits. They all had mortgages and children to educate and households to run, and all of them, like him, had in the past held senior positions in large companies and received high salaries. They had all found work through friends, all in similar situations. That made it much easier for Makoto to adapt to his new job. He felt at home.

In the meantime, we continued planning Kai's trip to Israel. The school year would end in six months, and he stopped going to the juku, agreed on after long negotiations with Makoto. The time freed up was spent online with a private Hebrew teacher. He never lost sight of his goal and made fairly good progress.

A Challenge for Kai

After a long series of negotiations Makoto agreed to accompany me to the Israeli embassy to fill out a form that would enable Kai to go to Israel, and I could tick off one of the many missions I had to accomplish. We spoke to the school principal in Tokyo and agreed that if studies in Israel were unsuitable Kai could take high school entrance exams and continue his studies, which would now be suspended. The principal, teachers and basketball coach all wished Kai good luck and his friends held a farewell party for him.

The school year doesn't begin in Israel at the same time as in Japan. In Israel it begins in September, while in Japan it begins in April, which later turned out to be important. Kai left Japan at the beginning of the ninth grade but in Israel he landed towards the end of the school year. That meant he had lost a lot of the year by leaving Japan on March 30, 2009.

There were still financial issues. We had to return money to Daniella and pay for Kai's tuition and someplace to live in Israel. Fortunately, I had begun earning a lot of money and could finance the flight by myself. Makoto paid for the rest and Daniella told me not to worry about paying back the loan, she dealt with it every six months and by playing with the exchange rate between the shekel, the yen, and the dollar, she had reduced the outstanding sum, which made me very happy. I was terribly emotional about Kai's going away. I wished him whatever he wished for himself, but I didn't like the idea of being separated from him for so long. The only thing that comforted me was knowing how happy he was, with his enormous motivation, excited to begin a new life at the Wingate Institute.

Between April and July all the ninth-grade students were busy with preparations for the end of the year party. They practically had no studies at all and spent most of their time at rehearsals without adult supervision. It took almost two weeks before I understood what was going on. The educational framework had broken down completely and I thought it would be a good idea for Kai to spend the time improving his Hebrew, but I couldn't find anyone responsible to talk to about it.

The Wingate coaches were mainly interested in the students' sports achievements, and they had no connection with the junior high school teaching staff. Kai told me he spent most of his time in coffee houses with his new friends. I was happy he had been accepted socially and was invited to friends' homes for the weekend, but beyond enjoying himself I could tell by his voice that he felt lost. I called the school principal and he said they had no system in place for absorbing new immigrants who were minors and had come without their parents, and I was responsible for his welfare. I spoke with the director, head of the Wingate boarding school, and he tried to help me but was stymied by red tape and bureaucracy. I felt guilty for having supported Kai's desire to go to Israel and my anxiety rose. It was a slap in the face, and I didn't realize how I could have made such an awful mistake. Who sends their 14-year-old child to Israel alone? I was petrified, and it motivated me to find a way out of the awful situation. The director continued trying to help me with paperwork, but it went nowhere. In the end he suggested I try enrolling him at the sports boarding school at a kibbutz in the north of Israel, because maybe the kibbutz environment would give him what he lacked in the center of the country. Besides, he added, the teens there played with a good team and studied at a school which put an emphasis on developing athletes, not just on achievements in sports.

I spoke to Kai about it, and he objected, angry I had even suggested the idea. That didn't surprise me because he had no interest in academic studies. He wanted to stay at Wingate and play basketball. But I knew Makoto would never forgive me if he found out Kai was just playing basketball and not studying. My concerns regarding Makoto made me tell Kai he either moved to the kibbutz or he came back to Japan.

The school was within walking distance from the kibbutz and the teachers were involved in the students' lives and had direct relations with the coaches. I took care of everything and sent Kai to an interview. Beforehand I spoke with a distant relative who had never met Kai, but who lived in Kibbutz about 20 minutes away by car. I told him the whole story and he promised me he would pick Kai up at the bus stop and take him to the school interview.

The school principal loved Kai from the first minute she

set eyes on him and was impressed by his motivation to play basketball. She later told me, "It was moving to see how his eyes shone when he talked about his playing basketball and living in Israel." She welcomed him with open arms and promised she would take him under her wing and fill out the new immigrant forms, which would give him some rights as a citizen. At our next conversation she told me the school year would end in two weeks and from an academic point of view there was no reason for Kai to remain in Israel. I decided to fly him back to Japan to spend the summer with us. He returned to Japan after having been in Israel for three months, which unfortunately hadn't been what we had expected. The only success was finding him a new direction. I didn't tell Makoto about everything, just that it had been recommended that we send him to a quiet kibbutz in Israel's north so he could invest his energy in studying as well as in basketball. That wasn't too far from the truth, and I knew it would satisfy Makoto.

Kai spent the summer vacation with his Japanese basketball team. We told the Japanese school principal he was dropping out, although I was very concerned when we made the announcement. I didn't know what was waiting for him in Israel and I was worried I was destroying his future, as Makoto kept telling me. However, now there was no turning back. The most important thing was to make Kai feel confident that everything would work out all right and he would like Israel. I told him that whatever happened, we would find a solution. There was one ray of light in his visit to Israel, because even though things hadn't turned out the way we planned, I could feel he had changed for the better.

He returned to Japan with much more self-confidence, he was in a good mood and best of all, for the first time he was open enough so I could talk to him seriously.

At the end of the summer of 2009 we flew to Israel. I decided this time he would have a softer landing. All my friends were recruited to help him. Daniella volunteered to be responsible for him while he was Israel, but only after my sister admitted she thought the responsibility would be too much for her. She would be his contact person and in charge of everything regarding Israel's national insurance institution, his HMO, and the boarding school. We met, all three of us, at the school, where Daniella received a detailed explanation of the implications of her responsibility for Kai. She signed a lot of documents and legally became his guardian in Israel.

We met Kai's new basketball coach, who was also a new immigrant. I liked the school immediately. Kai's room was within walking distance of the Jordan River and there was also a swimming pool. The grounds were lush and green, and the kibbutz members were welcoming. There were parents sitting with their children everywhere, and they all smiled and said hello. We had reserved a room at the kibbutz hotel. The visit to the north brought me back to the end of the 1980s, shortly before I left Israel for my big trip abroad. I looked at the green panorama around me and remembered when I came to visit the kibbutz with my family. I had the feeling I was leaving Kai in the right place. I also knew that my relative liked Kai and would help him, another reason I could be less fearful. He came to the school to meet us, and after he saw Kai's room, he promised to bring him a desk and a comfortable chair.

I wanted Kai to feel at home, so Daniella and I went to the department store and I bought him curtains and a rug. We had brought a TV with us from Tokyo together with the video games he liked so he could play with his new boarding school friends when he had free time. My sister bought him sheets, pillowcases and towels.

We also met the house-mother. She welcomed us and said, "Every time before you come to visit let me know. The kibbutz has a guest room, and you can always use it," which was very nice of her. I stayed in Israel until September 5th to make sure everything was all right. I attended several parents' meetings both of children in his class and of his basketball team, and I was happy to see the coach was friendly, not threatening like the coach in Tokyo. I also met some very nice mothers and they promised they would help Kai assimilate. When classes for the 10th grade started, I said goodbye to him and returned to Japan.

The year was a great challenge for Kai, and nothing was easy for him. I was happy that at least he made friends quickly, not only on the basketball team but in class as well. He had a private Hebrew tutor, and I could tell he was trying hard to adapt to life in Israel. On the basketball court life was very difficult for him. He said his teammates didn't feel they could rely on him and didn't pass him the ball, and the coach didn't let him on the court for games. He was frustrated; in Japan he had been team captain and played in every game. He was used to everything depending on him and his abilities. There wasn't a single team in Tokyo that didn't know who he was. But in Israel for an entire year, he almost never participated in a game. The team was already formed, the players were good, and it was hard for him to become one of them. Kai had been educated to obedience. He knew the rules, not how to fight for his rightful place. That made him very different from the Israelis, who regarded him as weak and not knowing how to be demanding to get what he wanted. It was hard for him and even at a distance I could feel his pain.

The house-mother did everything she could to make him feel at home in the kibbutz. She introduced him to the Paran family, lovely people who lived in the private kibbutz extension, where people from the city who wanted to enjoy what a kibbutz had to offer but who didn't want to be kibbutz members came and built their home. They agreed to be his adoptive family. The father, worked for an Israeli company that had Japanese clients and often visited Tokyo for work. His wife worked as a school counselor and was sensitive and could speak easily with Kai immediately. She listened to everything he said and made him feel comfortable in her home. The father's visits to Tokyo enabled me to send Kai clothing and food he liked. Kai joined them for Friday dinner, and they spoke to him every day, which helped him to get through a difficult phase. So, Kai was covered on all sides. It couldn't replace being at home, but I gradually worried less. The only time it was hard for me was on the weekends and during holidays. Kai wasn't alone, my sister and brother invited him to their homes every chance they had, but they lived three hours away in each direction by bus, which was enough for him to make him say thank you, but no. Instead, he went to my relatives or to the Parans or to friends in the kibbutz. He only went for a few hours and then he went back to his room because whenever he went visiting, he had to speak Hebrew, which was a real effort for him. He needed to rest on the weekends, distance himself from a foreign language, to watch his favorite Japanese TV shows, speak with his Japanese friends, and most important to catch up on his sleep.

I tried to take care all the technical details to make life easier for him. I paid for three meals a day in the kibbutz dining room, gave him an open account at the kibbutz store and paid for his laundry, which made me stop worrying he might lack for something. I could hear from his voice that he had found his place and I was happy the change in his life was making him happy. He told me that Israel was very different from Japan, and I understood he meant the closeness among Israelis, the hugs and kisses, the intimate conversations and the expression of emotions, things which made him flinch in Japan and which were regarded as weakness.

He had grown up with a cult of privacy and believed, like many Japanese, that everyone had to keep his weaknesses to himself. The Japanese believe that if you tell your troubles to someone else you are embarrassing and annoying them. Fourteen years is a long time to internalize ideology and beliefs, but Kai couldn't remain immune to the warmth of Israel. Within a few months he took his first steps into sincerity and intimacy, and even began to enjoy himself. His friends and even his teachers invited him to their homes, and it was hard for him to get used to the fact that the educational staff used a friendly, informal tone when speaking to students. In Japan that wasn't acceptable behavior. Students and teachers maintained their distance, both physically and emotionally, and students spoke to their teachers and with their coaches formally and with respect.

After a year Kai was much more fluent in Hebrew, had learned to read and write, and his spoken English has improved as well. I credited his impressive learning skills to the juku, where he had been taught memorization techniques. During his second year I began to hear signs of homesickness and longing for Japan, and he said he was thinking of coming home. I asked him what he missed, and he said, "My friends, the food, the big city...everything." I realized it didn't matter how well he adapted to Israel, he would always feel like a foreigner, and no one could understand that better than I could. He said that when it came to basketball, for instance, parents defended their children's right to play on the court, and he didn't have parents in Israel who would get angry with the coach or fight for him if he wasn't allowed to play. That was perfectly acceptable in Israel, but in Japan no parent had the right to intervene or question the coach's decision, we had no influence. He said, "Here it's different, a player who has a parent who invests in the team and contributes gets more time on the court, it has nothing to do with ability." He felt he wouldn't ever be a successful basketball player in Israel. He was far shorter than the others, not even 5'9", and most of them were already 6'2". I knew he was approaching the end of his Israeli adventure, and he also understood, without me having to tell him, that before he came home, he would have to make up for the time he lost if he wanted to go back to high school with his friends.

During Japan's winter school vacation, I went to Israel to visit him, and I was surprised by the young Israeli man I met. He dressed like an Israeli and swaggered like an Israeli. He wasn't a boy anymore; he had already started to shave. His teachers had nothing but praise for him. "If only we could clone him," they said. They were impressed by his upbringing, his discipline, his respect for his elders, his academic capabilities, and I couldn't help smiling to myself. They didn't know that was the norm in Japan, for better or worse. I wasn't always happy with Japan's strict educational system, and I was glad to see Kai was happy in Israel, free of discipline, without punishment and without intense studies. I was happy to see him free and more open, not afraid his teachers would punish him or hit him or be angry with him. He learned to talk back to his friends, say what he thought, and if necessary to fight for acceptance, and nevertheless hadn't and most likely would never become coarse like so many native-born Israelis. Both physically and mentally, they were stronger and more experienced than he was.

The Tsunami in Japan

On December 31, 2010, New Year's Eve, we received wonderful news. First, Tomonori told us that he and his girlfriend Mami-San were planning a summer wedding. They had been together for four years and seemed perfect for each other and very much in love. Then Michitaka told us he had been hired by a large company with branches all over the country, and he would start work immediately after the New Year's holiday. He would be in Nagano, which was three hours by train from Tokyo. The company had leased him an apartment and he said he wasn't sure how long he would live in Nagano.

Kai was in his second year of high school in Israel, and it seemed to be getting acclimatized to Israel and living in a boarding school. He came home for a visit over the summer holiday, and I visited him twice during the winter and once during the spring vacation. Makoto and I were suffering from the empty nest syndrome. However, I now had a lot of free time to perfect my website, and my business began to expand. The site was among the first results on the Google search. That led to a wave of interest and requests for information, and tour dates gradually filled my calendar, and I continued teaching in the morning and giving private lessons in the afternoon.

In the evening I sat in the dining room working on paperwork. When the date for the arrival of a group of Israeli tourists approached, I asked for time off from teaching. I loved my new occupation, and I felt I improved all the time, the feedback was very good, people saying things like, "We felt we were touring with a friend who taught us a lot about the Japanese people, things we would never find in Wikipedia." After the tour ended, they always said they wanted to keep in contact, which proved how comfortable they had felt with me, and suggested we meet when I came to Israel. I took it as a real compliment, and they also recommended me to their friends. For the first time in my life, I felt I had found the work I should be doing, and I hoped I could make it my main source of income.

Our financial situation improved and with-it optimism regarding our future. Makoto had a job, I had three jobs, the children were doing well, and we were both a lot more relaxed. I hoped we could keep on an even keel and repay Daniella what we owed her and finally begin enjoying life without tension and existential anxiety. But you never know what the future has in store.

On March 11, 2011, a date I will never forget, I finished teaching school at about noon, and as usual, on my way home, I went shopping at the local supermarket. While filling my cart I heard loud sirens I had never heard before, and the PA system announced an emergency and called on us to take cover because an earthquake was about to hit us.

We had had the occasional earthquake, but never

anything serious, nothing that justified an emergency warning. People panicked but did as they were told and sat next to a wall. Ten seconds later the earthquake hit and threw us from side to side, lasting longer than any other earthquake I had experienced. We later found out it measured 9 on the Richter Scale. Goods flew off the shelves and I was afraid the building would collapse. I sat on the floor in shock.

After the shaking stopped, I looked around and no one seemed hurt. We kept sitting on the floor, trying to adjust to what had happened only seconds before, and then everyone ran outside, leaving their shopping carts behind. I ran to the parking lot, got in the car, and drove home. On the way I felt the aftershocks. I entered the house and surveyed the damage. Potted plants that had been on the windowsills were on the floor, the pots broken, as were the bottles of alcohol and our wine glasses, all of them shattered and lying the floor throughout the house. I knew the small amount of damage to the house was nothing compared to what must have happened in other locations in Japan. I turned the TV on and learned there was a tsunami warning for Sendai and an enormous amount of damage had been done to northern Honshu.

It was already afternoon in Israel, and I called Kai to update him and to tell him I was safe before the radio reported anything that would frighten him. I told him there had been an earthquake, but we were all fine, which was how I summed up the trauma of the last hour. I had awakened him, and he didn't know what I was talking about. He mumbled something and went back to sleep.

The extent of the catastrophe became clear only two hours later. All the TV stations broadcast live from the city of Sendai, which had been hit by a tsunami. The sight of the destruction it had wreaked was terrible. Fifteen thousand people had died, and the government declared a national emergency. Within a short time, all the tourists and foreign businessmen had fled Japan.

Makoto called to tell me the trains weren't running, and he would sleep in his office. He said I should ask our neighbor for help in lighting the gas, which had automatically switched off when the earthquake hit. I did what I could inside the house and went outside to throw out the broken glass. I met our neighbor who, without even being asked, came with me, and showed me how to turn on the gas. With the gas on, the house heated up again. The telephone lines were down but the Internet was working so I could communicate with my friends and family in Israel. Through them I was contacted by Israeli TV and asked for an interview for the evening news. There wasn't much I could say beyond that I was in Tokyo. Like them I watched the tsunami on TV and all I could add was that no one in Tokyo had been hurt.

Later we found out that damage to the power lines in Fukushima had caused the systems that cooled the nuclear reactors to stop working and the temperature in the reactors rose. The electric company worked as fast as it could to repair the damage, but it wasn't fast enough and 48 hours later the reactors exploded leaking radioactive materials. The Israeli embassy sent all Israelis an email recommending we get as far away from Tokyo as we could.

The last formal message from them made me realize that Japan had a particularly serious problem.

In the days after the earthquake all the tours planned for the Passover vacation were cancelled because everyone was afraid of radiation. A week later the situation worsened, and Japan became a country no foreigner was prepared to visit. The Japanese were used to dealing with natural disasters and every household had a security kit with dry food, cookies, water, tissues, and a radio. The government invested efforts to limit the damages done by natural disasters, but they couldn't be completely prevented. The reactor explosions created a crisis of trust between residents and Japanese institutions, especially the electric company, which hadn't been able to prevent the immense damage to the nuclear reactors.

The streets were silent. No children cried and people spoke in whispers. Everyone enlisted to help the families who were evacuated from Sendai and Fukushima. Dozens of families were housed in Tokyo's schools and people who lived near the schools made sure they had food. I knew foreigners wouldn't understand Japanese restraint and would think people didn't care, but over the years I learned that that was Japan's strength. The Japanese had amazing self-control and helping one another reminded me of how Israelis behaved in emergencies. My friends in Israel, especially Daniella, pressured me to come to Israel two weeks earlier than planned. I told Makoto, and he tried to convince me to stay in Tokyo, telling me with conviction Japan was safe and I had nothing to worry about. However, I didn't share his certainty and after news about the radiation at Fukushima I couldn't sleep at night and began to think it might cause my cancer to return.

Israeli friends who lived in Japan started leaving as they became concerned about the government's lack of transparency. Everyone said the government didn't reveal the true extent of the radiation and there would be mass deaths. They encouraged me to leave as well. After a week I surrendered to my fear. Daniella, my good angel, told me a plane ticket was waiting for me at the airport. The schools closed for spring vacation, which would last until April, and I had no other work on the horizon, so despite Makoto's strong objections I decided to fly to Israel.

I arrived in Israel frightened, feeling everything was collapsing around me and I had no control over anything. In Israel I was treated like a leper. People kept away from me because they were afraid, I was radioactive. Israelis who hired me to guide their tours had made down payments and they called and wanted their money back. I called Makoto and asked him to contact all the hotels and bus companies I worked with and ask them to return the money. They said it would take a month, and the tourists didn't have the patience to wait even a day; they became angrier by the minute. I promised them it was being taken care of, but they weren't satisfied and demanded a refund immediately.

I realized I was losing one of my main sources of income, and I was thankful I at least had my teaching job and private students. Clearly, without my tours, both our incomes combined wouldn't cover our expenses, including repaying the loan, and as soon as I got organized, I would have to consider my next move. The feeling of being attacked from all sides depressed me, scared me, and humiliated me. I hated the idea of being a burden on everyone I knew and in need of help. My relatives did what they could for me without my even having to ask, and I was ashamed. My sister gave me an envelope with money and said, "This is just for the time you'll be here. Repay me when you can, and if you can't, never mind, forget about it."

I sat with Daniella to consider my options. The visit to Israel was terribly sad and difficult. The only ray of light was how my friends and family supported me with their love, which made me think about staying in Israel and finding temporary work. I even made tentative efforts to see what was available, but the salaries offered were very low. That surprised me because the cost of living in Israel was much higher than in Japan. A couple of friends asked me if I spoke Chinese, because Chinese translators were in great demand. The automatic connection people made between Japan and China always made me laugh and reminded me that I really couldn't stay in Israel.

To add to it all, as if all my financial problems weren't enough, Kai called to tell me he had been injured during a basketball game. He said that while he was preparing for a shot a player on the other team slammed into him, injuring his ribs and collarbone. His condition was serious, he was in terrible pain, and the coach told him he had to rest in his room for at least three weeks. He was terribly upset. He had been eagerly anticipating the upcoming season and now he would miss it. He didn't want to talk to me and was angry at the whole world. I wanted to go to the boarding school to see if there was anything I could do but he rejected the idea immediately. "Don't come here, I want to be alone, you'll only get in my way." I wasn't hurt or angry, I knew how distressed he was. Everyone around him tried to help, which made me feel a little better. His adoptive mother tried to talk to him; the boarding school house-mother encouraged him in her own way; and his teachers spoke with him and tried to ease his frustration. They all organized to take him to the school guidance counselor and doctors' appointments. Despite their kindness, he was blind to everything around him, sunk into his own unhappiness, while I was far from him and sunk into my own pain and sadness. It was an awful month for all of us.

In the meantime, the panic in Japan about radiation from the reactors subsided. The media reported that there had been very little leakage and nothing at all like what had happed at Chernobyl. After two weeks in Israel, I flew back to Japan. I didn't feel comfortable that life in Israel continued routinely and in Japan they were picking up the pieces and trying to get back on keel. My friends tried to cheer me up by taking me out for coffee, but they couldn't feel what I felt. I knew they were trying to help but I was light years away. Makoto told me the school in Japan had called him to ask if I would return for the new school year, and that was all I needed to remind me I had to get back to Japan as quickly as possible.

The day before I flew out, I met an old friend who was married to a Japanese woman, and like me, had fled to Israel to escape possible contamination. We discussed relevant employment opportunities for me in Japan, and he suggested he call his boss, who ran six kindergartens. He said that if I was interested, he could set up a meeting with him. I thanked him, and smiled for the first time in a long, long time.

Once back in Japan I met his boss, who turned out to be perfectly charming and a great fan of Israel. He said they were looking for English teachers and staff for his kindergartens. I would have a one-month trial period, and if we agreed I was suitable for the position we would talk about employment. My friend told me he had an excellent salary, and I would be making more than I made teaching school.

I went to work at a kindergarten relatively close to my house, about 40 minutes away by train. I was nervous on the first day because I wanted to make a good impression on the director. She was a young woman, about 35 years old, and I relaxed when she smiled at me. She introduced me to her staff, all unmarried women between the ages of 20 and 35. I was the oldest one in the room, 42 years old, and the mother of a 14-year-old boy. For a month I learned the work, my performance was satisfactory and at the end of the trial period I was hired with the same salary my friend received. Between what I earned at the school and what I earned at the kindergarten; I had a decent income.

I began filling my calendar with the parts of my jobs, mornings at the school, afternoons at the kindergarten, and holidays and national vacations full-time work in the kindergarten, since they didn't break for vacation.

Once I began to understand the organizational side of the kindergarten, I understood how important the teacher's demands and instructions for the parents were.

When Kai was in kindergarten, I found all the rules useless and unpleasant, I couldn't understand the notebook we had to fill out every day or why I had to pack his bag every day with his name embroidered on every article. Suddenly it all seemed very important. The mothers worked full-time jobs and were rushed in the morning. They said goodbye to their children at the kindergarten entrance and disappeared. The scenario repeated itself in the evening, they came, collected their children, and rushed home to make dinner for the older children who were waiting for them. I understood that the only way they would know what their children had done during the day was by means of the notebook.

The Kindergarten, Home Away from Home

The kindergarten staff was made up of a group of very dedicated women and provided an extremely high level of service to both parents and children. The kindergarten really was a home away from home and the children received loving, devoted care. I remembered how much Kai loved his kindergarten and always came home clean and polished and in a wonderful mood.

According to Japanese law there must be a kindergarten teacher for every three children and no more than 20 children per class. There were five classes where I worked, divided among children from the age of four months to six years. There were 22 workers, kindergarten teachers and helpers, 15 on every shift, and since the kindergartens were open all week long, they director was responsible for assigning shifts.

Every grade had six teachers, three with teaching certificates. They were the only employees permitted to speak to parents and had most of the responsibility. They had six helpers who dealt with the routine daily work, arranging the children's clothing in their cubbyholes, changing diapers, setting the tables before meals, etc. In the afternoon the teachers filled in the first part of the forms. Everything went like clockwork. Everyone knew exactly what to do and worked tirelessly. The children were happy, I almost never heard a child cry because all their needs were met immediately. I came to understand the tremendous influence the kindergarten teachers had on the children's characters and education. The children entered the framework as infants sometime in the first year of their lives and the mechanism raising them worked perfectly. Within a short time, they adapted to their environment and obeyed its rules. It was so very different from the educational systems in Israel.

Tomonori Gets Married

In July of that year Tomonori and Mami got married. He knew what our financial situation was and didn't ask Makoto for assistance. He and Mami organized everything and paid for it all themselves. He asked me not to get dressed up for the ceremony because it was Mami's day, and she had to be the center of attention. Only a hundred guests were invited, a far more modest number than what was usual in Israel, where most of the guests were friends of the bride and groom. In Japan, anyone who wasn't a relative didn't bring a date with him; Kai of course, arrived from Israel for the wedding.

Surprisingly, despite Makoto's being the father, we sat at a side table with Norio. When I asked Makoto why, he said the parents of the bride and groom didn't have the same status as the guests. We were hosts and had to act like hosts, that is, to go from table to table, pour drinks and be welcoming. The bride's parents sat at their own table as we did, but on the other side of the room. Very strange. I promised myself that when Kai got married his wedding would be different. I had been asked not to draw attention to myself and to dress modestly, but there was nothing I could do about people's curiosity, especially Mami's friends and family, about the only foreigner in the room. I felt very uncomfortable. Guests came up to me, shook my hand enthusiastically and spoke to me in English.

Tomonori and Mami both worked for large, well-established companies. Tomonori didn't like his work and remained only to please his father. He worked around the clock, and because he and Mami were well-paid they got a bank loan to buy a house at favorable rates, and the house was only a 15-minute ride away from us.

I was happy things had been easy for them and that they were independent. Our current worry was Michitaka, who was unstable, drank a lot and showed no signs of settling down any time soon. Makoto had to be his guarantor with the bank and sometimes we had to give him money when he couldn't make ends meet by himself.

Money Worries

Throughout 2010 and 2011 I had no work either guiding tours or translating, but thanks to our various salaries we managed to cover expenses, including repaying the loans for Kai's schooling. But we still hadn't fully paid back Daniella, I couldn't stop worrying about it and it kept me awake at night. I couldn't bear the thought of not being able to repay her, and I was ashamed and embarrassed. When I told Daniella she told me to calm down, saying she trusted me and had patience.

She knew about everything that had happened during the past year and said she believed everything would work out in the end. On one occasion she said maybe we should sell the house to pay off our debts. I knew Makoto would jump off a skyscraper before he would sell the house, but when I realized we had no choice I broached the topic; all I wanted was not to be in debt anymore. His response was that when Daniella asked for the money we would sell, now wasn't the time. When I asked why he was dead set against something that would solve our financial problems he said I didn't understand that if we sold our house, we would never have the money to buy another house. No bank in Japan would give us a loan. When I was ill Makoto fell behind in credit card payments, and that automatically put us on the banking blacklist. That meant he could only get credit when he had repaid all his debts, and after that there would be a five-year cooling-off period, and as his wife I was automatically on the same list and subject to the same conditions.

Makoto's explanation was logical, but I was angry at his lack of practicality and inability to solve our problems. He was working, but his salary was low. In my opinion he could have done several things to solve the problem, like finding a second job or a relative who could lend us the money we owed Daniella. The problem had dragged on for many years and we fought a lot about money. I wanted to know where the money was going, why we never had any to spare at the end of the month and how we could both work so hard and not have anything to show for it. Makoto saw how hard I was trying financially and realized he had to tell me everything.

One evening he asked me to sit with him at the computer and he showed me a spreadsheet with all our updated financial data for the year. I could see that our debt to banks was shrinking, and that if we continued within three years, we could pay off our mortgage and other big debts. For the first time I could see the whole picture and understand what Makoto was thinking, and that reassured me a little. I asked him to send the spreadsheet to my computer so I could study it. I wanted to become like a Japanese wife and tried to think the way he did, but first I had to relax and be able to think clearly. I spent a long time studying the table of our income and expenses, but no

294 • Tokyo Tales - My Journey

matter how hard I tried to be creative, I couldn't find a way out of the mess we were in.

In the middle of 2012 I started receiving inquiries from my website, and some were interested in trips to Japan. They showed interest and asked questions, but nothing came of it. In the spring of 2013, there was a significant rise in the number of hits on my site and finally I returned to what I considered my true calling and was reminded of the days before the tsunami. I asked the kindergarten director to let me work fewer days. She asked for the reason and I told her that before the tsunami I had my own tourist and translation business. She was surprised and impressed and said, "You were a company president. I am so proud of you!" She said whenever I needed time off, I should just give her notice in advance.

When the trickle of interest in my website became a substantial stream, I quit my job at the school because it was the least profitable. The police once again requested my services as a translator, and I felt the cork was out of the bottle and things were returning to normal.

Working Around
the Clock

One evening, after working in the kindergarten and having dinner with Makoto, I sat down in the living room to answer all the questions on my website. Constructing a tour according to the personal demands of each client demanded a lot of time. I recommended everything that could make it easier for them to plan a trip. I knew that Japan was not the country Israeli tourists usually picked, and it demanded a huge investment of time and money.

At the beginning of 2014 I could no longer deal with the quantity of appeals on my website. I worked all evening until two in the morning and I was up again early and enroute to the kindergarten, answering clients' questions on the way; I spent my lunch breaks the same way. The telephone became my workplace because I always had to be available. I worked around the clock, and it soon became clear that if I didn't get help with office work and tour guiding, I would collapse. I put a notice on an Israeli Facebook page asking for people interested in working as tour guides in Japan during the vacation to contact me. I held interviews with people who were intelligent, pleasant, and liked Japan. In the end I chose a student named Sarah, who knew a lot about Japan. Even during the interview, I could tell she would be up to the task. She came to my house twice a week and I gave her a list of tasks. She was experienced in using word processors and spreadsheets, and she prepared impressive, professional-looking documents for me. Managing an office seemed like second nature to her, and she easily performed tasks I struggled with.

From her first day at work our services improved amazingly. She contributed her office-managing skills, I dealt with finalizing business on the phone, and Makoto with service providers like hotels and travel agencies. We created a digital work environment that was suitable for all three of us. In addition, I contacted an Israeli graphic designer to brand the business, improving the website I had created by myself.

Sarah became my right-hand woman. From the beginning, she understood the way I thought, and as time passed the division of labor between us became clearer, each of us doing what she did best. We both began to understand better what Israelis wanted, like always being available to answer questions and solve problems. In addition, Israelis always wanted free information, and would only be willing to pay after they trusted us completely.

Initially I communicated with them by email and telephone calls, and once they authorized the trip and sent me their flight information, I transferred everything to her and she took over from there. She constructed an orderly plan with price quotations, and as noted, Makoto was responsible for arranging transportation and hotel rooms.

With Makoto's help, that year we opened a business in Japan. Objectively, he was surprised by my abilities. He was used to my being the little woman he had to placate on occasion. He never thought he would see me running my own successful business. I could tell he was proud of me, but my own growth made me see him in a different light. For the first time he didn't seem like the strong, successful man I thought he was when we met. He found it hard to be flexible and adapt to new situations, especially when he had to operate under pressure. Our relationship changed completely. I already knew I couldn't lean on him for support, and that made me stronger and more determined to do things as I saw fit. I understood I couldn't do things like a Japanese because our clients were Israelis and I had to operate in a way familiar to them. I was flexible, responded to all their requests by saying "Yes," even when the groups had families with children and the religiously observant. I accepted every project and didn't stint.

However, I still needed Makoto's help, and our approaches to business were often different, mine Israeli and his Japanese. I tried to explain that Israelis couldn't be spoken to as if they were Japanese, an Israeli client wanted immediacy, friendliness, and transparency. Makoto couldn't stand that I worked with my heart and not with my head. Either it was profitable, or it wasn't and if it wasn't it had no place in a business. When people cancelled at the last minute he was stressed and didn't understand that it happened sometimes, claiming forcefully that when clients created problems, we shouldn't do business with them.

Struggling with him on such issues exhausted me and kept Sarah and me from doing our jobs. At the beginning I was afraid to tell him about a change or cancellation and ask him to deal with the service providers because it infuriated him. I knew it would be a waste of time trying to convince him there were other approaches and did my best not to get into fights with him. When something good happened, I made sure to say something to raise his morale and make him feel important because I knew how much his ego was involved. I was also careful to involve him as little as possible in what went on behind the scenes and to share things with him on a need-to-know basis.

On the good days when we could discuss things calmly, reading between the lines I understood he felt under pressure because of my success and because I was earning more than he was. He was afraid I would value him less and leave him. As soon as I realized that was what was bothering him, I started signaling that everything was fine, it made him feel better. I understood I had to make him a manager so he wouldn't feel extraneous. I gave him full access to the company's bank account and let him be the CFO, and in any event, he was much better at such things than I. In many respects it was the best thing I could have done. The financial side of the business was taken care of in the best way possible and his fears subsided. From then on, he was totally invested, did everything he could to get us better deals from hotels and transportation companies, and our profits increased.

I had the feeling we were finally succeeding. My nephew joined us twice a year when there were holidays in Israel. That was when we had the most requests for guided tours, and he not only knew Japan well, but he loved the country and he loved being a tour guide. It wasn't long before I made him the company's representative in Israel, and he found his niche with people who wanted to meet in person and consult about a trip.

One of the best things that happened during that year was that I could repay Daniella a significant part of the money we borrowed from her, and for me it was like a dream slowly coming true. Fear of the future dwindled and for the first time I could breathe freely and look ahead with optimism, smile more, and enjoy life more.

Family and Business Matters

In the summer of 2014 Kai finished high school in Israel and waited to be enlisted in the IDF. He used the time for a long vacation in Japan, occasionally joining me for a trip with Israeli tourists. He was popular with them, and some groups extended their stay in Japan on condition he accompany them on the tour. People told one another about him, and I started getting requests from people who asked to reserve tours he would accompany. He loved the work and was particularly successful when the groups included families with teens.

In the meantime, I found out that without my knowledge Makoto had begun a project to keep Kai in Japan and prevent him from going into the IDF. Without consulting me he began investigating programs for him at several Japanese universities. He sent emails to the best ones asking for appointments for entrance exams. Two very high-ranking universities answered him, and when Kai found out he was surprised because he hadn't gone to a high school in Tokyo. He also was frightened by the way his father pushed him to take the exams, saying, "How do you expect me to pass the exam? I haven't prepared for it, and I haven't written Japanese for four years." Makoto explained that because he had been overseas for a long time, he wouldn't be examined like a student who had just finished high school. Makoto had done his homework and found that local students who hadn't gone to Japanese high schools didn't have to take the standard exam, all they had to do to be accepted was write a composition and pass an interview. Kai was angry, and told me, "He's pressuring me again. I don't want to take the exam." However, here I supported Makoto, and said, "What do you care? It can't hurt to try."

Things changed when he came home smiling in the afternoon after the exam, and he was no longer angry and irritated. He said the examiners had been nice and polite and the interview was different from what he had expected. To his surprise they asked him a lot of questions about Israel, his high school there, basketball and his personal life. After such a long time in Israel Kai had no problem with personal questions and answered them freely and fully.

After a week we were notified, that Kai had been accepted by Keio University, one of the best in the country. We were taken by surprise, and never believed we would be so lucky. Makoto rejoiced. The acceptance letter was the realization of his dream after his two elder sons had refused to pursue academic education. Clearly, Kai owed a lot of his success to his four years in Israel, which made himself confident, trilingual, full of good spirits and ready to do what he wanted with his life.

Kai was now at a crossroads. On the one hand, he wanted to serve in the Israeli army, but on the other hand he wanted to go to university; it was a difficult decision. His Japanese friends told him it would be a shame to give up a university education, his Israeli friends suggested he postpone his military service and do it later, once he had finished studying, his father begged him to go to university and his brothers were also in favor. With so many different people advising him of the same thing, he decided, finally, to take their advice.

I filled out a form for the Israeli embassy requesting a postponement of Kai's military service. After a month we received a reply from the IDF rejecting the request; he had to report for induction on the given date. I appealed to a lawyer who had been recommended and he tried to arrange a postponement. It was a long, drawn-out process which included an endless procession of letters to the IDF's manpower and other units. In the meantime, the lawyer informed us that Kai couldn't reenter Israel until the matter had been settled. It took half a year to settle it, symbolically close to the outbreak of the war in the Gaza Strip in 2014. Finally, his status was changed from new immigrant to son of immigrants.

Kai's university studies cost $72,000. Makoto said it was the first time he enjoyed paying for something. It was his dream come true and nothing could have made him happier. He preened like a peacock and told everyone who was willing to listen that his son was a student at Keio University. Kai decided on his own to stop playing basketball and devote himself to his studies.

That same year Michitaka informed us he was planning to marry a girl named Miho-San whom he had met in Nagano, where he was working and living. He didn't want a formal wedding like Tomonori and the couple went to the city hall to get married. When he was alone with Makoto, he told him Miho was pregnant. Makoto was furious but said nothing to Michitaka. I didn't say anything either, privately thinking that history was repeating itself.

Just around that time Kurako's health deteriorated, and Norio called to tell us she had been taken to the hospital. The doctors, he said, weren't optimistic. She was 89 and we knew we would unfortunately have to say goodbye to her. I knew how hard it was for Makoto. His mother had always been a significant figure for him and had supported him financially until she became ill. Being sick didn't prevent her from worrying about him, and because she was aware of his financial situation, she was sensitive to his facial expressions. Makoto told her she didn't have to worry because he was making ends meet. That wasn't the truth, but it was important for him not to let her know.

Kurako died when she was 90 years old and had an impressive funeral like the one she had given her husband. The customary rites were observed but this time I knew what was waiting for me, and I participated in the ceremonies reserved for family members.

Business was booming for us and after years of counting pennies we could again allow ourselves to enjoy things we had almost forgotten. Our relationship also improved, and we returned to showing affection for each other. Now, without arguments or tension I could again go abroad with friends and visit Israel. It was like waking up from a nightmare that had lasted for ten years.

The friends I had had since I came to Japan, Cai, Sophie and Sandy, had all left the country. Cai met a man from France, married him and went to live with him in his own country, informing me over the years that she had given birth to two daughters. Sophie had met a man from Spain and gone to live with him; she didn't want children. Sandy returned to Israel after having lived in Japan for two years and was living with her Israeli husband in Israel's southernmost city of Eilat; they also had two daughters. I maintained contact with them regardless of the distance, and every now and then on my way to Israel I stopped off in France or Spain for a visit, and I usually went to visit Sandy when I took my annual vacation in Eilat.

With encouragement from Makoto, I spent more time on vacations in Israel than previously. While my main purpose was to meet with friends and family, I also had business in mind. I met with travel agents who had contacted me after tourists I had worked with recommended me. They were very interested in an Israeli representative in Japan because so far, they had only dealt with Japanese tourist agencies, and not only was communication difficult because of the language, there was also the difference in time zones. Tourist agencies in Japan worked from Monday to Saturday and closed in the afternoon, when it was morning in Israel, and the Israeli week began on Sunday and ended on Thursday. That left only a small window of communication. Most requests from Israel were answered only after two or three days, making it difficult to arrange trips to Japan.

I was glad of the opportunity and promised I would be available even when the Japanese agencies were closed. Once back in Japan I answered them immediately, even if it was midnight. That opened the door to working with Israeli tourism from Israel, which changed over time. Initially the tourists were mostly adults who wanted to see "classic Japan." That changed to a much younger audience, people who didn't want to see the routine sites and were more interested in having a contemporary Japanese experience. That forced me to learn a lot about young, unconventional Japan. In consultation with Makoto and with Norio's agreement, I took some of the tourists to see their parents' home. Both brothers were proud of their legacy and welcomed the opportunity. I added an authentic touch with a stop at the local supermarket. The tourists loved meeting people and seeing how they lived, where they did their shopping, they felt they were experiencing the real Japan. Most of them bought only sushi, and then we continued the tour.

Inside the house Makoto and I had them sit on the floor on tatami mats and they ate sushi while looking out the window at Kurako's marvelously kept garden. Every single one of them was deeply moved and when we left, they said it had been the trip's best experience.

The years 2013 to 2018 were wonderful and challenging. I grew as a person and learned something new every day. Sometimes I had something to say about the way the office was being run, sometimes I had an insight into my relations with clients or with the guides. I knew I had to change my status from tourist guide to tourist agency owner, quit my job at the kindergarten and deal exclusively with the business. I also realized I had to re-examine my relationship with Makoto and look at motherhood differently.

During those years I found a new group of friends, all of them Israeli women ten years younger than I. What bound us together was that we were all married to Japanese men. Since I had the most experience, I became their mentor. I also made random friends through work; I was always happy to meet Israelis. I was beginning to be happy again.

In 2014 a representative from a manpower company called me; I had contacted them when I was looking for work. She said they were looking for Israelis who would be willing to participate in a TV show that would be filmed at the end of the following week. I said I would check with all the Israelis I knew and asked the tour guides who worked with me and my friends the Israeli wives, but not one of them was interested. I called the company back and said my son was a student, half Japanese half Israeli, and if she still needed people for the program, I could bring him with me. She said yes and the two of us went to the studio. The program was a panel talk show with ten Israelis and ten Germans, and the topic of discussion was the story of Anne Frank.

About a week later the manpower company called again and asked to meet with Kai. The producer had been impressed and offered him a permanent spot on a sports show that featured Japanese marathons. The shows were filmed on Saturday and broadcast in the middle of the week. Kai was excited by the offer and agreed immediately. He not only enjoyed himself, but he was paid far more than the going rate for student employment. Every Friday he went to the marathon site with the crew, returning Saturday evening or Sunday morning. His exposure was phenomenal because the show was popular and had very high ratings. Between university studies and the TV show on the weekends he was busy all week long. We only met during university holidays, when he worked as a tour guide along with me, so I could be with him all day long.

Kai wasn't the only one who was busy. Sarah, Makoto and I worked into the night almost every day. Requests from prospective tourists were challenging and we had to become familiar with places we had no knowledge about. They wanted to visit places further far afield than Tokyo and Kyoto. At the end of the season my nephew and I went to visit new tourist sites and studied them from an Israeli tourist's point of view. Every time we put a new pin in the map Sarah and I calculated what the new tours would cost.

In the summer of 2016 Miho and Michitaka had a little girl named Ayane and Makoto became a grandfather. Two months later Michitaka told us he and Miho were getting a divorce. Makoto tried to get Miho to tell him what the problem was, and she said Michitaka "does not respect me." Personally, having known him for years, I wasn't surprised. Makoto tried to speak to him as well and asked him to try to repair their relationship, but she decided to return to her parents and wanted nothing more to do with him. When a Japanese couple divorces the relationship ends completely.

That same summer, I went to visit Israel. I got a phone call from the Chabad representative in Tokyo. He wanted help for an Israeli tourist agent who specialized in tours for religiously observant Jews. The agent had quarreled with his usual Japanese tourist agency and everything they had agreed on had been cancelled. The trip was scheduled for the cherry-blossom season, the tourists had already paid, and they couldn't be expected to pay more. They had been promised a tour including places to sleep, a bus and a local guide who spoke Hebrew, and there was very little time to put a new tour together; I said I would help him. I called Makoto and asked him to find out about prices and I spoke with an Israeli guide I hadn't been acquainted with previously, who had an immense knowledge of Japan, its geography and history. He had studied Buddhism, was charming, and knew a great deal about art. When it turned out he also had experience with guided tours I knew I couldn't ask for anything better. We agreed to guide the tour together, he would talk about Japan's history and religion, and I would talk about modern Japan. In the meantime, Makoto had arranged all the practical details. He finalized reservation with the hotels, hired buses, arranged for workshops and a geisha show, and a reception venue with kosher food.

The travel agent confirmed the price and for the first time I produced a tour I had taken complete charge of. I had to overcome many difficulties, including providing times for prayers, keeping the Sabbath and kosher food. The tour lasted for two very intense weeks, but it was a success from beginning to end. From that day we went from being a boutique agency specializing in guided tours to a company providing total service for large tour groups.

The change in the company's orientation meant we needed more guides, so I created a reservoir that made it possible to have ten one-day tours in progress at the same time. One of the new guides was a good friend who had lived in Japan for 15 years before moving to Thailand, and she was happy to come to Japan twice a year to help me out. My family and the friends I trusted the most became the nucleus of the staff I relied on, and I also employed students living in Japan for reinforcement during the high season and during Israeli holidays.

Time to Make a
Dream Come True

In 2017 I gave Daniella the remainder of the money I owed her and managed to convince Makoto to fly with me to Guam. It belonged to the United States but most of the tourists were Japanese or Korean. It had been ten years since Makoto had set foot outside Japan after I forced him to participate Kai's bar mitzvah. I wanted this vacation to be a success so that after so many years we could feel close to one another again, because over time we had grown apart. I couldn't remember the last time we had talked about something that didn't concern the business, something about what we felt or thought. His strictness in dealing with the way I ran the business made me keep my distance from him. He was so introverted and stubborn I preferred not to share my indecisions or plans, and to keep the information to myself. I hoped that finally paying Daniella would mean the end of the punishment he had inflicted on himself for the past decade, and maybe let us start anew.

The vacation in Guam exceeded my expectations. The color returned to his cheeks, his eyes were like those of someone who had just woken up, and he told all his friends about Guam, posting pictures to the social media. When I saw how much he had changed I became optimistic about our relationship.

That year Kai finished his university studies and came home. His first day home he handed his father his diploma and said, "Now that I'm a graduate of one of the best universities in Japan like you wanted, leave me alone and let me live my life the way I want to." Makoto still hoped Kai would find a job in one of the large companies, earn a lot of money and learn Japan's business culture. "You'll never make a good living working for TV," he claimed. Kai had other plans. His agent offered him an interesting job on a new TV show interviewing people who lived in far-away corners of Japan as well as abroad. He and his crew went to a different location every time and interviewed people who were living by themselves in the wilderness. The producers were impressed and promised him new challenges.

When he was working less intensely, he continued working as a tour guide, enjoying the interaction with Israeli tourists, who warmed up to him immediately. Clearly, he was a tourist magnet. Makoto wasn't pleased, complaining again and again that Kai had made a terrible mistake. Kai felt he was being strangled by his father and begged me, "Mom, get him off my back. I got him his dream, now I want my dream." I tried to broaden Makoto's horizons and show him how happy his son was, and how important that was, but it did no good. He was inflexible; he couldn't be any other way. The gap between our concepts of Kai's future was enormous. He kept saying, "What kind of mother lets her son work as a tourist guide and participate in B-list TV shows? Why don't you encourage him to work at a respectable place and develop a serious career?"

Weirdest to me was that when Makoto spoke to his friends he always boasted about Kai, and when the programs aired, he not only watched them, but also recorded them. However, whenever he spoke to Kai, he told him he was wasting his time on an insignificant TV show. I was happy Kai had the backbone not to cave into his father's wishes but to continue doing what he really loved.

In 2018 Makoto and I celebrated our 25th wedding anniversary. Five years previously our financial straits were as bad as they could have been, and we dreamed of celebrating our 25th anniversary in Hawaii, in the same place we spent our honeymoon. I told him, "Don't worry, I'll make it happen," because something inside told me everything would be all right and that when the time came, we would no longer be in debt. When my promise was kept Makoto became very emotional and took care of all the details for the trip. That told me that we were halfway on the road to complete recovery.

It turned out to be the best trip we had ever taken together. Our relationship strengthened and we were happy. We flew to Hawaii, and I was glad to see there were fewer Japanese than I remembered from our last visit. Nature bloomed all around us, and our hotel room had a balcony with an ocean view. We rented a car and drove around the island. In the morning we lay on the beach, ate in good restaurants and at night talked until the early morning hours. I told Makoto I had finally been released from the guilt and shame that had plagued me for a decade, and although I had tried to hide the truth from my friends and family, everyone knew how bad the situation was.

While we were on vacation Makoto made an important decision concerning his work. According to Japanese law, since he was almost 65, he could retire and receive his pension or, if he liked, continue working. He decided he would tell his employer he would work until he was 70. Even though in the past he had objected to working for a lower salary than what he received at the insurance company, he discovered he liked where he was working. Financially we were doing very well, but I knew the change was a great boost to his ego, and I was happy for him.

Things around me were also falling into place and I was happy in every aspect of my life. My sister's sense of being responsible for me never left her and even though our financial situation was good she continued acting as a mother. She took courses every year and remained the perennial student. She had two university degrees in education and dozens of diplomas. When she registered for a course in guiding relaxation, I was her first guinea pig, and gradually I also learned about spiritual matters. Talking to her all the time, even back when I had my health and economic crises, helped me to take small steps to ease the awful suffering I endured. I learned to tap into the enormous power I had inside me and believed in myself again. I understood that if I didn't make significant changes in my life I would fall again. So, I also marked the milestones that taught me how to listen to myself and do what I liked and be in the company of only people whose presence was beneficial. In 2008, on my 40th birthday, I prepared a list for the next ten years, arranged according to importance:

1- To keep healthy, including regular physical activity.

2- To be successful at work.

3- To help Makoto pay off his debts, including the debt to Daniella.

4- To work on our relationship.

5- To renovate the house.

Now, 12 years later, I could be proud I was healthy, thanks to proper nutrition, physical activity, and a positive outlook on life.

Releasing Tension

The dream of getting my old life with Makoto back came true only around 2017 after we paid off most of our debt to Daniella. The vacation in Guam was a turning point in our relations. Part of it was due to a change in my approach to life. I understood the debts were what pushed me to wake up and act, making a drastic change in my professional career. I think that without the debt I would have remained taking whatever job presented itself, a man's wife, and nothing more, dedicated to home and children, living a completely different life.

I could see I had changed completely. During the past ten years I had learned to release tension, letting the universe rule and show me the way. I learned that money was not a reason to be angry or upset and put it aside. I began standing on my own two feet and my self-confidence returned. Full of optimism I could transfer those feelings to Makoto. He also discovered that we couldn't control everything and taking hesitant steps he learned to believe, as I did, that the universe would take care of us.

We began renovating the house dealing with the most important things first. We crossed off one thing after another on the list of what needed to be done. We replaced all the air conditioners, installed a new kitchen, and bought new beds for all the rooms. Twenty-five years was a long time between mattress changes. He got a smart TV set and bought a washer and dryer, and our quality of life improved considerably.

Makoto had always wanted to visit the United States, and we realized that dream as well. He had often spoken of his desire to visit relatives in Seattle, and we also went to visit my relatives in New York.

Working with tourists was a good opportunity to acquaint Makoto with new sights in Japan. There were towns and cities I had been in dozens of times that he had never seen, like Hiroshima, Naoshima, Takayama and Kanazawa; he came along as our driver.

I was happy and supremely satisfied that I managed to do most of what I had planned ten years previously. I celebrated my 50th birthday in Israel with friends and family. And now to list goals for the next ten years.

The Year of the Corona Virus

One evening in March 2019, I got a phone call from my friend Daphna who told me her daughter Lia was planning to arrive in Japan at the end of April. She asked if Lia could stay with me for a week and I said I would love to have her. I had tours planned for that week, but Makoto and Kai would be home so there was no problem. Somewhat later I found out that Kai and Lia had a lot in common and a lot to talk about and had spent the week together. Lia returned to Israel full of stories for her mother, telling her about the wonderful time at our house. A month later Daphna told me Kai and Lia had fallen in love when she was in Tokyo. We couldn't have been more pleased. Kai had told me nothing, and when I asked him, he smiled and said yes, they were a couple. He said Lia was coming to Japan to learn Japanese and was planning to get a student visa. It reminded me so much of my early days in Japan, and how much I wanted to stay there.

Lia returned to Tokyo in June the same year and enrolled in a Japanese language school. From that minute on she spent most of her free time with Kai. I was happy for them both. When school finished her visa expired and she returned to Israel. Her short time in Tokyo was enough for her to decide she wanted to move to Japan to continue her studies. Since she had already been in Japan for six-month in the same year, she had to wait several months before she could enter the country again. Kai and Lia had to maintain a long-distance relationship until January 2020, right before we had heard of the corona virus outbreak. A month after she entered Japan, the Israeli government declared travel warnings to a list of countries including Japan. In the following weeks, the corona virus also increased in Israel, and within few months spread in Europe and around the world rapidly. Not long after, The World Health Organization has declared the novel corona virus outbreak a global pandemic. One country after the other, had decided to lockdown their borders, in order to avoid spreading the virus.

The government in Japan took a different approach than governments all over the world. They only tested 0.2% of the population, that's why reports indicated a very low number of infected people. This trend continued as long as the question of holding the Olympics was on the agenda. But after the final decision was made, that the Olympics would not take place in 2020 as planned, a strict lockdown was not imposed, as in other countries, and although the number of patients increased, the number of patients hospitalized due to severe symptoms were still quite low.

In Japan, businesses continued to operate almost as usual - people went to work, the shops were crowded, public transportation operated as usual, and the restaurants and bars continued to provide services until 7 in the evening. Looking from the outside, and also from the point of view of the foreigners who lived in Japan, there was sharp criticism towards the Japanese government. Some have argued that the government is hiding the real situation from its citizens, and that it is much more severe than reported. The forecast for Japan, as it sounded from the outside, was that Japan was facing a catastrophe, which at that moment it had no idea was about to happen, just like in Italy.

I was aware of the test fever that was being done in Israel, I also heard about the long lines for the tests; and for a moment I didn't think there was any need to panic unnecessarily.

I believed in the way Japan chose to deal with the pandemic, and I believed in the Japanese government that would know how to deal with this crisis professionally, as it has proven many times in the past.

I have often heard Israelis whispering during the tours: "How cold these Japanese are", and continued: "How do you live with such coldness? They are not human; walking robots... I would never live here". I was already used to these statements, and I used to tell them: "Enjoy Japan; accept it as it is. There are many things that are difficult to understand from the outside, as in any country."

The irony of fate, I thought to myself, this culture that many misunderstand actually saved Japan from mass contagion. This happened thanks to their being "cold and distant", avoiding hugs and kisses, and even not shaking hands, and keep a distance to respect each other person's personal space. In Japan there was no need to force citizens to wear masks. Long before the pandemic, masks were part of the daily routine. In winter, the mask prevented infection with the flu virus; And in the spring and autumn seasons, the mask is intended to protect from various allergic phenomena. As the government ordered, they behaved in the streets obediently, and kept the rules. The residents took responsibility in the public space - the traffic on the streets decreased and the rules were kept.

I entered this period much more relaxed and confident in myself and my abilities to deal with what is happening outside. I strongly believed that everything would be fine, and it was only a matter of time. Unlike the tsunami crisis and the fear of radiation in Japan, this time I did not listen to the comments coming from outside; From the media and social media, where I knew that the outlook was always moving towards catastrophe. I adhered to the instructions of the Japanese government, and I trusted their ability to take control of the situation.

In perfect coordination, we finished renovating the house, as if we knew that the house would accommodate us for an extended stay. Everything was new and clean, and ready for us. We felt that the renovation paid off and improved our lives.

The company Makoto worked for continued to work as usual; And we were happy that they didn't fire anyone. He was calm and relaxed, and told me several times: "Enjoy your time off; don't worry, your business will return to activity when everything calms down. I have no doubt about it." I was surprised to hear him give me a reassuring message and show such great confidence in my business. Until that moment I was not aware that he trusted me in such a way. It was also a completely different experience to hear him talking so calmly, for the first time he was the calmer of the two of us. The wheel turned again, and Makoto was happy to return to the position of the main breadwinner at home.

People rarely walked around the streets following the instructions, we also stayed at home. The feeling was that the pace slowed down and became much more pleasant. Kai, Lia, Makoto and I spent time together at home, we cooked a lot in the new kitchen, baked, watched movies and went for walks in the park and did only necessary errands. Since the flights to Israel and other destinations were stopped, Lia was automatically granted, like many foreigners, an extension of her tourist visa from the immigration department. Japan, like many countries, closed its doors to foreigners.

Kai started his own YouTube channel called KaiTube, where he explained in Japanese about the life in Israel and talked mainly about the cultural differences between the two countries. He found a huge community of Japanese who were pro-Israel and who followed his channel, and within a few months his videos were getting hundreds of thousands of views, which surprised Makoto no end.

Who would believe that one day we would receive one hundred percent cancellations and a whole year's worth of work went down the drain. Sara and I sat for several months to refund all the travelers' payments and cancel all the reservations we had made.

I realized very quickly that I would have to think about an alternative source of income, until further notice. At that time, I was optimistic and believed the tourism to Japan would return soon.

I found myself more interested in social media than before and formed a Facebook community.

In the beginning I uploaded videos from the city and the places I had gone to with Makoto. The feedbacks were excellent and motivated me to continue. People were interested in the daily life in Japan and loved when I talked about my personal journey over the past 29 years.

I was interviewed by several tourist agencies and podcasts. I spoke about my life in Japan and about the differences between Japanese and Israeli culture. The only difference was that this time the audience was online, from anywhere all over the globe. That made me realize that my mission was to tell my story explaining how I dealt with living between two such very different cultures.

Unlike Kai, who told the Japanese in his YouTube channel about Israel and their way of dealing with the outbreak of the corona virus, I did the opposite and spoke to the Israeli audience.

I started walking around the city with my camera, filming live on Facebook and showing my group what was happening in real time in Japan. I never imagined there would be such a response. People who were in lockdown in their houses in Israel were so moved by the sights of the streets of Japan and later I realized that it gave them the opportunity to travel to Tokyo without leaving the house. For a year I walked around the city with an audience of more than 6,000 people watching my broadcasts, some in real time some watched later in a recorded one. They were so interested in the daily life that it got me thinking that it was time to sit down and write my story and publish a book. I had notebooks in which I wrote for many years, and I decided to go through them and add experiences from recent years. I knew that there were costs to publish a book and that right now the time was not so suitable. I decided to talk with my Facebook community about it and share with them the path I'm about to go through. Some asked for my bank account to send me tips to show their appreciation for the time I spent on the virtual tours. Little by little, I turned from a frontal tour guide into a virtual tour guide. I discovered that the field had become popular around the world and that quite a few guides earned their living through virtual tours. I started receiving inquiries and requests for tours for large companies, schools and many nursing homes in Israel. This is how I made a living then.

When I almost finished writing the book, after a professional editing and before printing, I asked them if they would be willing to purchase it before its launch and to my surprise a lot believed in me and were happy to support me. And that's how the book *Tokyo Tales: My Journey* was born. Before the launch of the book I already sold few hundreds of copies that helped me to complete the book.

I traveled to Israel to promote the book and discovered I was good at lecturing and that got me another source of income and a way to finance my visit to Israel.

Still More to Come

Next year will mark my 30th anniversary of living in Japan. Thinking about all the years Makoto and I have lived together, and all the crises and challenges we dealt with, individually and as a couple, fills me with pride. Life taught us its best clichés, that every time we stumbled and fell, we got up stronger than before. We learned after every storm to prepare for the future and know that not everything depends only on us. Learning to accept and respect the profound differences between us became the source of our strength. I am curious to find out if I will achieve what I desire during my sixth decade of life and live in tranquility and harmony in the two worlds I have chosen.

It took me years and an enormous amount of work to write this book, and I hope it will interest readers, many of whom are good friends of mine, but mainly I hope it will form a bridge between people wherever they are. It doesn't matter if you are Japanese or Israeli, European or American, we are all people and we all want to live and be happy.

Acknowledgements

My thanks to Moshe Alon, who produced this book.

This project would not have been possible without Danielle Nehl, for proofreading and editing so professionally.

I cannot begin to express my thanks to Shanee Azran who spent hours working with me on this project.

To Haya Ne'eman, my sister, who is an integral part of my life.

To my friends, Samantha Tsunezumi and Mihal Indyk, who invested time and effort reading the book beforehand, editing and giving me the confidence to publish it.

To Makoto and Kai, the people closest to my heart and most important in my life, who allowed me to share our story and most personal events.

Thanks to them, I am who I am.

Made in the USA
Middletown, DE
04 November 2022

14124403R00186